Andrew Simms is Policy Director of the New Economics Foundation (NEF) and has been described by *New Scientist* magazine as a 'master at joined-up, progressive thinking'. He is the author of the hugely successful *Tescopoly, Ecological Debt: Global Warming and the Wealth of Nations,* and *Do Good Lives Have to Cost the Earth?*

David Boyle is a fellow of NEF and the author of a series of books about history, social change and the future, including *Authenticity: Brands, Fakes, Spin and the Lust for Real Life*, *The Tyranny of Numbers* and *The Sum of Our Discontent*. His book, *Funny Money: In Search of Alternative Cash* launched the time banks movement in the UK.

Nick Robins, who contributed chapter one, is the author of *The Corporation that Changed the World.*

D0417891

Eminent Corporations

The Rise and Fall of the
Great British Corporation

by

Andrew Simms and David Boyle

with Nick Robins

Constable
London

Constable & Robinson Ltd
3 The Lanchesters
162 Fulham Palace Road
London W6 9ER
www.constablerobinson.com

First published in the UK by Constable,
an imprint of Constable & Robinson Ltd

A copy of the British Library Cataloguing in Publication Data is
available from the British Library

ISBN: 978-1-84901-049-8

Printed and bound in the EU

CONTENTS

INTRODUCTION

A KIND OF PRIVATE GOVERNMENT

Concentration of economic power in all-embracing corporations . . . represents private enterprise become a kind of private government which is a power unto itself.

Franklin D. Roosevelt, 1936

It is not by the direct method of a scrupulous narration that the explorer of the past can hope to depict that singular epoch. If he is wise, he will adopt a subtler strategy. He will attack his subject in unexpected places; he will fall upon the flank, or the rear; he will shoot a sudden, revealing searchlight into obscure recesses, hitherto undivined. He will row out over that great ocean of material, and lower down into it, here and there, a little bucket, which will bring up to the light of day some characteristic specimen, from those far depths, to be examined with a careful curiosity.

Lytton Strachey, *Eminent Victorians*, 1918

Wealthier than nations, outliving empires and whole political systems, corporations have become so important, so eminent, that some, we are told, are too big to fail. It is the great irony of our economic era. Where corporations are most worshipped as flagships of market forces and the private sector, as in the United States and the United Kingdom, the public sector bailed them out, pouring unprecedented billions into failing banks and the economy. Yet, in the

1

process of patching up a market failure, the public sector – that's us – mortgaged our own future. But were the corporations worth it? Was good money thrown after bad?

Are we now living through the twilight of the corporation as we have known it and the resurgence of many different ways to organize our economic affairs? We demand trust, transparency, accountability, involvement and, perhaps more than anything, humanity from the world of business. The opportunities should, then, be enormous for mutuals, co-operatives, social enterprises and community interest companies.

These are big, hard-to-answer questions. But the great spiral of history may give us hints about how to approach them.

'Concerning the Age which has just passed, our fathers and our grandfathers have poured forth and accumulated so vast a quantity of information that the industry of a Ranke [Leopold von Ranke, the German historian] would be submerged by it, and the perspicacity of a Gibbon [Edward, author of *The History of the Decline and Fall of the Roman Empire*] would quail before it,' wrote Lytton Strachey at the beginning of his book *Eminent Victorians* (1918). This book is based on the conceit that we have an absolute avalanche of information about the corporations that dominate our lives, for good or ill – rather as Strachey and his Edwardian friends had about the giants of the Victorian age – but very little actual knowledge.

Strachey's book came out in 1918 to wide acclaim. The philosopher Bertrand Russell read it in prison and laughed so much that the guards had to remind him that prison was supposed to be a place of punishment. A short biographical note introducing a modern edition describes the author as 'chronically frail and, in later life, an unapologetic homosexual'.[1] Set aside the curious antithesis this

2

conjures, how did someone apparently so weak, who failed at school and in academia, manage so successfully to rip apart a nation's image of itself, drawn down from the empire's iconic public figures, people such as Florence Nightingale and General Gordon?

Timing was one issue. The First World War was ending. Not only had the fields of France and Belgium taken a pounding from unimaginable amounts of military ordnance, so too had the automatic deference formerly given to figures in authority. People were less prepared to forgive incompetent leadership on the battlefield. That experience, and the social fluidity created by wartime, primed a society for iconoclasts.

Strachey, like Russell a conscientious objector during the war, raised a droll, astute hammer and brought it down on the reputations of individuals who defined Britishness. By the end of the war, the nation's pre-eminent political role in the world was permanently changed. By Strachey's hand, so too was the image of the people who helped build it.

But as one age defined by the imperial power of states was coming to an end, a new one grew from the emerging power of corporations. Many of them were British. The boundaries of formal empire shrank back, but the reach of the corporation would, for decades more to come, sustain the nation's power and influence around the world. International standing seemed once again secured. Yet in a few short decades that would change as well. Many of the corporations which both made and reflected an image of Britain in the twentieth century would be torn apart. Not, this time, by the elegant prose of a chronically frail writer, but by the inexorable man-made forces of economic globalization – forces that once did the bidding of Britain's national interest, before they turned against our 'eminent corporations'.

Following in Strachey's footsteps is a high-risk venture. He was one of the great stylists of the century. We are not in his class. Russell's laughter is less comprehensible now, reading *Eminent Victorians* a century on. It probably bubbled out as much from seeing icons broken, the shock value of what Strachey was saying – or at least implying – about the sturdy figures of the past. Even so, nobody would want to compete with his wit. We are not trying to.

But there are parallels between corporations and the great Victorians, especially when it comes to their history. There are obscure tomes of corporate history which only academics read and there are cursory notes – written by the marketing department – that appear on websites. Otherwise that's it. Yet history is important.

The great corporations are treated as if they were people in courts of law. They have similar rights to us. But in other ways they are very unlike real human beings – they have no emotions, often no morals and worst of all they have no life histories. For these reasons, in his book *The Corporation*,[2] Joel Bakan made the case that large corporations were inherently sociopathic in character. While they enjoy a kind of personhood, they also display a cold, commercial disconnection which means they relate to you and me in a way fundamentally different from that in which you and I relate to each other, our friends, neighbours and other people we meet. In place of empathy there is direct, self-interested economic calculation.

Without accessible, critical corporate biographies, we often do not know where most great brands came from, what they mean and where they are going. Manipulated by advertising and lacking easy, alternate sources of information, we fall for their latest makeovers time and time again.

We live in an age where the PLC is almost the proudest institution on earth. But actually, seen through an historical perspective, PLCs become flimsy, fragile, insubstantial things, which flower briefly and then disintegrate into their constituent bits – a few brands there, a vice-president here, an office block there: more like multinational mayflies than megacorps.

In fact, the Fortune 500 – the emperors of our age, a roll-call of power and pomposity if ever there was one – includes only one company (General Electric) which was on the list half a century ago. All the rest have gone, broken, bankrupt, merged and raided for their parts. All those teak-lined boardrooms and mahogany tables where they signed their environmental promises, those giant offices which keep the modernist architects in work, those logos and slogans which the world's three-year-olds repeat before their own name, proved so insubstantial.

It is a peculiar thing, but – because there are no histories of these corporations, no back stories, no roots – we let them control our lives with stories about what they are for conjured out of the air by whatever director of marketing they last employed. We remember almost nothing about them before their last CEO, or their last sweatshop scandal but one. The result is our strange, one-dimensional view of corporations. We suffer under the delusion that the great names of corporate power – Coca-Cola, Procter & Gamble, Walmart – were knocked together by God some time on Day Six of the creation of the world. We do not know where they came from; we do not know why. We do not know what they really are. *Eminent Corporations* is intended as the first dose of an antidote to all that. We hope others will provide more.

When Strachey's experiment in biography was published during the First World War, most biography – or so he believed – was suffering from problems similar to those outlined above. He wanted to tell the truth about the suffocating legacy of Victorian England, but all that was available was heroic hagiography of the titans of the generation before. Strachey decided to tell it how it was, at least about Florence Nightingale, Cardinal Manning, General Gordon and Dr Thomas Arnold. We wanted to do the same job for the titans of British business, not so much to take pot shots at the companies everyone loves to hate – Tesco, Rio Tinto or BAE, or those who can't see an animal without experimenting on it for some new shampoo. Anyone can see the problem with them.

No, we wanted to look at some of the pillars of British life – those corporations which have wheedled their way into our national consciousness – and to set out their history for better or for worse while trying to uncover the real narrative that holds them together.

The corporations whose histories we have dared to set out here have little in common, on the face of it. The BBC is a state-sponsored corporation, more like the chartered companies of the past, such as the East India Company. Rover has ceased to exist in anything but name. Yet these are the names which – in the absence of any other kind of culture – we have used to define ourselves as British over the past few generations: buying vests and socks from Marks & Spencer, watching Morecambe and Wise on the BBC, feeling the shiny purple Cadbury packing with chocolate melting inside in our pockets on a summer's afternoon, filling our petrol tanks at a BP station, putting our faith in the reassuring dullness of Barclays and Rover and, more recently, rolling our eyes at the brashness and cheek of Virgin and Richard Branson. These are specifically British experiences.

But there are also other things they have in common. One is their sheer fallibility: how some visionary can create something fresh and new, a whole new chapter in human organization, how they can reach for the great prize – sustainable profits, changes in lifestyle – and maybe touch them briefly, only for them to slip away again.

And there are bigger tragedies here: how a company based on Quaker values of equality and social justice such as Cadbury could morph into an American conglomerate dedicated to fizzy drinks, struggling to avoid the taint of slavery; how a Quaker bank dedicated to upright financial management could play such a role in the financial crash of 2008; how a retail chain dedicated to supportive relationships with British suppliers could turn on those suppliers and destroy them.

These are tragedies in the sense of disappointments, but also of moral endeavour.

They explain another theme of this subject: the gap between appearance and reality. These iconic British brands often became something completely different from what their founders intended. Maybe it is a hopeful sign that such a shift is possible. Maybe, though, we need to become more clear-sighted as we look, for example, at the reassuring blue Barclays logo, the utility that looks after our money, and realize that there is another side to it which is more at home in the international casino.

Another continuing theme is how those moral ambitions are undermined by corporate financing. Even the BBC's unique method of raising money locks it into a problematic relationship with the government and its audience. But the problem of financing is even more evident for Marks & Spencer, BP, Cadbury and others. For them there has been a fatal moment of taking the company public, of handing over control to faceless and distant analysts and traders – who will punish innovation unless it provides short-term profit.

This last theme raises the question, especially now that the survival of modern corporate finance is suddenly in doubt, having failed so spectacularly on its own terms in the great financial crash of 2008, of whether corporations in their current form can survive at all. And, if they cannot, what will replace them.

But this is to get ahead of ourselves. Time to step back. Let's begin with the mother and father of all great British corporations. One which set the mould for the many that followed, and contained the seeds of both the greatness and tragic failings of our eminent corporations: the English East India Company.

CHAPTER 1

THE BIRTH OF THE CORPORATION – THE ENGLISH EAST INDIA COMPANY (1600): THIS IMPERIOUS COMPANY

by Nick Robins

I mean not to throw any odious imputation upon the general character of the servants of the East India Company ... It is the system of government, the situation in which they are placed, that I mean to censure.

Adam Smith, *An Inquiry into the Nature and Causes of the Wealth of Nations*, 1776

Loot

Like Ozymandias' statue, little now remains of the great hulk of a building on London's Leadenhall Street that was once home to England's East India Company. Richard Rogers' postmodern Lloyds Building currently stands where the Company's classical headquarters was sited for over 200 years. London is a city of full of plaques, but none marks the spot where the world's most powerful corporation was once based. It was here that the Company's famous quarterly auctions were held, and so fierce was the clamour for the riches that its ships had brought back from

Asia that the noise of howling and yelling could be heard through the thick stone walls on the street outside. It was also here that the Company's board of directors met each Wednesday to oversee their global import-export business – and to push and prod their subordinates to further glories in the East.

Founded on New Year's Eve in 1600, the English East India Company is the mother of the modern corporation. With a monopoly of all seaborne trade with the East Indies – effectively all of Asia – the Company grew rich on the import of first spices then textiles and finally tea. Starting out as a highly marginal player in the well-developed commercial networks of the Indian Ocean, John Company, as it was colloquially known, also initially lagged behind its Dutch namesake, the Vereenigde Oostindische Compagnie (VOC). But through persistence and luck, force and fraud, it built itself up into a corporate colossus, alone accounting for between 13 and 15 per cent of all Britain's imports between 1699 and 1774. Every seventh pound of goods brought into Britain would be carried on Company ships, unloaded at Company docks and then consumed at home in Britain or re-exported across the world. For modern comparison, think of the retailer Tesco, which takes around one pound in every eight spent by British shoppers.

At its height, the Company's empire of commerce stretched from Leadenhall Street around the Cape to the Gulf and on to India and China. Trading posts were established at St Helena in the mid-Atlantic, where Napoleon would later drink Company coffee in exile. 'Factories' were also established at Basra and Bandar-Abbas in the Middle East. But it was in India that the Company's impact was most profound, establishing thriving centres on its coasts, not least at Bombay (Mumbai), Calcutta (Kolkata) and Madras (Chennai). From here, the Company sourced the wondrous variety of Indian silks and cottons – bandanas, chintz, ginghams, humhums, seersuckers and taffeta – creating a lifestyle revolution in Europe as well as prompting riots and protectionist trade barriers against cheap Asian imports.

Beyond these coastal ports, the Company progressively established a huge inland empire, first as an opportunistic quest for extra revenues and later as an end in itself. With an eye to the share price at home and their own prosperity, the Company's executives in India combined economic muscle with their small, but effective private army to establish a corporate state across large parts of the sub-continent. The Battle of Plassey in June 1757 was the turning point, when the Company's forces defeated the Nawab of Bengal and placed its puppet on the throne. Plassey is often regarded as the contest that founded the British Empire in India, but it is perhaps better viewed as the Company's most successful business deal. Over the next 100 years, the Company would grow into an extraordinary anachronism, administering huge swathes of India for a profit, paying out dividends to its European shareholders from the taxes on Indian peasants.

Yet, the Company's footprint did not stop there, but stretched on to Southeast Asia, where it had established its first outposts to access Indonesian pepper, nutmeg and mace. Penang and Singapore were both ports purchased by the Company in an age when territories could be bought and sold like commodities. And if India was the site of the Company's first commercial triumph, it was in China that it made its second fortune. The Company's 'factory' at Canton was the funnel through which millions of pounds of bohea, congo, pekoe and souchong teas flowed west. Mixed with slave-grown sugar from the West Indies, the Company's tea provided the foundations for a novel afternoon meal that eventually grew to cover the whole of the British Empire.

ANDREW SIMMS & DAVID BOYLE

Yet its tea was also an ingredient in revolution and catastrophe. It was Company tea that was dumped into Boston harbour in December 1773 by American patriots protesting as much about the intrusion of a corporate monopolist into their markets as about taxation without representation. And it was opium grown under Company monopoly in Bihar that would be increasingly smuggled into China to avoid having to ship hard cash to pay for China's tea. Proudly bearing the Company chop (or logo), some 2,000 chests were exported in 1800, rising to over 50,000 by the 1850s. When China's Commissioner Lin Zexu clamped down on the trade in 1839, complaining that 'the barbarians may not necessarily intend to do us harm, yet in coveting profit to an extreme, they have no regard for injuring others', the result was war. Twice the Company provided Indian troops to back the gunboats that enforced Britain's right to a free trade in poison. Yet by the time the Second Opium War was over in October 1860, the Company itself was no more, victim of a rebellion across northern India.

For the Victorian historian, poet and Indian administrator, Thomas Babington Macaulay, the Honourable East India Company was simply 'the greatest corporation in the world'. In its more than two and a half centuries of existence, it bridged the mercantilist world of chartered monopolies and the market era of corporations accountable to shareholders. The Company's establishment by royal charter, its monopoly of all trade between Britain and Asia and its semi-sovereign privileges to rule territories and raise armies certainly mark it out as an institution from another time. Unlike today's globalized world of air freight and instantaneous communication, for the Company a round trip from London to India and back could take up to two years. The operational risks the Company faced were equally acute, not just from shipwrecks and pirates, but also from disease. Over half of its employees posted to Asia died while in service.

Yet in its financing, structures of governance and business dynamics the Company is undeniably modern. It may have referred to its staff as servants rather than executives, and communicated by quill pen rather than email, but the key features of today's corporation are there for all to see. As with the modern corporation, the Company's share price was its heartbeat, communicating to the world the market's estimates of its future prospects. For the jobbers clustered around Exchange Alley in London, the Company's stock – along with its bonds and annuities – became the bellwether for the market as a whole. From the 1690s, when a clear time-series is available, its share price is dominated by a series of peaks and troughs, reflecting both the state of its commerce and the health of its relations with governments at home and abroad.

Following the Glorious Revolution of 1688, when the Parliamentarians and William of Orange overthrew King James II of England, the 1690s was a period of ferocious speculation. For the Company, its share price peaked in 1693, and then fell for the next five years as successive parliamentary inquiries exposed corruption and proposed potentially disastrous remedies. In January 1697, thousands of Spitalfields' weavers marched to Parliament to lobby for protection against Indian textiles – and on their way home attacked what they saw as the source of their problem, breaking open the doors of East India House and forcing the intervention of the local militia. The low point was in 1698 when a rival company was established, sending the Company's shares with a nominal value of £100 down to a mere £39. By the turn of the century, however, the threat had been seen off, the two companies merged to maintain market dominance and prices had returned to well over £100 once more, rising to over £200 in 1717.

Along with the rest of the market, the Company's shares then became caught up in the market mania, subsequently known as the South Sea Bubble, which followed the end of war between several European states, including Britain, in 1713. The price of Company stock doubled from £200 at the end of 1719 to £420 in June 1720, before collapsing to £150 in the following summer. Yet while this spike was extreme, the underlying vitality of the East India Company can be seen in the way that its share price continued a slow but steady climb once the South Sea crisis had abated. In many ways, the two decades that followed can be seen as the Company's 'golden age' – an unremarkable time of steady trading and regular returns. But this comfortable pattern was shaken in the aftermath of Plassey. As soon as news of the victory reached the London markets in 1758, its shares more than doubled to reach £276 in 1769. But this was a 'Bengal Bubble' which eventually imploded, revealing corporate corruption, insider trading and the irrational exuberance of financial markets. The Company experienced its own 'Northern Rock' moment, begging the government for a bail-out in return for state-appointed representatives on the board of its most important subsidiary in India. The Company's share price continued on a downward path for the next fifteen years, ultimately halving in value.

Not marked on the share graph, however, are the human consequences of the Company's malpractice, most horrifically in the form of the Bengal famine of 1770. As Horace Walpole wrote at the time, 'we have murdered, deposed, plundered, usurped – nay, what think you of the famine in Bengal, in which three millions perished, being caused by a monopoly of provisions by the servants of the East India Company'.[1]

The big fear that drove the market downwards was that Parliament would take savage revenge on the Company, even removing the board of directors and replacing it with its own appointees. But the Company's friends at Court ultimately won the day, and when this threat was finally removed with the passage of Pitt's East India Act of 1784, the Company's financial fortunes recovered, and its shares began to rise once more. Paradoxically, deepening state intervention in the Company's affairs brought some surprising benefits for the Company's shareholders, with the government increasingly guaranteeing a high level of dividends, making the stock an attractively secure investment after the mayhem of the 1760s and 1770s. Buoyed by the surge in share prices that followed the end of the Napoleonic War in 1815, the Company's shares reached a third peak of £298 in April 1824.

By now, the Company was trading less and operating more as a profit-making administrator in India on behalf of the British Crown. In 1833, the spirit of free trade prompted Parliament to remove the Company's monopoly trading privileges, in return for a guaranteed dividend. From this point on, the value of the Company's stock rarely slipped below £200, the generous level at which the government had agreed to buy out Company stock.

The Company's end as an operational force came in 1858. Generally known as the Indian Mutiny in Britain and the First War of Independence in India, the rebellion against corporate rule provoked a fierce backlash in Britain against a Company managed by 'obstinate old clerks and like odd fellows' in the words of the London correspondent of the *New York Daily Tribune*, Karl Marx. The Company's most senior executive, John Stuart Mill, pleaded with Parliament for a stay of execution, but in the India Act of 1858, the Company was effectively nationalized; the British Raj had begun. East India House was demolished four years later, a sign of the City's lack of architectural sentimentality. However, the Company lingered on as a zombie corporation, paying out dividends for the remaining years of its last charter. Eventually, time ran out. Each £100 block of shares was exchanged for £200 in cash or government bonds, and on 30 April 1874, the stock was liquidated and the Company's financial heart stopped beating.

John Company may have ceased to exist, but its financial shadow stretched deep into the twentieth century. In the shape of continuing interest payments on the government bonds that its shareholders had received in 1874, 'the Indian people are virtually paying dividends to this day on the stock of an extinct Company', wrote Romesh Chunder Dutt in 1908. This ghostly drain ceased only with independence in 1947. For India's first prime minister, Jawaharlal Nehru, the Company's imprint was deep and lasting. Looking back at the Company's conquest of Bengal, Nehru charged that 'the corruption, venality, nepotism, violence and greed of money of these early generations of British rule in India is something which passes comprehension'. To underline his distaste at the Company's practices, Nehru then added, 'it is significant that one of the Hindustani words which has become part of the English language is "loot"'.

The pursuit of profit

Imperial rule was certainly the final outcome of the Company's adventurism in Asia. But it was the hunt for personal and corporate profit that had drawn the Company inexorably on. The results of this enduring dynamic were world-shattering.

Starting out as an insignificant importer of Asian spices, the Company eventually became the agent that changed the course of economic history, reversing the centuries-old flow of wealth from West to East. From Roman times, Europe had always been Asia's commercial supplicant, shipping out gold and silver in return for spices, textiles and other luxury goods. European traders were attracted to the East for its wealth and sophistication at a time when the western economy was a fraction the size of Asia's. And for its first 150 years, the Company had to repeat this practice, as there was almost nothing that England could export that the East wanted to buy. First in Bengal in the 1750s, and then half a century later in China, the Company broke the regulatory authority of the Mughal and Qing empires and disrupted this longstanding flow of trade and wealth. By the time of its demise, Europe's economy was double the size of those of China and India, a complete reversal of the situation in 1600. There are clearly many elements in this turnaround, but the East India Company was certainly one of the institutions that engineered this great switch in global development which marked the birth of the modern age.

Throughout its career, the Company confronted many of the timeless questions facing business enterprise: how to keep employees motivated, customers satisfied, shareholders happy, governments sweet and society content. Its success at matching supply and demand along lengthy supply chains whether for textiles or tea proved to be one of the secrets of its enduring commercial success. In its heyday, the Company demonstrated a sophisticated and focused approach to sourcing, marketing and finance that brought the consumer quality goods, earned the investor regular dividends and yielded healthy tax revenues for the state at home and abroad. But once it had attained market and political power in India, corruption, speculation and war followed in its wake, corroding the Company's commercial purpose and laying waste the livelihoods of millions.

In ways that are immediately familiar, the Company lay at the centre of a web of relationships. Internally, the interactions between owners, executives and employees set the fundamental direction of the business. Externally, fiscal and regulatory arrangements with states in Europe and Asia defined the Company's scope for action, while in the marketplace, its standing with customers, competitors and suppliers determined its chances of success. Ultimately, however, it was the Company's ability to maintain a basis of trust with society at home and abroad that decided its fate – and once this trust was broken, protest, litigation, regulation, rebellion and, ultimately, closure would follow.

For us today, the lives of four contemporaries from the eighteenth century can perhaps best explain the metabolism of this almost unimaginable corporate beast. Robert Clive and Warren Hastings were both Company executives, initially successful in promoting their employer's (and their own) interests in the East, but ultimately brought low by corruption and sleaze. Adam Smith and Edmund Burke were both Celtic critics of the Company, the first seeing it as the enemy of open markets and the second regarding it as a threat to political liberty in Europe as much as in Asia. The conflict among these four characters helps to reveal not just the Company's own story, but also the deep dynamics of the modern corporation and the enduring tensions between enterprise, justice and development.

Statues of a sheep-stealer

If you walk to the Foreign and Commonwealth Office in

London from St James's Park, you will climb up 'Clive Steps', named after the larger-than-life statue of Robert Clive that stands outside the old India Office building. It was to here that the governance of India passed after the Company's demise in 1858, but it took another sixty years for this monument to the great 'nabob-maker' to be erected. The reasons for this delay say much about his contested record and the Company's place in British history.

From Shropshire gentry stock, as a boy Clive earned a reputation for being 'out of measure addicted' to fighting, and when he joined the Company's service in India he soon switched from the dull formality of clerking to the excitement of war. For his defence of the Company's acquisitions in southern India in the early 1750s, Prime Minister William Pitt the Elder described him as Britain's 'heaven-born general'. The Plassey coup brought him even greater fame as a much-needed national hero during the bitter Seven Years' War. Placing his puppet on the throne of Bengal, Clive ordered the contents of the Bengal treasury at Murshidabad to be loaded on to over a hundred boats and sent downriver to the Company's base at Calcutta. In one stroke, Clive had netted £2.5 million for the Company and £234,000 for himself – equivalent today to £232 million for his employers and a cool £22 million personal success fee. Aged thirty-three, Clive had suddenly become one of the richest men in the world. Lacking the racist sense of superiority of future British rulers, Clive celebrated his victory by making an offering at the feet of Durga, Calcutta's local deity. Writing in triumph to the Company's directors on 26 July 1757, Clive concluded that 'this great revolution, so happily brought about, seems complete in every respect'.

Once more, Clive was feted back home in England, becoming Baron Clive of Plassey, a title that carried a sting, however, as it was only an Irish baronetcy, with a distinctly second-class status. Returning to India as president of the Calcutta operations in 1764, Clive delivered his master-stroke, engineering the outsourcing of tax collection in the Mughal provinces of Bengal, Bihar and Orissa to the Company. Known as the office of the Diwani (the right to collect taxes), it was as if the Inland Revenue had been taken over by Walmart. When all the costs of the Nawab's administration had been deducted, Clive calculated that the takeover would yield sufficient revenues to pay for all the Company's purchases of both Indian textiles and China tea, leaving a healthy balance besides.

Clive also ensured that he benefited once more from his ingenuity, instructing his agents and friends back in Britain to 'lose no time in purchasing all the Company stock you can, for I am persuaded it must be doubled in three years', one of history's more accurate share tips. When news of this coup reached London, the response was rapturous, with the *Gentleman's Magazine* forecasting in March 1767 that:

> the prodigious value of these new acquisitions may open to this nation such a mine of wealth as not only in a few years to pay off the national debt, to take off the land tax, and ease the poor of burdensome taxes; but to add to the dividends upon the Company's stock such a proportion of the increased revenue as will astonish Europe and exceed the most sanguine expectations.

The Company's share price soared, attracting the attentions of investors across Europe.

When Clive left India for the last time in February 1767, he believed that he had endowed the Company with an 'unrivalled estate'. For some, Clive was a single-minded genius, for others an unethical plunderer. Of course, he was both and more. It was his guile that had won the Battle of Plassey, humbling the authority of the Bengal state, smashing the Asian merchant class and eliminating the competitive threat from France. He was the great 'revolutionist', the 'nabob-maker' extraordinaire. But Clive was not just a powerful individual; he was the chief representative of a corporate machine that worked with remorseless logic to achieve its ends. Wrongly portrayed as an agent of the British Empire, Clive was always 'actuated by a sincere desire to promote the prosperity of the Company' according to James Mill, writing in 1817.

The problem was that the internal logic of the corporate state that Clive had established was wholly at odds with both effective internal governance, as well as human justice for society at large. A three-fold crisis hit Bengal. First, the acquisition of the Diwani meant that its fiscal surplus, rather than silver bullion from Britain, paid for the Company's exports, an 'unrequited trade' that impoverished the region. Second, the Company was able to act without restraint as a monopoly power, driving down the prices of the goods it bought and abusing its position to demolish the living standards of the weavers. According to William Bolts, one of the Company's fiercest critics, among the winders of raw silk, called *nagaads*, the Company's oppression resulted in a horrific form of self-mutilation, whereby 'instances have been known of their cutting off their thumbs to prevent their being forced to wind silk'. Third, the Company's takeover of the Mughal economic apparatus was not matched by any countervailing social investment. So, when drought struck Bengal in 1769, the traditional Mughal systems of relief and intervention were no longer operational. Not only did the Company's executives corner the market in the limited stocks of grain, driving the price up higher, but the Company actually increased the rate of taxation in the ensuing famine to maintain its revenue levels. Looking back, the Bengal famine stands out as perhaps one of the worst examples of corporate mismanagement in history.

Like so many mergers and acquisitions since, the Company's conquests in Bengal proved to be a step too far, driven by personal ego and corporate aggrandizement. On the streets of London, Clive was lampooned as Lord Vulture, and even King George III protested at Clive's 'fleecing' of India. Hauled before Parliament to explain his actions, Clive resented being treated like 'a common sheep-stealer' and declared himself 'astounded at my own moderation'. He may have been cleared in the vote that followed, but he committed suicide shortly afterwards, with Dr Samuel Johnson observing that he had 'acquired his fortune by such crimes that his consciousness of them impelled him to cut his own throat'. Clive's reputation would remain tarnished for the next century, with his military exploits on behalf of the Company outweighed by his underhand methods and single-minded corruption. It was only in the run-up to the 150th anniversary of Plassey in 1907 that his memory could be rehabilitated at the height of imperial jingoism. Another hundred years later, it remains a peculiar anachronism that Britain's greatest corporate rogue should still have pride of place in the heart of Whitehall.

Eminent talent and integrity

Across Parliament Square from Clive's statue, Westminster Abbey is famous for its Poets' Corner, commemorating Chaucer, Shakespeare and Dickens. Directly opposite in the north transept is what could equally be called Company Corner, marked by extraordinary monuments mixing the classical and the oriental to praise two of Clive's comrades in arms at Plassey. On the wall nearby is a discreet memorial to Warren Hastings, who had been appointed Bengal's first governor-general in the wake of the East India crash. Installed by his widow, the tablet praises his 'eminent talents and integrity'. This was a distinctly different message to history than that proposed by Hastings' contemporaries. The utilitarian thinker, Jeremy Bentham, for example, proposed that the Company's shareholders should erect a special statue to Hastings with the following inscription: 'Let it but put money into our pockets, no tyranny too flagitious to be worshipped by us'.

The career of Warren Hastings highlights the conflict within corporations between ethics and opportunism. Fluent in local languages, he was a great philanthropist, sponsoring the first English translation of the Hindu *Bhagavad Gita*, supporting a new madrasa for Muslim students in Calcutta and ordering the construction of a Buddhist temple on the banks of the Hugli. Nehru himself argued that 'India owes a deep debt of gratitude' to Company executives such as Hastings and William Jones for helping to rediscover India's heritage. Like Clive a product of down-at-heel West Country gentry, Hastings developed a quite different reputation in India, seeking out a more principled basis for British commerce. He told Parliament: 'If our people, instead of erecting themselves into lords and oppressors of the country, confine themselves to an honest and fair trade, they will everywhere be respected, and the English name instead of becoming a reproach, will be universally revered.'[2]

Yet, these essentially cultural interventions were always secondary to Hastings' primary task of generating wealth for the Company and its shareholders. When Hastings took over as governor of Bengal in 1772, his chief concern was to restore order and return the Company's operations to profitability. He started by commercializing the tax system, farming out revenue collection for five-year periods. Moving to the lucrative opium trade, he gave the Company exclusive rights to buy all the opium grown in Bihar, thereby enabling it to drive down prices. Soon compulsion was being used to force the *ryots* (tenant farmers) to grow opium against their will.

Hastings took a similar approach to salt, imposing a Company monopoly and farming out production to contractors, a system that would remain almost unchanged until the end of British rule in 1947. A final source of cash for Hastings was to look outside Bengal, hiring out the Company's army to help the neighbouring principality of Awadh to conquer Rohilkhand. He also annexed Varanasi, which he presented to the directors back in London as yet another 'valuable acquisition to the Company'.

Hastings' drive for cash typifies the dilemma of good men forced by institutional circumstances into doing bad things. This tension was beautifully laid out by Macaulay in his 1840 essay on Hastings. In essence, the Company directors wanted Hastings to simultaneously enhance financial performance and improve ethical standards. 'Govern leniently and send more money,' the directors urged, according to Macaulay, adding 'practise strict justice and moderation towards neighbouring powers, and send more money'. Ever the practical administrator, Hastings recognized that 'it was absolutely necessary for him to disregard either the moral discourses or the pecuniary requisitions of his employers'. He chose the safest course and decided 'to neglect the sermons and to find the rupees'.[3]

What added to Hastings' stress was the dramatic change in governance brought about by the 1773 Regulating Act to curb the Company's excesses. The new Act ended the Company's operational independence, establishing a five-man council in Bengal, with three of the members appointed by Parliament – John Clavering, Philip Francis and George Monson – to represent the public interest. From the start, tensions were high, with Francis writing of the Company's rule that 'the corruption is no longer confined to the stem of the tree, or to a few principal branches; every twig, every leaf is putrefied'.[4]

The first clash came in 1775 when the parliamentary trio backed the accusations of corruption levelled at Hastings by Raja Nandakumar, former governor of Hugli under the Nawabi regime. Hastings was not to be outdone and revived an ancient fraud case against Nandakumar, bringing him to trial at the new Supreme Court where Hastings' ally found him guilty and sentenced him to death.

A clear case of judicial murder, Nandakumar's execution stands in sharp contrast with Clive's extensive use of forgery to win at Plassey: where Clive was applauded and ennobled, Nandakumar was hanged. Back in London, the Company's directors voted to recall Hastings, but they were overruled by their shareholders. Parliament then voted that Hastings had 'acted in a manner repugnant to the honour and policy of this nation', but once again, the Company's shareholders refused to budge, exposing the weakness of the Regulating Act which gave Parliament no right to recall the governor-general.

The obstinate axis of corporate executive and shareholders drove Philip Francis to despair, resulting in an extraordinary boardroom battle. At dawn on 17 August 1780, Francis travelled to Hastings' Calcutta mansion, Belvedere House, for a duel. Beside the 'trees of destruction', the two rivals stood fourteen paces apart. Francis fired and missed; Hastings then shot, hitting and wounding his opponent, who returned to England a bitter man, vowing revenge.

The Belvedere duel was more than just an exotic skirmish between two irreconcilable individuals. It epitomized a deep-seated battle for control of the Company: on one side were the corporation's executives and shareholders and on the other the rising power of the British imperial state. Round one had gone to the Company and, with Francis gone, Hastings had carte blanche to run affairs as he wished. Seeking an outlet for the Company's opium, Hastings ordered two ships to smuggle 3,450 chests into China. When the Company's directors heard of the escapade, they were horrified, stating that it was 'beneath the Company to be engaged in such a clandestine trade'. In its place, Hastings extorted cash from neighbouring Awadh and tightened the fiscal screw in Bengal. The result was a raw combination of rebellion and famine. By the time Hastings left Calcutta to return home, peace had been restored, but Hastings' remorseless focus on raising corporate revenues had left his reputation in tatters. His one-time school-mate, William Cowper, captured the mood with his 1782 poem, 'Expostulation':

> Hast thou, though suckled at fair freedom's breast,
> Exported slav'ry to the conquer'd East
> Pull'd down the tyrants India serv'd with dread,
> And rais'd thyself, a greater in their stead?
> Gone thither arm'd and hungry, return'd full,
> Fed with the richest veins of the Mogul,
> A despot big with pow'r obtain'd by wealth
> And that obtain'd by rapine and by stealth?
> With Asiatic vices stor'd thy mind,
> But left their virtues and thine own behind;
> And, having truck'd thy soul, brought home the fee,
> To tempt the poor to sell himself to thee?[5]

Hastings would be impeached in Westminster's Great Hall a few hundred yards from where his memorial would eventually be placed next door in the Abbey. After seven long years, the initial outrage that had driven the case had ebbed; imperial conflict with revolutionary France was now uppermost in the mind of the British establishment. Hastings was cleared, like Clive, an outrageous example of corporate impunity. He lived to the ripe old age of eighty-six at his country estate, Daylesford, now home to Anthony Bamford, head of the JCB business empire.

Nuisances in every respect

Hastings' record in the East had prompted Adam Smith to update his masterpiece, *An Inquiry into the Nature and Causes of the Wealth of Nations*. Smith had little place for the corporation in his vision of economic liberty. Published in 1776, *The Wealth of Nations* had been written at the height of public interest in the East India Company's impact both in India and back in Britain. For Smith, the Company held the secret to one of the greatest puzzles of his time: explaining the unequal distribution of benefits from the rapidly increasing integration of the world economy. Smith argued: 'The discovery of America, and that of a passage to the East Indies by the Cape of Good Hope, are the two greatest and most important events recorded in the history of mankind.'[6]

Smith's belief was that the full potential of this dramatic opening had not been realized, owing to a combination of colonies and corporations. For the natives of both the East and West Indies, 'all the commercial benefits have been sunk and lost' in a series of 'dreadful misfortunes'. In Asia, the agents of this pain were the Dutch and British East

India Companies, monopoly corporations that he condemned as 'nuisances in every respect'.[7]

Earlier than most, Smith recognized that commercial success often comes not just from meeting consumer demand, but also from building up market power to generate excess profits. 'To widen the market and to narrow the competition is always in the interest of the dealers,' Smith argued. The result of this anti-competitive behaviour was to raise profits above the natural level, amounting to 'an absurd tax upon the rest of their fellow citizens'.[8] More dangerous still was the establishment of exclusive corporations, such as the East India Company, which destroyed any pretence at competition. Not only did the inhabitants of England pay 'for all the extraordinary profits which the company may have made upon those goods in consequence for their monopoly', but they also suffered from 'all the extraordinary waste which the fraud and abuse, inseparable from the management of the affairs of so great a company, must necessarily have occasioned'.[9] The Company's descent into malpractice was therefore no accident, but the inevitable and necessary product of a faulty institution.

According to Smith, corporate scale serves to magnify an underlying problem of behaviour. When it was small, the damage that the Company could inflict was relatively limited. When it grew in size to dominate whole markets and territories, its potential for harm grew correspondingly large. Monopoly thus did not just create economic injustice, but it was also 'a great enemy to good management'.[10] In Smith's vision of an open economy, entrepreneurs could not afford to displease their customers as these could easily choose alternate sources of supply.

Outside the state sector, few companies today have similar monopoly privileges, except those managing utilities, such as energy, telecoms, transport and water. But two decades of global deregulation have resulted in increasing levels of corporate concentration. Over 60 per cent of international commerce now takes place within corporations rather than in the open marketplace, making it somewhat idle to talk of free markets. For all the efforts to liberalize the world economy, the current pattern of global commerce is perhaps better described as one of corporate trade – a situation with great similarities to the Company's own day. Adam Smith was certainly a believer in open markets. But freeing the world for corporations formed no part of his vision.

For Smith, the Company was not just flawed as a commercial institution. After Plassey, political tyranny was added to the mix through the 'strange absurdity' of a joint stock corporation holding sovereign powers. Corporate rule stunted the natural growth of Bengal 'to what is barely sufficient for answering the demands of the Company'. Sick of the callousness this engendered, Smith described the way in which the Company's executives sought to make a fortune in Bengal and then leave as quickly as possible, 'perfectly indifferent though the whole country was swallowed up by an earthquake'.[11] In the form of the Bengal Famine, this earthquake had already struck.

Smith, like many others, soon realized that the reforms contained in the 1773 Regulating Act were unable to rein in the Company. After 'a momentary fit of good conduct', Smith observed in 1783 that the Company was 'in greater distress than ever'. So in May 1783, as his contribution to the resurgence of public and political interest in corporate reform, Smith wrote to his publisher, William Strahan, that he planned to add a new section to *The Wealth of Nations* giving a full exposition of 'the Absurdity and hurtfulness of almost all our chartered trading companies'.[12] This counter-blast appeared in the final book of the new volume, dealing with 'the Public Works and Institutions which are necessary for facilitating particular Branches of Commerce'. In Smith's opinion, however, the joint stock corporation was a deeply flawed piece of public policy. A particular danger was the impetus for hazardous speculation created by the separation of ownership and management in the joint stock arrangement.

By limiting the liability of shareholders to the nominal value of their investments, excessive risks would be taken. Known today as the 'agency problem', Smith asserted in the 1780s that corporate executives would never look after shareholder funds with the 'same anxious vigilance' that they would in a partnership where ownership and control were in the same hands. The Company's boom-and-bust cycle in the Bengal Bubble is still eerily familiar – the same passion for aggressive acquisitions, the same obsession with exclusive perks for corporate insiders and the same focus on executive self-preservation as ordinary shareholders started to suffer the consequences of excess. The conclusion for Smith was stark: 'negligence and profusion must always prevail, more or less, in the management of the affairs of such a company'.[13] Hoping for shareholders to act with 'more dignity and steadiness' was unlikely to yield results, he felt. Instead, Smith's prescription for these dire ailments was simple: recognize that the Company would never be 'fit to govern' its possessions in India and make the trade between Britain and India 'open to all'. In addition, the use of corporations should be limited to financial services (banking and insurance) along with infrastructure (water and canals).

Smith's scepticism about the corporation did little at the time to rein in the Company. And today, he would probably be appalled at the way in which an ever smaller number of corporations dominate the world's commercial and financial landscape. But his theories of free trade would be used both by campaigners against the Company's monopoly of trade with Asia, and also against government interference in markets during times of famine – to devastating effect in both India and Ireland. This position was later strongly supported by the East India Company's own resident political economist, Thomas Malthus, who taught at its Haileybury College. For the modern corporation, Adam Smith remains one of the most powerful investigators into its flawed metabolism. It would be his friend, Edmund Burke, who would try to bring the Company to book.

Making the company accountable

If Adam Smith analysed the economic roots of the Company's failings, Edmund Burke confronted head on the political framework that enabled its negligence to flourish. Born in Dublin in 1729, Burke is today seen as the father of modern conservatism for his passionate defence of the *ancien régime* during the French Revolution. Yet he can also be viewed as one of the first champions of corporate accountability, seeking to bring the East India Company to justice for its crimes thousands of miles away in India. Indeed, for Burke, there was a close connection between his two enduring campaigns. Like Marx half a century later, Burke regarded the corporation as a revolutionary institution, whose pursuit of market domination led it to overturn the rights of both princes and peasants. For Burke, this was something to be opposed, even in the face of impossible odds.

Author of *The Sublime and the Beautiful*, Burke was a rising star of the Whig faction in Parliament. Initially, Burke defended the Company, opposing the 1773 Regulating Act as an unjustified infringement of the Company's chartered status. But in the early 1780s, Burke became increasingly involved in the intense parliamentary scrutiny of Hastings' management of Bengal, authoring the Select Committee's Ninth Report. The conclusions were damning. India had been 'radically and irretrievably ruined' by the Company's 'continual Drain' of wealth – a phrase that would haunt the next 150 years of British presence in India. Burke exposed how the traditional 'commercial circle' which had ensured that trade between Britain and India brought mutual benefit was now broken. With the Company able to use Bengal's own fiscal resources to pay for its imports of Asian goods, the model of exchange had become simply 'intercourse for it is not Commerce'. Burke estimated that India was suffering 'what is tantamount to an Annual Plunder of its Manufactures and its Produce to the Value of Twelve hundred thousand Pounds'. In effect, India was being screwed.

The only solution to the crisis, argued Burke, was to re-establish the Company on a 'Bottom truly Commercial', dismantling the corporate state in Bengal and overhauling its systems of governance. Rather than acting as a restraint on executive malpractice in Bengal, the 'Negligence of the Court of Directors has kept pace with, and must naturally have quickened, the Growth of the Practices which they have condemned'. The unstable political situation in Parliament gave Burke the opportunity to put his analysis to work. In the summer of 1783, Burke's great political ally, Charles James Fox, formed a coalition government with Lord North and high on the agenda was a new piece of legislation to rein in the Company.

Drawing on the rich Whig tradition of legitimate resistance to tyrannical government, Burke argued that 'every description of commercial privilege [is] all in the strictest sense a trust, and it is of the very essence of every trust to be rendered accountable'.[14] Burke continued with a rhetorical flourish: he mused 'to whom then would I make the East India Company accountable? Why, to Parliament, to be sure.' For Burke, the only way to confront this impunity was to recast the Company's charter so that it became accountable once more.

Speaking to Parliament in defence of his India Bill in December 1783, Burke made a clear distinction between political and commercial rights. The 'Magna Charta is a charter to restrain power and to destroy monopoly'; but 'the East India charter is a charter to establish monopoly and to create power'. Burke believed that he had a strong case for making the Company and its executives accountable for their actions: 'they themselves are responsible – their body as a corporate body, themselves as individuals – and the whole body and train of their servants are responsible to the high justice of this kingdom'. The grant of a corporate charter carried with it intrinsic duties, according to Burke, since 'this nation never did give a power without imposing a proportionable degree of responsibility'.[15]

The India Bill framed by Burke aimed to enforce this accountability by replacing the Court of Directors with a body of seven commissioners appointed by Parliament. In effect, the Company would be decapitated, its shareholders remaining as nominal owners, but disenfranchised of any voice in the management of their assets. It is said that when Sir William James, one of the Company's oldest directors, read the bill, he died of shock. The Company's shares also suffered, falling some 13 per cent on the news of the bill.

But the Company was not going to give up without a fight. It marshalled the best propagandists of the day to warn of the concentration of patronage that the bill would place in Fox's hands. The directors also played on the king's deep personal hatred of Fox. Ultimately, this combination of City and Court was able to force Fox from office. William Pitt the Younger became prime minister, winning a devastating general election in March 1784. Pitt soon passed his own act for the 'Better Regulation of the Government' of India, giving the British state effective control over the Company, while leaving the directors with their powers of patronage.

Edmund Burke was not one to call an end to his pursuit of justice simply because of a lost election. What depressed Burke most was his belief that 'all the tyranny, robbery and destruction of mankind practised by the Company and their servants in the East is popular and pleasing to the country'.[16] Yet Burke was severely hampered by the poverty of legal instruments at his disposal to bring the Company's executives – notably Warren Hastings – to account. He could press for a parliamentary vote of censure – tried ineffectively against Clive in 1773 – or revive the ancient practice of impeachment. In an impeachment, the House of Commons first had to vote on the charges and then the House of Lords would sit as a court and decide the case. The flaws in such a process are obvious, with political loyalties rather than evidence or law likely to decide the matter.

Nevertheless, Burke chose this route, and in 1786 commenced the impeachment process against Hastings in the Commons. It is a testament to Burke's mastery of his brief that he managed to win majorities in the House for his charges. In all, twenty charges were laid against Hastings when the full trial opened on 13 February 1788 in Westminster Hall. In his four-day opening speech, Burke accused Hastings of 'high crimes and misdemeanours', and impeached him 'in the name of the people of India' and 'by virtue of the eternal laws of justice'. Burke and his legal team, which included the playwright/politician Richard Brinsley Sheridan, certainly had rhetoric on their side. In a memorable phrase, Sheridan portrayed the Company as combining 'the meanness of a pedlar and profligacy of pirates . . . wielding a truncheon with one hand, and picking a pocket with the other'.

This was all good knock-about stuff, but what made the trial so significant for the accountability of corporations was the principle upon which Burke based his case. For him, natural law meant that all humans should be accorded equal rights to justice, wherever they may be. He declared on the third day of the trial:

> The laws of morality are the same everywhere, and that there is no action which would pass for an act of extortion, of peculation, of bribery, and oppression in England, that is not an act of extortion, of peculation, of bribery, and oppression in Europe, Asia, Africa and the world over.[17]

Against the corrosive relativism that increasingly viewed India as an inferior land in which different standards of justice should be applied, Burke unfurled the standard of absolute values. 'I must do justice to the East,' he declared, for 'I assert that their morality is equal to ours.' Full of contempt for what he saw as Hastings' 'geographical morality', Burke denounced the view that 'the duties of men are not to be governed by their relations to the great governor of the universe, or by their relations to men, but by climates, degrees of longitude and latitude, parallels not of life but of latitudes', adding in a wonderful image 'as if, when you have crossed the equinoctial line, all the virtues die'.

Yet, for all the sophistication of this analysis and the extent of this verbal prowess, the prosecution case was a muddle and a mess. Even though the trial lasted a full seven years, the Lords sat for only 149 days, often for less than a few hours a day. To no one's surprise, Hastings was acquitted of all charges in April 1795. Many years later, Burke wrote to his young friend and literary executor, French Laurence, to communicate what he still valued in his long political and literary career. Known today for his conservative defence of social hierarchy during the French Revolution, Burke told Laurence that everything apart from his work to bring justice to India should be forgotten.

His outrage burning once more, Burke damned the way that the Company had turned its relations with India into 'nothing more than an opportunity of gratifying the lowest of their purposes, the lowest of their passions'. Unlike Macaulay, with his bitter scorn for all things Asian, Burke continued to argue for an ethical equality between East and West which had been violated through the Company's acquisition and subsequent oppression of India. In the process, Europe had incurred an enormous moral deficit. 'If ever Europe recovers its civilisation', Burke concluded, then his 'work will be useful'. And summoning his own generation and those to come to face the full reality of the East India Company, Burke calls out from the eighteenth century, 'Remember! Remember! Remember!'

'This imperious Company'

The Company's demise in 1874 ended the era of the chartered corporation. These leviathans of mercantilism were no longer suited to the new empire of free trade that Britain was establishing across the globe. Where the Company and other chartered companies had once married the functions of overseas sovereign and trader, these were now prised apart, with the Royal Navy taking up the role of commercial enforcer, as it had done in the Opium Wars. The decline of the slave trade had brought the end of the Royal Africa Company in 1821, and two years later, the ancient Levant Company was wound up.

Strangely enough, the South Sea Company that had caused such panic in 1721 had lingered on for another century and was closed only in 1853. The Hudson Bay Company continues to this day, but surrendered its territorial rights in 1869 for a future in retail. In parallel, the longstanding restrictions on corporate expansion were progressively removed, with the repeal of the 1721 Bubble Act in 1825 and the passing of the Joint Stock Act in 1844 allowing companies to be set up through simple registration. Finally, in 1862, a year after the demolition of East India House, the comprehensive Company Act was placed on the statute-book, swiftly followed by a stock-market bubble and the collapse of Overend, Gurney and Co., a major bank, in 1866.

The precise legal form embodied by the East India Company may have died, but its systems of administration and governance live on in the modern multinational. Its ability to match supply and demand over lengthy supply chains, whether of textiles or tea, proved to be one of the secrets of its enduring commercial success. In its twin 'golden ages', first in the 1670s and early 1680s and then in the 1720s and 1730s, the Company managed to bring bullion and growth to its host countries, offer the customer quality goods at a reasonable price, deliver regular dividends to its investors and provide welcome tax revenues for the state.

Yet, in each case, boom was not just followed by bust,

but also by a deliberate attempt to achieve unwarranted wealth and power. For Philip Francis, newly arrived as the public's champion in Bengal in the 1770s, instead of securing a 'moderate but permanent profit', the Company seemed hell-bent on producing 'immediate and excessive returns'. In fact, John Company's example shows us that open markets and corporations do not necessarily mix, and that economic diversity and enterprise are likely to flourish best where corporations are kept in check. According to Adam Smith, the East India Company highlighted the folly of allowing over-mighty corporations to dominate the economy, creating stock-market bubbles at home and oppression abroad. For Edmund Burke, the Company exposed the need to make corporations accountable – and thereby subservient – to the will of the people as expressed through Parliament. And his quest to impeach Hastings revealed the need for effective legal instruments to counter corporate impunity.

Much can be learned from the critique and campaigns launched by the Company's contemporaries to curb its excesses. But there is also one inspirational case where its victims not only exposed the Company's malpractice, but won their fight for compensation. As part of the Company's drive to establish commercial dominance in Bengal following Plassey, Clive's successor Harry Verelst eliminated competition from commercial rivals, and in 1768 summarily arrested and imprisoned four Armenian merchants: Gregore Cojamaul, Melcomb Phillip, Johannes Padre Rafael and Wuscan Estephan. After five months in jail, all four were released without charge or explanation. When they regained their freedom, they found that the commercial landscape had been turned upside down: all Armenian, English and Portuguese merchants were prohibited from operating in Bengal's internal markets.

In an extraordinary move, two of the four – Cojamaul and Rafael – sailed all the way to England to seek redress. First, the two petitioned the Company's directors, complaining of the 'cruel and inhuman' manner in which they had been treated. Next, they appeared before Parliament to tell their story before the Select Committee investigating the Company. When all this failed to move the Company to voluntary recompense, the Armenians turned to the courts seeking civil damages from Verelst. Amazingly, in December 1774 a jury at the Guildhall found Verelst guilty of 'oppression, false imprisonment and singular depredations'. In spite of a retrial, Verelst was ordered to pay £9,700 – over £800,000 in today's money – plus the Armenians' legal costs. Verelst died in exile in Paris, while the Armenians sailed back to India never to be heard of again. Thousands of miles away from the scene of the crime, the principle of extraterritorial liability for corporate malpractice had been established in 1770s London.

The East India Company's story is ultimately a warning, a tale of an institution that generated great wealth, but also great harm, an institution that was ultimately doomed by the flaws in its own corporate design. For its contemporaries, it generated great passion and fear as well as awe. As the Company rose to a position of unbridled power after Plassey, the *Gentleman's Magazine* concluded in April 1767 that the issue at stake was 'whether the freedom or the slavery of this island shall result'. Its remedy for 'this imperious company of merchants' was to cry out 'down with this rump of unconstitutional power, the East India Company!'[18]

Across London, the Company's immense physical presence has been largely erased from the docks and the City where it once ruled. However, in the more glamorous West End, an Indian entrepreneur has just relaunched the

East India Company as an outlet for luxury teas, coffee and chocolates, with a store in Mayfair. As its website proclaims:

> We're pioneers, inventors, explorers and dreamers.
> We're honourable merchants.
> We're The East India Company.
> Reborn and renewed.
> A company re-invented for today.[19]

CHAPTER 2

BARCLAYS (1690): THE EUTHANASIA OF CAPTAIN MAINWARING

[Bankers] have pleasant voices, but you do not catch what they say, and all that is expected of you is to bow when they have completed a sentence.

J.M. Barrie, 'How I joined Barclays bank', 1931

The modern financial services industry is a utility attached to a casino.

Professor John Kay, *Prospect*, 2009

The Great Fire of London in 1666 turned the matchwood, half-timbered houses of London's Lombard Street into ashes. In its place, where the medieval goldsmiths from Lombardy had first set up their tables, a new street of brick and stone sprang up over a decade or so, and the bankers were back. Among them in the 1680s, under the sign of the Bolt and Tun, was a prosperous banker called Job Bolton.

Bolton, like so many of his profession, was an outsider from the establishment: he was a Quaker. He could hold no public office. He was barred from the army, navy and universities. His fellow Quakers were a persecuted minority, especially in Gloucestershire, where a number of them were languishing in prison. Bolton, as a senior Quaker, was particularly concerned about them. He therefore made his way west out of London to Rickmansworth, now a London suburb, then a wealthy village within reach of the metropolis, and also the country seat of the bishop of Gloucester, to plead for some of those who had been imprisoned for their beliefs.

Here we get some inkling, first why Quakers so irritated the establishment with their rigid Puritanism, and second why that rigidity gave them such an advantage as bankers. Because Quakers remove their hats for no man, Bolton immediately torpedoed his cause by refusing to take off his broad-brimmed Quaker hat. The bishop was so furious at this slight that he stormed across, grabbed it from Bolton's head and flung it across the room. You did not have to be a Quaker to want a man so principled and so rigid to manage your financial affairs.

If you had financial affairs in the 1680s, you did need somebody with a cool head, even if it was covered with a wide-brimmed hat. The nation was all but bankrupt. The merchants of the City of London had been the cheerleaders of the so-called Glorious Revolution in 1688 which had catapulted the Catholic James II from the throne in favour of his daughter Mary and Dutch protestant son-in-law William, restored the privileges of the City and upheld the privileges of the Church of England.

As those momentous events were still echoing around, Bolton's apprentice, a twenty-one-year-old called John Freame who was the son of a textile merchant from Cirencester, came to the end of his term under Bolton's tutelage, became a freeman of the City of London and set up shop himself as a goldsmith in Lombard Street. It was 1690. Freame was also a Quaker, and as such could have been in two minds about the new regime. As a non-conformist he might have supported James II's policy of equality for all religions before the law – the main reason for his removal – but as a Quaker, he might also have deplored James' Catholicism. But Freame knew which side his bread was buttered and William and Mary were prepared to give the financiers what they wanted.

Still, it was a time to keep your head down, to marvel at the new Bank of England which would create the national debt to pay for William's continental war, and to make your reputation dealing in jewels and coins and broking bills. This is exactly what Freame did, along with his partner Thomas Gould, and their partnership under the sign of the three anchors formed the basis of the company that became Barclays Bank, for some time the biggest, and later the most profitable, bank in the world. For the next three centuries (until 2005), Lombard Street would also be their headquarters address.

Gould came from Kent and seems to have been a relative of Bolton. Like Freame, he was – apart from the handicap of being a Quaker in an Anglican world – very well off. You had to be to set up as a banker. You needed capital and a supportive, well-connected family. The complexity of Freame's family in the generations that followed would provide his bank with not one family that dominated its management, but a whole series of inter-connected cousins and marriages, which would provide Barclays with its chiefs right up until the present day.

Freame began this complex set of alliances in 1697 by marrying Gould's sister Priscilla. Gould in turn married Freame's sister Hannah (this is not the only example of men marrying each other's sisters in this book). Both families lived above the shop until they were successful enough to have houses in the country. Even then, they lived next door to each other in Enfield and set off to town together by horse along Green Lanes to get to work on the morning commute.

By then the powerful London Quaker meetings were depositing their money with Freame and Gould. These were respectable men with enough leisure time in the great days of the early eighteenth century to write, as Freame did, a book of instruction for children warning them to 'be sensible of the ill consequences of vice and immorality'.[1] You get the overwhelming sense that Freame had something more than the usual Quaker horror of vice.

Their bank financed the Welsh Copper Company and the London Lead Company, and lost a packet shipping goods to North Carolina and bringing back Virginia tobacco when their ship was captured by French privateers and had to be ransomed.[2] In fact, Freame went on to rescue the London Lead Company, which was threatened by fraud after the South Sea Bubble, and handed over the bank to his son Joseph.

Joseph was not joined at the head of the business by Thomas Gould's son (also called Thomas), who had used his inheritance to set up his own business in Cornhill, speculated in the shares of the London Lead Company and went bankrupt. But going bankrupt was the great Quaker sin: it was the ultimate betrayal of your word. His mother paid his debts, cut him off and a generation or so later, his descendants were living in poverty in the East End. A sad story of banking folk.

Meanwhile, Joseph Freame bought a building, 54 Lombard Street, from a scrivener who used the sign of the Black Eagle. Freame adopted this for his own bank, now called Joseph Freame & Co., and it has been there ever since. He also took on a new partner from an eminent Scottish Quaker family, called Thomas Barclay. The Freame and Barclay family trees then became hopelessly jumbled, for which some explanation is required even if we don't have to remember too many of the details. Thomas' son David Barclay married John Freame's daughter Priscilla. David's son by a previous marriage, James Barclay, married Priscilla's youngest sister Sarah, who became both his sister-in-law and his daughter-in-law simultaneously. With us so far? The only explanation of all this intermarriage is that the pool of potential rich Quaker suitors was very small indeed.

By 1745, when Bonnie Prince Charlie was marching south and when the first John Freame died, the intricate links between the Barclay and Freame families included some very wealthy individuals indeed. Joseph Freame and Thomas Barclay were pioneers in the business of discounting bills sent by provincial bankers to London – taking the surplus savings from the country banks and lending them to the areas which needed money for investment. This was the model which financed the Industrial Revolution, still a generation away. David Barclay meanwhile had made such a success out of his linen drapery in Cheapside, exporting linen from America and the West Indies, that he was now one of the most successful merchants in London.

There was a major hiccup in the family progression in 1766, which explains how the bank became Barclays and not Freames. Both James Barclay and Joseph Freame died in the same week, leaving Joseph's insipid son John Freame in charge. He bought a farm in Norfolk and wandered around Europe in search of a cure (it was never quite clear what for). And here we plunge into the complex Barclays genealogy for the last time, we promise: young John Freame married his widowed Quaker cousin Christina Gurney, the daughter of David and Priscilla Barclay and, when Young John died two years later, his son Joseph moved with his mother to Bath, leaving the Barclays in charge of the bank.

Also marrying into the family were the Welsh Quaker Silvanus Bevan, and the Wandsworth brewer's son John Tritton. Tritton was a partner in the bankrupt bank next door in Lombard Street, which should have ruled him out as a husband for the Quaker Mary Barclay. However, Tritton had proved to be more upright, and perhaps more elusively romantic, in his response to the disaster. 'I would rather lean on John Tritton's arm than ride in a coach and four,' said Mary in 1782, so the marriage went ahead.

So it was that, by the end of the eighteenth century, the bank was called – after various permutations – Barclay, Bevan, Tritton & Co. By the 1980s, two centuries later, the board still included a Barclay, a Bevan, a Tritton, a Tuke (another offshoot) and a Gurney.[3] Mary may not have been right about Tritton's elusively romantic nature: he became the very model of an upright, not to say uptight Quaker, who 'lived in the entire subjection of his natural temperament and passion', according to one contemporary.[4] Such was the downside of marrying a Quaker banker.

As the combined families became more affluent, some of these Quaker principles began to wear a little thin. George II and Queen Charlotte chose to watch the 1761 Lord Mayor's Parade through London from David Barclay's balcony in Cheapside. Distant relatives joked about the compromises that the family was prepared to make to their accustomed Quaker plainness for the occasion. It already seemed a long way from the days, nearly a century before, when soldiers had locked the doors of the local Quaker meeting house, forcing Bolton, Freame and their colleagues to meet outside in weather so cold that the Thames had frozen for three months.

They still wrestled with their consciences as Quaker bankers. Refusing to pay tithes was one thing, but it often made sense just to leave the money where the bailiff could find it. But they would not let their ships carry guns, a risk in the pirate-infested waters of the Caribbean. They refused military and war finance, the source of so much profit among their rivals in the Rothschild and Baring families. They refused even to prosecute their employees for fraud, in case they were hanged, even though they might then be accused themselves of compounding a felony. Nor could they marry outside the Quaker circle. But most of all, in those very early beginnings of the campaign against the slave trade, they would not finance slavery.

Barclays' precise involvement with slavery has remained an issue until the present day, but it was always bound to be complicated. David Barclay the Younger foreclosed on a debt in Jamaica in 1774 and found himself the unhappy owner of thirty-two slaves. The local agent refused to release them, so Barclay shipped them to Philadelphia and freed them there. It was hard, being a banker, not to face some compromises, even if it was only holding the accounts of people who did transport or own slaves. What could you do? – or so they reasoned.

But if being a successful Quaker banker had its difficulties, there were also advantages. There was the broadening network of information from other Quakers, especially from the Quaker communities in Pennsylvania. It also meant some protection during panics and bank runs. Liquidity was available from the various Quaker cousins and their banks, such as the Gurneys in Norwich or Backhouses in Darlington.

Joint stock banks were illegal until 1826, so these family partnerships provided the mainstay of English banking until after the Industrial Revolution. The Barclays and their cousins were among those financing the Stockton to Darlington Railway, Battersea Bridge, Regent's Canal and other great engineering projects, but always in partnership with other cousins. For two centuries, the inter-connected Quaker banking families enjoyed their busy but comfortable lives, commuting to Lombard Street by coach, exercising razor-sharp judgement, spreading information ('If in, get out; if out, stay out,' said one message), plus a little riding to hounds. It was a gentle life.

Yet throughout the nineteenth century, the Quakers were in decline, and not least in Barclay, Bevan, Tritton & Co. By 1850, their Gracechurch Street Quaker meeting house was empty, used by clerks as a temporary office, with the bank ledgers kept in the galleries. David Barclay the Younger had died in 1809. His grandson, Hudson Gurney, married back into the Barclay family – the snobbish Margaret Barclay – and stopped banking when he was fifty-seven to devote himself to society and collecting books. He became an Anglican.

There were also family strains. Overend, Gurney & Co. were by then the biggest dealers in bills in Europe, and their Quaker zeal had become a little rusty. They tried to organize a disastrous run on the Bank of England in 1860 and made a series of dubious and probably fraudulent loans. On 10 May 1866, known as Black Friday – it is amazing how many 'black' days the City of London has endured during its history – rumours began to spread that they were insolvent. The rumours grew until Overend Gurney stopped payments. They were prosecuted by an Irish lawyer called Edward Kenealy, acquitted of fraud, but left the court – horror of horrors – bankrupt. Their Barclay cousins refused to bail them out. Robert Bevan, by now a Conservative-voting Anglican, married to the daughter of the bishop of Chichester, urged the Bank of England not to try any kind of rescue.

By now the Barclays partnership was the most profitable bank in the country, with a new office building in Lombard

Street in Portland stone, and hundreds of staff writing out the ledgers in ink every night and operating the electric telegraph that was beginning to replace the personal links that had made banking such a matter of personal judgement. Communications tools like this meant that decisions became more about rules, rather than relationships. It meant that partners could increasingly delegate to junior staff and go hunting. It was the beginning of the old tradition about banking which dubbed it 'three-six-three': borrowing at 3 per cent, lending at 6 per cent, on the golf course by 3 p.m.

Yet change was in the air. The new joint stock banks could issue shares and were now big enough to buy up any struggling family partnerships they found. The Scottish banks were opening branches across northern England. It was the beginning of the theme that would dominate Barclays for the next century or more: how could they deal with the competition without getting like them? How could they stay personal and local and yet be big enough to see off the opposition?

By the final years of Queen Victoria's reign, the bank was already growing fast enough to expand its name: it was called Barclay, Bevan, Tritton, Ransom, Bouverie & Co. – known in the City as the 'long firm'. In 1896, they persuaded nine smaller banks to join them, mainly in the east and north, in a major enterprise to secure Barclays for the future. The banks that joined them included now forgotten names like Molineau, Whitfield & Co. in Lewes, Woodhall, Hebden & Co. in Scarborough, and – strangely – the Anglo-Catholic Goslings and Sharpe in London. Together, the new bank would have a total of seventy-one partners, 190 branches and a share capital of £5 million.

This was also intended as an answer to the question about keeping up with the vigorous new competition: the new bank would hold a quarter of all the deposits in the private banking sector. Barclay & Co. was a big fish, under the quiet chairmanship of Robert Bevan's son Francis, and would operate on the principle of local diversity, with the local boards still in existence, with their local knowledge and decision-making power: 'Local management will remain in the same hands as heretofore, the private character of the Banks being thus preserved.'[5]

It was a unique arrangement – a merger which kept the local flavour and knowledge in place, a compromise with the future, preserving its own aristocracy in London, but with local gentry in the form of the local directors. It was a very English kind of bank.

The great banking cull

Francis Bevan might not have had the drive of his ambitious father. He might not have had the radical reforming zest of Edward Holden at his rivals, Midland Bank. But it was a period of enormous change for banking in Britain, as the new middle classes flocked to open accounts, and the local banks which had served their forefathers disappeared month by month into the corporate beasts of the City of London. During this time, Bevan had one attribute which gave him an advantage over his rivals: his sheer dullness.

Not that he was humourless as a person. Quite the reverse. He was always easy-going and he boasted a grand walrus moustache, turned up at the ends to indicate joviality. But when Bevan was chairman, retreating at regular intervals to his family home in Trent Park, Enfield, the Edwardian middle classes knew that he would never surprise them. They knew they could expect nothing pushy and imaginative, nothing clever or rash or decisive, nothing bold, and they loved him for it. That was the kind of place they wanted to keep their money. Nothing faddish or ambitious. It felt, in other words, entirely safe, like the great granite portals of one of Barclays' burgeoning branches.

There were more and more of these. By the outbreak of the First World War, the new bank had doubled its branches, mainly by the most frenetic merger activity, starting straightaway in their first year with the Newcastle bank, Woods & Co. The biggest takeover was the Consolidated Bank of Cornwall in 1905, itself a recent merger of family banks. The most dramatic was the United Counties Bank, giving Barclays a major presence across the Midlands. Its most controversial was J. and J.W. Pease, an old Quaker bank in Darlington, which turned out to be insolvent. Bevan went ahead with the takeover but refused to accept the liabilities. Old Sir Joseph Pease was left relying on a guarantee fund, which in turn relied on the personal generosity of some of the national directors of Barclays.

In 1902, Barclays was quoted on the stock exchange, its shares divided into 'A' and 'B' shares – 'A's for the sons of a family, with extra risk and extra returns; 'B's just earning a basic risk-free income, intended for the daughters to inherit. Barclays still regarded itself as a complicated family enterprise. A and B shares survived until well into the twentieth century.

When Bevan stepped down, during the First World War, Barclays had quadrupled in value and was the thirty-eighth most valuable company in Britain. Barclays' history has been one of the banking aristocracy, effortlessly inheriting, while the outsiders behind it drove the business of real change. And so it was in the first decades of the new company. Behind safe, conservative Bevan was a thrusting modernizer, Frederick Goodenough, a serious outsider – born in Calcutta, educated at Zurich University, and recruited as the company secretary in 1896.

By 1903, Goodenough was general manager and when questions arose which made the inter-related directors uncomfortable, they were more than happy to leave the answers to him. By 1916, when Bevan retired, Goodenough towered over everybody else, knew everything – family skeletons and all – and he was the obvious choice as successor. Behind Bevan, Goodenough had been managing the mergers, and once he was safely in the chair – he was even known as 'chairman' in his own home – there was no stopping him. A staggering twenty-seven banks were snapped up by Goodenough by the end of the decade.

By 1918, even the government was worried about this merger mania and appointed a committee of inquiry which urged it to legislate immediately. Being the British government, trained in the art of taking no action for decades at a time, it never quite got round to it, and agreed to drop the idea of anti-trust legislation – which was bitterly opposed by the banks – on condition that there would be no more mergers between the big ones, and any others should be submitted to the Treasury and Bank of England for approval.

Desperate to get under the wire, Goodenough just had time to snap up the massive 601 branches of the London, Provincial and Western Bank. By 1920, he had 11,000 clerks, ten times the branch network Barclays had when Goodenough joined in 1896 – a massive 1,783 branches – and an increasing presence in the suburbs where the wealthier tradesmen were encouraged to open accounts, despite the murmurs of disapproval from the more snobbish banking directors. There were now five big banks left standing, Midland, Westminster, Lloyds, Barclays and National Provincial. It was already the most concentrated banking infrastructure in the world. Six-sevenths of British banks had disappeared during the half century to 1920.[6]

The orgy of consolidation had also provided Goodenough with a bitter rival. The London, Provincial and Western's aggressive chief Sir Herbert Hamling, now vice chairman of Barclays, set up court in his old headquarters in Fenchurch Street and began plotting and intriguing against Goodenough, or so he believed.

There was space for this kind of thing now. The Big Five were protected by their own new oligarchy, which was smiled on by the Bank of England because it looked strong. In a conservative industry, Barclays was the most conservative of all, each branch filled with young men in starched collars and black coats who would never find promotion, writing laboriously in ink the entries in their daily ledgers. It was a world where the informal rules against employing left-handed people – presumably because they might smudge the ink – were made formal in 1929. It was a world where the important jobs locally and nationally were all given to sons and nephews of the directors. Where women were dismissed when they got married. Where board minutes were still written by hand. Where ledger clerks were issued with special ink designed to clog any new fountain pens, of which the aristocracy deeply disapproved, almost as much as adding machines, which were used 'experimentally' for nearly two decades from 1914. In Manchester, they were still transferring cash across the city using the last horse-drawn cab as late as 1940. It was a world where, once you were employed at Barclays, no other bank would ever give you a job: it was considered bad form for the Big Five to employ each other's staff.

Barclays was conservative also in its attitude to money, believing in the lost gold standard for moral reasons – that it was wrong to pay debts in money which was worth less than it was when the loans were agreed. Goodenough therefore agreed with the disastrous decision of the Chancellor of the Exchequer Winston Churchill in 1925, egged on by the Bank of England governor Montagu Norman, to return to the gold standard at the pre-war rate of $4.87, the decision which almost led to national bankruptcy in 1931.

Except for that flutter of sound money, Barclays was also staggeringly cautious. It had local directors who could provide some local knowledge about small businesses and loans, but it had no technical knowledge to help it work out the significance of new technologies. It understood very little about the kind of risks that small businesses represented, and where it could lend, especially when the nation was plunging into the Great Depression. William Morris, the motor car manufacturer, faced an uphill task persuading Goodenough, via the local Barclays affiliate in Oxford, to keep his overdraft facility in place until he had been paid for the cars he had exported. He only just succeeded, but failed to persuade him to offer hire purchase through the branches to buy cars.

The Macmillan Committee, set up in 1931 with a starring role for John Maynard Keynes, found there was a serious gap for smaller companies needing long-term finance below the threshold of a stock market issue. The banks were certainly not helping, regarding that as the responsibility of the investment banks, which barely existed. As a result, Barclays' massive fund set aside for bad debts in the Depression had barely been touched. There were two possible explanations for this: one was that they were so skilled in assessing loans that they got it right every time. The other, much more likely, was that they were actually taking no risks at all. Barclays lent to small business, using the contacts and knowledge of the local directors, but only to the dead certs. They did not really regard the fledgling enterprise economy, and the new technologies behind it, as their problem.

Give the Bank of England their due. As many as 5,000 banks in the USA shut their doors in early March 1933 as Franklin D. Roosevelt was inaugurated. Not so in England, where they were carefully protected by the semi-monopoly and the high interest rates they were able to charge as a result. On the other hand, was there any point in these protected rates given that they were hardly oiling the wheels of the economy at all?

The Macmillan Committee gave Barclays and the other members of the Big Five a thorough jolt, and involved them in a joint venture to finance new business. They gave in to Bank of England pressure that they should help reorganize the steel and cotton industries. They began to lend money at lower rates to the special areas designated in 1934, mainly to German refugees because – or so they said – there was so little demand.

And here we find ourselves at the heart of the great mystery about British banking. The banks have little interest, traditionally, in technology or industry. The idea of backing innovation bothers them if the outcome is less than certain, and when is that not the case? But the enterprising individuals of the nation instinctively shun them in any case, perhaps because they were deliberately forbidding – the pen on the end of a chain, next to a grille (then), or (now) the impersonal international call centre with software which might possibly include the answer to your query.

Other countries have banks that thrive on backing regional industries and support them through the long term, some becoming involved in joint ventures with regional government. However the trick has been managed, the Germans and Dutch have been able to finance their industry in a way that the British have not, at least in the inter-war years. But then, the customer pool was much smaller then. A century ago there were about 200 million pledges to pawnbrokers to raise money every year, and only 10 million savings accounts in banks.[7] The affluent working classes used post office accounts, not banks. As a result, the banks were facing increasing competition from before the Second World War from the new sectors catering to the working classes: hire purchase companies and building societies.

Goodenough confirmed many people's fears when he gave evidence to the Macmillan Committee, explaining that the banking cartel meant they were not forced to 'take too great risks'.[8] Sure enough, when the United States Federal Reserve quite wrongly reported in 1932 that Barclays was close to collapse – it was then the biggest bank in the world – their weight of reputation allowed them to avoid a panic. Their sheer dullness had saved them.

The new aristocracy

Montagu Norman bestrode the British economy between the wars. In two decades as governor of the Bank of England, wearing his distinctive wide hat and cloak, he dominated politicians and bankers alike. He was a patient of the pioneering therapist Carl Jung, who believed he was insane. He was also colourful enough to be blamed by conspiracy theorists for personally causing the Great Depression, thanks to a secret agreement with Benjamin Strong of the Federal Reserve, stitched up in mid-Atlantic by Norman travelling under the alias of Mr Skinner. The story is probably too good to be true, but Norman certainly believed with every fibre of his being in the moral authority of the gold standard, and consulted Goodenough – who agreed with him – on a political strategy to return the pound to what he saw as its rightful place as the guarantor of global stability. But he would not be crossed, and he thoroughly disapproved of Goodenough's policy of global expansion.

Barclays had bought banks in Antwerp, Cologne and Rome after the First World War and they had been thoroughly loss-making (its only foreign subsidiary before had been the British Army's bankers on the Western Front). Goodenough was a bitter opponent of American economic power and he looked instead to the British Empire, then in its dying days covering a quarter of the earth, with its potential to provide safe, global trade between its dominions (a doctrine known as 'imperial preference'). He bought the Anglo-Egyptian Bank, hoping it would help finance raw cotton imports to help the Linen Bank that Barclays had just bought in Manchester. He also had good relations with the South African leader Jan Smuts and, when the National Bank of South Africa ran into trouble in 1925, Goodenough snapped it up too. Then he merged the whole caboodle into a new company, Barclays Bank (Dominion, Colonial and Overseas), known as Barclays DCO.

Barclays DCO, or Barclays International as it became, was an extraordinary mixture, a cross between a bank and a branch of the diplomatic corps, with a dash of modern international charity about it. This was the one remaining corner of Barclays where the old Quaker values remained intact, and it was always a source of deep suspicion back home, where the traditional bank managers – those stiff and upright people immortalized by the role of Captain Mainwaring in the TV series *Dad's Army* – looked askance at any Barclays banker who claimed they had to ignore their precious operating handbook. It was a widening rift that never really healed and left the Barclays branches around the world doling out car loans and financing local businesses while Citibank and Chase Manhattan were making use of their much smaller international networks to do global mega-deals.

Barclays DCO was a massive operation: it gave the Barclays group more branches around the world than all the American banks put together. It experimented with financing intermediate technology. It also managed to hold together in the most bizarre circumstances. Two managers were shot by rioters. Many more were rescued from angry mobs. Some of them resorted to issuing their own cash. One new portable bank in Nigeria was stolen by a disgruntled employee, lock, stock and safe deposit box.

The ambition to make a difference in racially divided South Africa would eventually give Barclays the biggest political headache in its three-century history, but that is to leap ahead in the story. The one person the creation of Barclay's DCO absolutely enraged was Montagu Norman, who was fearful that overseas links would undermine the bank just when his favoured Big Five needed to be strong enough to withstand the coming economic meltdown. Norman did his best to torpedo Goodenough's lobbying efforts to get the proposed mergers through Parliament, and when he failed he did the only thing he could do. He closed the Barclays DCO account at the Bank of England. It stayed shut for two decades.

When Goodenough died in 1934, the bitter row was still going on. One commentator who happened to see Norman getting out of a car at his funeral service said the governor was probably just checking that Goodenough was really dead. In fact, Norman knew what he was doing: he was getting out of a car belonging to the Tuke family – another of the great Barclays aristocracies – knowing that they were about to inherit.

The Bevan family were by then temporarily out of the picture. Francis Bevan's fourth son, the arrogant and untrustworthy Gerard, had left Barclays, bought the City Equitable Insurance Company, speculated with their money, lost it and then turned to fraud to cover it up. When he was confronted by the other directors, he fled, owing Barclays £240,000, and was arrested in Vienna. At the end of his seven-year prison sentence, he thanked the prison governor 'as one Old Etonian to another'.[9]

So it was that William Tuke took over in 1934, handing over to a former Birmingham local director Edwin Fisher to take the company through the trauma of the Second World War. Tuke and Fisher were less autocratic than Goodenough, but if Goodenough had managed to defy the clear wishes of the Bank of England, the war years would do away with that kind of independence for good.

Wartime posed peculiar risks for banks. They were told to shift their banking operations out of London, in case of invasion, and Barclays moved its backroom operations to Staffordshire. Every branch also had to send a duplicate of the day's transactions to another branch every night in case they were bombed. As many as thirty-six Barclays branches were destroyed by bombing, though the Lombard Street headquarters was barely scratched, even though a third of the buildings in the City of London were flattened. This infuriated the directors who had had wanted to demolish it in 1939 and hoped for an excuse to build something spanking new.

But the biggest change was what the banks saw as the insidious embrace of the state. They had become used to doing what they were told by Montagu Norman in return for being protected from too much competition. Now the banking industry became an unofficial arm of the government, lending three times as much to them as they did to their own business customers. Barclays and the others paid only 1 per cent interest on savings accounts and lent them on to the government at a small mark-up. It was a guaranteed profit, and – unless the Nazis arrived – a safe investment. When Keynes was asked what he thought of Labour plans to nationalize the banks, he said he thought they had already been nationalized.

The financial authorities had been terrified of a repeat of the inflation which dogged the country during and after the First World War. Keynes had set out one solution, which rather oddly appeared first in the German newspapers in the first weeks of the war: compulsory savings. But it was still important not to create too much money to slosh around the economy. Prices were kept down by rationing and agreements with the trade unions, and it was made known to the banks that they were not really expected to lend much money to businesses, unless it was somehow in the national interests.

The war finished, Hitler had died, but nothing changed for the banks. They were still expected to control their lending, and there was another nasty surprise. When the Bank of England was nationalized in 1946 there was an obscure clause which said that the governor might 'issue directions to any banker'.

This was another very British compromise. The Bank of England could determine interest rates. That was their function. Otherwise, the banks were independent, but maintained in that independence by a cartel which protected them from competition, and allowed them to agree not to waste money on advertising to steal customers from each other. They were even independent of the Bank of England. The governor had powers, but of course he would never do anything so brutal as to use them. But he might raise an eyebrow occasionally to remind them who was boss. It used to be said that the banks were ruled by the eyebrows of the governor of the Bank of England.

It was only in 1958 that the eyebrows finally allowed the banks to start lending as much as they wanted. It was the era of washing machines and 'you've never had it so good'; the result was a balance of payments problem which caused a frightening economic boom and scared the financial establishment. This was the story of post-war Britain: boom, bust and the occasional peep at a different kind of world, only to dash back under the bedclothes, fearful of the implications.

Even so, the boom lasted just long enough to give the aristocratic Barclays directors the confidence finally to demolish their Lombard Street offices and build a new one, complete with squash court and rifle range in the basement. By 1962, it was already a year behind schedule and £1 million over budget. Why is it always like that?

The rifle range was not really an aberration. That was the kind of bank Barclays was: it recruited gentlemen steeped in banking, from Winchester or the Brigade of Guards, but prepared to pop home at the weekends for a spot of hunting. It was so old-fashioned that the Gurney family still took their hounds into the office with them in Norwich. As late as the 1930s, the Newcastle branch had let in livestock men on market days to send their dogs down the trapdoor looking for rats. One local director in York famously carried on attending meetings until he was ninety-seven.

It was still a cosy regulated life. Barclays still paid no interest on current accounts. It still fought shy of lending to anything in the least risky, which included anything too technical to understand. From 1945–62, the money set aside for writing off bad debts was only 0.1 per cent.[10] Apart from the money the government wrung out of it for the motor and aircraft and nuclear industries, Barclays was still using little or no imagination when it came to lending. These were the great days of Captain Mainwaring:

reassuringly dull, unexciting and absolutely reliable. It was all very English, and – given that they employed almost no graduates – a little anti-intellectual.

When Edwin Fisher died in 1947, while he was at Buckingham Palace, his next five successors were all from the great Barclays families, who were known in the bank as the 'uncles'. The uncles included Goodenough's son William, who exhausted himself and retired at the age of fifty-one because of ill-health. He was succeeded by another Tuke: Anthony Tuke was shy, formidable, conservative and terrifying. He was known as the 'Iron Tuke'. 'Frightened of me?' he said about one employee. 'Nobody has ever been frightened of me.'[11] The Iron Tuke and his colleagues regarded progress, as Anthony Sampson put it, as something 'rather vulgar and regrettable'.[12]

It was still an enchanted world, especially for the uncles. They called each other by their first names and called their general managers by their surnames. It was a privileged world in more than one way: banks were allowed, in effect, to keep their profits and other financial details secret. But it was all about to change. The secrecy about their profits ended in 1970. The new Conservative government that year under Edward Heath began again to risk loosening the restraints. In the wider world, the inconvenient half-truth that the dollar was based on gold was about to be abandoned by Richard Nixon and the various currencies of the world began to float freely in value against each other, rather than against the value of gold. Aggressive American banks began appearing in London seeking whom they could devour. The regulations about liquidity ratios – how much of the money deposited with the bank they had to keep available (30 per cent in 1960) – were being relaxed, which meant there was a very great deal more money available to lend. Even the weekly meetings with the governor of the Bank of England began to dwindle to monthly. It was a new world, but at first it was not very clear how new.

The first sign was the way that commentators began to turn on the bankers. When it was revealed in 1980 that Barclays was the most profitable bank in the world, the *Economist* also mentioned that they 'are not very much liked'. 'Something is seriously wrong with Britain's retail banking system,' it said. 'It is class-based, diverse and sleepy . . . badly in need of a shake up.'[13] What was happening to good old British respect?

Going global

The first result of the change in monetary policy was the so-called Barber Boom, the massive expansion of credit, and the secondary banking crisis, which ended with more controls at the end of 1972. A year later, interest rates had shot up to 13 per cent, by which time Barclays had lent heavily to help the Bank of England stave off a run on the banks and had led the bail-out for Cedar Holdings in an eighteen-hour meeting at the Bank of England.

Fearful of the new American giants, Barclays launched a whole new round of banking mergers by snapping up the last of the independents, the ancient Liverpool-based Martins Bank with over 700 branches. Barclays cleverly secured a deal with the Bank of England whereby Westminster could take over National Provincial (creating NatWest) and both deals would not even be referred to the Monopolies and Mergers Commission. The Big Four were now in place and would remain so until the disasters of 2008 began to unfold.

Barclays also oversaw some radical diversification, as the uncles finally woke up to the non-banking competition around them, setting up their own insurance company and buying unit trusts, but in the great tradition of the British establishment, they stayed suspicious of competition. Chairman Sir John Thomson said, 'Without being a traitor to private enterprise, we can admit that competition can sometimes lead one to act against one's better judgement.'[14]

The architects of the big changes inside Barclays were not uncles at all, but outsiders: Derek Wild, who had joined the bank at the age of sixteen and risen to become Thomson's general manager, and Deryk Vander Weyer, a former Indian Army officer who came in to run the new marketing department. Wild and Weyer between them made Barclays the most innovative bank in Britain, using a mixture of marketing and technology. Their 'robot cashiers', the first cash dispensers, were based on an idea the managing director of De La Rue Instruments, John Shepherd-Barron, had in the bath. He telephoned Wild who arrived the next day in a limousine and bought into the idea immediately. The first 'hole in the wall' appeared in 1967 at the Enfield branch.

By then Wild had already seen the first Bank of America credit cards, which had been famously test-mailed to every household in Fresno, California. Barclays launched their own Barclaycard in 1966, backed by Weyer's first massive advertising campaign and Barclay's first massive direct mailshot, distributing the cards unsolicited to 1.5 million likely customers. There were not enough envelopes the right size in the whole of the UK and more had to be brought in from Germany.

A third of those with Barclaycards were customers of other banks. Real competition had arrived, and if you could go into debt immediately using a Barclaycard, why would you need those delicate negotiations with a bank manager?

In the early 1970s, only two-fifths of the population had bank accounts; by the late 1980s it was two-thirds. Britain had gone from the lowest personal debt in Europe to the highest.[15] It was the first nail in the coffin of bank managers like Captain Mainwaring, upright, stuffy, dull and incorruptible.

There was also a flurry of consultancy. Urwick Orr management consultants recommended a whole new structure, finally getting rid of the local boards and directors and local independence for Barclays branches. Barclays DCO became the subsidiary, Barclays International. The brands guru Wolff Olins urged Barclays to get rid of the eagle symbol and change its blue to a lighter shade. The story that he wore a pink suit for the presentation is apparently not true, but for the effect of his presentation, he might as well have done. He told the old Barclays aristocrats that he wanted Barclays 'to be regarded as a financial supermarket'.[16]

When Thomson handed over to the next Tuke in line, the son and grandson of previous chairmen, Barclays was already becoming a different animal. It was fearful, as ever, of the prospects of another Labour government, but it was still comfortable in its old certainties. The main source of discomfort was the embarrassing business of Barclays' continued presence in apartheid South Africa. The argument that they were there to make a difference meant confrontation with the growing transatlantic campaign – beginning with the American churches – to disinvest to force political change. Barclays argued that it had bucked the system already by paying equal pay for equal work, but a House of Commons committee in 1973 found that actually nearly all their 1,600 black workers were cleaners.

The argument began to unravel seriously by 1977 with the murder of Steve Biko and the invasion of Mozambique, especially when it was clear that the Barclays National

Bank of South Africa had bought South African defence bonds. Barclays struggled to respond, but there were more embarrassments to come.

The real pinch point was in the universities, where Barclays became a symbol of African oppression. Their share of the vital student market had fallen to just 17 per cent by 1985, the year that Oxfam withdrew their account. The following year, Barclays caved in, forced into the worst of all worlds. They sold the South African bank at a massive loss at £80 million, and sold it to powerful white South African interests too. By the time Nelson Mandela was president, it was worth £350 million.

The Conservative government was furious. In the event, as always, the previous Labour government had been a pussy cat compared to the aggressive revolution imposed on the banks by Prime Minister Margaret Thatcher. A few months after her victory, regulatory controls on lending were swept away along with foreign exchange controls, together with the thousands of bank staff who used to administer them. The new administration made no secret of the fact that they regarded the banks as hidebound dinosaurs of a previous age.

Barclays refused to guarantee export deals, despite the government's request. It also infuriated ministers by breaking inflation-busting guidelines in its pay rises for staff. The Chancellor, Sir Geoffrey Howe, got his revenge. He looked at various kinds of privileges which the banks could be punished for – including their ability to create money in the form of loans and their continuing failure to pay interest on current accounts – and hit them with a one-off tax on non-interest-bearing deposits in the 1981 budget. It cost Barclays £94 million.

But the real revolution came in 1986 with the end of fixed commissions in the City of London, ending the distinction between brokers and jobbers, and the other reforms that came to be known as the 'Big Bang'. Money poured into the financial services industry in London. The tiny stockbroking partnerships which had managed so much of the City were snapped up by foreign companies, many of the British investment banks – tiny affairs compared with the American and German giants – were swept away into foreign ownership. It was clear, as so often, that once more the interests of the establishment and the interests of the biggest players in the market coincided. Both preferred their organizations to be big, and it was hard to see how the small ones could survive without some kind of regulation, which never came.

What should Barclays do? Their profits were falling in the face of foreign competition, but they had to keep the branch network and other infrastructure they needed for the basic utilitarian business of looking after people's money. The answer was to take a minority stake in a stock-jobbing company called Wedd Durlacher Mordaunt & Co., plus the stockbrokers de Zoete. The two companies drove a wonderfully hard bargain and Barclays was forced to spend £129 million, the most expensive investment by any bank in the whole Big Bang business.

So was born the most controversial and troublesome of all the Barclays ventures, Barclays de Zoete Wedd or BZW, the British candidate for world domination of the investment banking world. It set up its headquarters in an old multistorey car park and immediately ran into trouble. In the Stock Exchange crash of October 1987, BZW managed to lose another £60 million, which led to a hefty loss in its first year. How was old reliable Barclays going to deal with the new global dispensation, requiring a whole shift of focus towards the burgeoning speculative economy?

Towards the Big Bang

'The process by which banks create money is so simple the mind is repelled,' said John Kenneth Galbraith.[17] Banking is a peculiar business, especially in Britain where it is usually outside political debate, particularly opaque and so establishment, and where our fantasies about it are so rooted in a bygone age. Most obscure was the very simple business of creating money in the form of loans, which was enormously lucrative to the banking industry. But this is done by the banking system as a whole: when you lend deposits to someone else, the money appears as a credit twice, once in the borrower's bank account, but also still in the bank account of the person who deposited the money in the first place. Of course, as the banks say, once the money is repaid it is deleted, but by that time the credits have been lent on and on in a thousand different ways, the money supply has grown and the banks are fatter than before.

That was the privilege which Sir Geoffrey Howe identified when the government was looking for a way to tax the banks in 1980–81. But it was hard to pin down exactly what benefits went to which bank, which left them – as we have seen – with those current accounts which pay no interest.

Once Lloyds Bank had dared to break ranks and start paying interest on current accounts in 1988, leaving only a fifth of their accounts profitable, it was clear that the business of banking was going to have to change. They could close more branches, fend off the less profitable customers – the poorer ones – with high-tech, online or call centre solutions, then maybe the whole business of being a money utility could still pay. Certainly, Captain Mainwaring would have to go.

You can see, in that way, how the fatal decisions were taken – as the finance professor John Kay puts it – to chain the utility to a casino. The vast financial conglomerates were earning fantastic sums, hyping their own clients' stock, fuelling the various booms, lending vast amounts to dodgy Third World regimes, from the striving to the downright brutal. By 2000, $2 trillion were hurtling across the global wires every day. How could the little English utility banks, even those with a long aristocratic history of Quakerism, hold back from the trough? Even by 1980, Barclays was getting a third of the money it needed to lend, not from its own depositors, but from the money markets.

Barclays was still instinctively conservative. Faced with the choice for chairman in 1980 between the innovative Deryk Vander Weyer and a Barclays uncle, the parachutist and ocean racing enthusiast Tim Bevan, they instinctively chose Bevan. Weyer drank a whole bottle of whisky in the office of the head of Barclays Merchant Bank, Lord Camoys.[18] It was a serious defeat for the modernizers.

Bevan closed the local head offices and redoubled the branch closure programme. He set aside vast sums for the bad debts lent abroad to foreign countries in the 1980s. He even raised the rates to longstanding customers. The Quakers, who had banked with Barclays since 1694, withdrew their account. The belated foray into business start-up was an expensive failure. Manufacturing loans were down to just 10 per cent by 1992. It was as if, without the infrastructure of local branch managers and directors, they could not generate the skills to lend to small business, and their loans to them were turning bad by 1991 at the rate of £1 million a day. Vast sums were also lent to Robert Maxwell in the early 1990s. Bad debt provision had to be doubled in 1990, and the result was a shocking pre-tax loss in 1992 of £242 million, only a little over the sum they had lent to Maxwell in 1990. Yet the Barclays board was still presided over by the chairman sitting on a dais, above the massive thirty or so board members, who were not given papers to read in advance.

The truth was that the bank's attention was not really on the business of lending small sums through retail banking any more, but on the emerging froth and fury of the speculative market. Barclays, and many of their competitors, took a languid, British approach to modernization. They left the details to those who understood the complexities of global finance. In the case of Barings, which collapsed when Nick Leeson made a massive error of judgement in the Singapore office, their checks (such as they were) missed the problem altogether. The old guard happily colluded with the myth that money was still sound, Captain Mainwaring was still in his place, and all was right with the world. They gave the impression that this was all fair competition, when so much of what was happening in the City of London and Wall Street was actually the emergence of rapacious greed.

They welcomed the demutualization of their former competitors in the building societies, at great personal profit to the people running them, and then swallowed them up. Bank of Scotland merged with Halifax to create HBOS, but Barclays bought Woolwich and cynically closed it down. Within a decade, nearly the whole of the demutualized sector had gone, the sad successors of all the local banks which had once populated Britain's high streets, and still populate the high streets of Germany, France and the USA.

The remaining UK banks presided over a generation when the best and brightest were tempted into the City of London, starving productive enterprise of imagination, talent and investment. Financial services made up a respectable 13 per cent of British GDP in 1970; by the 1990s it was running at a quarter. By the 1980s, Barclays had more staff than the total of everyone employed by financial services in the UK in 1900.[19] It was almost as if financial services were driving everything else out. Big Bang was massively successful in one way: it gave London the pre-eminent place in the bull market that followed. Barclays was there, and its high street operations were clearly in difficulties, so of course it was going to get involved. But the immediate problem was how to staunch the losses.

To do this, Barclays recruited a new team at the top, with Andrew Buxton as chairman (the Buxton family had been brought in to help rescue the Gurney Bank in Norwich a century or so before). It was Buxton who happened to be in the Bank of England when the news broke that Barings Bank had collapsed at the hands of Leeson, and chaired the meetings which tried to mount a rescue operation (it failed and Barings was bought for £1 by the Dutch bank ING). As chief executive, Barclays chose a cerebral former financial journalist, Martin Taylor from Courtaulds. Taylor was outspoken about Barclays' plight when he took up the job: he told the *Financial Times*, 'Losing large amounts of money ought to make people angry, but they've got used to it. It's decadent.'[20]

Taylor set about his task with a vengeance, setting up a special committee to identify bits of the company that could be sold, mainly loss-making parts of Barclays' American empire. This had been instructed to lend, lend, lend, only to find that their customers tended to be those who had been turned down by the more knowledgeable local banks. But he also became increasingly sceptical about the sound and fury that was issuing from BZW, a hotbed of ego and ambition, its new headquarters in Wall Street, with its gilded taps, still empty because the basement was full of water.

Not only were BZW executives paid up to ten times as much as their colleagues in retail banking, but there was an irritating jockeying for prominence between Barclays and BZW in places such as Tokyo. This was the background to the very un-Barclays slogan, coined by BZW chief Bill Harrison: 'A weekend with the family is a missed marketing opportunity.'[21] This was the background to the widening divisions between the old-fashioned bankers and the vast salaried speculators and investors at BZW. Buxton used to go down to the street at lunchtime to tell the taxis waiting to take BZW traders to lunch in the West End to go away.[22] It wasn't enough to stem the expense.

The problem was that to speculate on equal terms with their American rivals, BZW would need a huge injection of investment. In the end, Taylor was not prepared to do that and decided to sell it. The added difficulty was that, once the numbers had been crunched, with a share of central costs, they showed that the equities and corporate finance departments of BZW had never made a profit. Martin Vander Weyer, Deryk's son, estimated in his book *Falling Eagle* that BZW had probably cost Barclays a total of £2 billion.[23]

The break-up of BZW marked the end of the last British investment bank capable of taking on the great houses of Wall Street, and it was widely criticized in the press. 'I am sorry to announce the demise of the City of London,' wrote Christopher Fildes in the *Daily Telegraph*.[24]

After the sale, even the rump of BZW – Barclays Capital – ran into trouble when they invested heavily in Russian stocks just before the rouble crisis in 1998 which reduced the entire Russian stock market to about the same value as Sainsbury's. When Taylor suggested a demerging of Barclays Capital, at a notorious board meeting at the St Regis Hotel in Manhattan in October 1998, only one board member spoke in favour. Taylor was left with his head in his hands. Eight weeks later, he resigned.

By the end of the decade, Barclays had still not clawed its way out of difficulties, despite cutting 7,000 jobs in retail banking in 1999 and closing another fifty branches. Taylor's successor, a former US marine called Michael O'Neill, never started work to draw down his massive promised salary because of heart problems, but he did exercise his right to invest £5 million in Barclays shares and made a large profit.

It was still a decade before the great banking collapse, but some of the reforms were possibly responsible for the scale of the disaster that was to come. The central advances department that took decisions about major loans was abolished, and replaced with a computer program called Lending Advisor. Other computer programs which claimed to measure the probability of defaults, called Economic Capital and Risk Tendency, were set up. Both removed human oversight and replaced it with IT that only analysed default patterns back some decades to make decisions about risk in the future.

Perhaps it wasn't just a British faith. The American hedge fund Long Term Capital Management, run by two Nobel Prize winners in economics, placed an astonishingly naive belief in their risk software and consequently ran so spectacularly foul of the Russian economic crisis that their losses threatened to bring down the whole banking system, in a dress rehearsal of the crisis of 2008, exactly a decade before. Perhaps it was the same software which convinced Barclays to lend them money and paved the way to their involvement in the £2.2 billion bail-out.

The truth was O'Neill's appointment was a symptom of a bigger shift that was going on. As Barclays turned its attention to the speculative economy, with Barclays Capital in the foreground, it may have looked like the old, safe, aristocratic English bank of the mid-twentieth century, but it was actually increasingly American.

A decade later, the paradox was even more pronounced. On the outside, this was a safe retail bank with the familiar British logo – the trustworthy utility to look after your money – presided over by chief executive John Varley, who had married into the Barclays aristocracy and was a man so traditional that he still wore detachable collars. On the other side was the equivalent of the casino, taking ever increasing risks, managed in the USA by American Bob Diamond and his American cohorts. On the one side was the Barclays retail operation, promising to go carbon neutral in the UK and increasing its use of green electricity to 50 per cent. On the other side was the San Francisco-based Barclays Global Investors, the world's biggest investor – strap-line 'quietly conquering the world of finance' – which was busy voting down environmental proposals in companies they part owned, including Exxon, ConocoPhillips and ChevronTexaco.[25]

Behind the safe facade, so reminiscent of Captain Mainwaring, was the American investment bank. That was what Barclays had actually become, and was making strenuous efforts to become more so.

The efforts were so strenuous that it forced an exhumation, not just of the whole apartheid debacle, but of ancient fears about the involvement of banking in slavery in the eighteenth century. Barclays' bid to have the new basketball stadium for the New Jersey Nets in Brooklyn called the Barclays Center was described by one local campaigner as 'eating the fruit of a poisonous tree', on the grounds that Barclays had been founded by slave traders called Alexander and David Barclay.[26] This was not true, but it was a useful tool for increasing Barclays' contribution to the local community. It was also a public relations disaster.

When the campaigners threatened to reveal their research at a local press conference, all they could come up with was that one of the forerunners of Martins Bank – bought by Barclays in 1968 – had been the slave-trading Heywoods Bank. But such were the perils of being more American.

Also, behind the retail banking facade, it was Bob Diamond's Barclays Capital – known to its friends as Barcap – that was earning the profits, nearly half of their £7 billion profits in the boom year of 2006. Varley asked after the disaster of 2008: 'Would it be true to say that for a lot of this decade we were overly dependent on Barclays Capital for growing Barclays group as a whole? I think that would be a fair comment.'[27]

When the credit crunch bit, Barclays seemed to be safe, despite dipping into Bank of England emergency funds twice in the autumn of 2007. It also issued a flat denial that it would have to write off £4.8 billion in sub-prime loans, as its share value plummeted 17 per cent. 'There is absolutely no substance to these rumours,' it said.[28] In fact, of course, there was. When the bank finally began to come clean, it was couched in such obscure language that it simply confirmed the suspicions of commentators: 'ABS bonds, CDOs and sub-prime residuals, are valued by reference to observable transactions including the level of the ABX indices and on a pool-by-pool basis, implied cumulative loss projections. RMBS backed CDOs have been valued consistently to the ABS CDO super senior exposure as noted above.'[29]

The truth was that Barclays Capital had been heavily involved in creating the notorious SIVs (Special Investment Vehicles) that included the dodgy sub-prime mortgage loans, and which were proving valueless and therefore causing all the trouble.[30] It stepped in at the eleventh hour to rescue Lehman Brothers as its shares nosedived in September 2008, as it became increasingly clear that the British government would never guarantee to underwrite the losses of an American bank. Diamond contacted the veteran investor Warren Buffett asking if he could insure the deal, but Buffett could not work his voicemail system and did not get the message for ten more months.

When Barclays withdrew from the deal – before even formally asking the British – it was inevitable that Lehman Brothers would collapse, and that it might take down the rest with it. It was a high-risk strategy, but it had also become obvious to the Barclays negotiators that all they had to do was wait a few days, and the valuable bits of the defunct Lehman Brothers could be snapped up for a song. So it was that before it became clear how huge the banking disaster was – the destruction of most investment banking in Wall Street and the City – Barclays stepped in to buy the capital markets division of the collapsed Lehman Brothers in New York, plus $68 billion in liabilities. Barclays is still facing legal action from Lehman's lawyers saying that the deal was deliberately structured 'to give Barclays an immediate and enormous windfall profit'.[31] Barclays is fighting the action.

Despite this windfall, once the scale of the collapse was becoming obvious, people began to wonder out loud if Barclays had over-reached itself. There were already worries that Barclays had not solved its own toxic debt correctly. The collateralized debt obligations (CDOs) which it had bought – the dodgiest end of the market – had been written down by 31 per cent, while other banks had cut the value of the same assets by half.

Barclays was represented at the famous meeting with the Chancellor of the Exchequer and Bank of England officials, described by the chair of beleaguered Royal Bank of Scotland as 'more like a drive-by shooting', but almost alone among the big British banks it refused to submit to government control. Varley and his directors believed that, if they could escape the constraints that government investment would bring, Barclays would be at a major advantage when the economic climate got better. But where would they get the recapitalization they needed?

The controversial answer was that they negotiated a deal with the sovereign wealth funds, the national oil reserves, in the Middle East, and in particular with the crown prince of Abu Dhabi, a country where there are serious questions about democracy and forced labour. It was a peculiar fate for a bank which had once been set up by Quaker anti-slavers.

Commentators inevitably claimed that it was a way to carry on paying big bonuses without government intervention, and certainly Barclays Capital employees were given bonuses on average of £182,000 each for the previous disastrous year. Eight employees taken on from the defunct Lehman Brothers were locked into salaries of between £10 million and £25 million.[32] Bob Diamond himself took away £20 million in 2008 alone. No wonder Barclays needed an injection of capital. But for the major Barclays shareholders, like Legal & General, the injection was just a bad deal. Barclays would pay 14 per cent a year in interest to the Middle East for the £5.8 billion, more than was being offered by the British government and for longer. Not just that, but it would pay £300 million in fees to intermediaries for arranging the loan. But for Varley and Diamond, it was worth it to stay out of the hands of the government, aware that – when business began again – companies would tend to choose those banks which were strong enough to have avoided the need for state rescue, even if they had enjoyed huge indirect benefits from the public bail-out of the rest of the banking sector. So it proved. It was a skilful game they had played, and they had nearly lost everything.

The global monster

In the early weeks of 2009, a letter arrived at the parliamentary offices of the then Liberal Democrat Treasury spokesman Vince Cable from a whistleblower, presumably from inside Barclays. 'Hidden away on the top floor of 5 The North Colonnade sit the formidable Barcap SCM (Structure Capital Markets) team,' said the letter.[33] It transpired that a team of 110 people were working at Barclay's Canary Wharf offices to help Barclays avoid tax and passing on that advice to other multinationals around the world. The work was entirely legal, but devastating, given that two-thirds of international corporations in the USA paid no tax at all between 1996 and 2000. As many as 90 per cent of the rest paid less than 5 per cent of their earnings. The result is that small companies pay their taxes, but their global competitors generally don't, with a huge impact on the services that governments can afford.

The UK tax authorities promised to investigate, and there were demands that Barclays should be given no taxpayers' money if they were not themselves paying their fair share of UK taxes. Given that most Revenue & Customs officials ranged against them were earning as little as £45,000 a year, while the Barclays advisers were earning multimillion-pound bonuses, they seemed likely to continue their worthwhile work – and Barclay's plans to set up a new tax haven in Ghana were revealed shortly afterwards.

Thanks to the juiciest chunk of Lehman Brothers, Barcap doubled their huge profits for 2008. The bank as a whole was not yet completely safe, and they decided to bolster the balance sheet by selling Barclays Global Investors for just over $13 billion. The sale went through in 2009, taking Barclays finally out of reach of the regulators. But there were implications from the sale. Diamond stood to earn a huge £22 million in profit from his own shares.

Nothing quite so exemplified the new world of banking. Why should Diamond earn such a bonus when it depended on decisions that he was making? Why should he have been given the shares, from an employee incentive scheme, when he was more than adequately incentivized as it was? As the economy crumbled in recession, the bankers carried on earning, and earning at a rate beyond the reasonable demands of anyone, however successful. Does anything remain at all of those upright, Quaker roots, or anything else about Barclay's long history? It is hard to discern, and our economies are more volatile as a result.

CHAPTER 3

CADBURY (1831):
CHOCOLATE CAMELOT

A small outpost of civilisation, still ringed around by barbarism.

> J.B. Priestley, *English Journey*, writing about the
> Cadbury company town of Bourneville, 1934

> Don't let it be forgot
> That there was once a spot;
> For one brief shining moment
> It was known as Camelot.
>
> Alan Jay Lerner, *Camelot*, 1960

Head west for an hour or so from Stonehenge on the A30, the ancient western road used since the days of the Celts, and you find your way to one of the most spectacular hillforts in the country. You can see Glastonbury in the distance. You can even glimpse the sea on clear days, when your glasses are free of the incessant rain. You can let the breezes brush past you while you ponder the idea that, if King Arthur's Camelot was anywhere, then it was here.

It certainly is not called Camelot any more: it is wind-swept, deserted and covered in sheep droppings. This is

Cadbury Castle in Somerset, close to the villages of North and South Cadbury, and it has another claim to fame as well. It is at least close to the original roots of the family which shares the name, and which became a byword for chocolate in the English-speaking world. In fact, the Cadbury family was steeped in West Country nonconformity for centuries before the staunch Quaker and anti-slavery campaigner Richard Tapper Cadbury made his way to Birmingham to seek his fortune as a draper.

It is one of the ironies of the chocolate business that his children and grandchildren founded that it has such roots in opposition to slavery, yet it was dogged for a century by the hideous link between its chocolate and forced labour. It would certainly have astonished Richard Cadbury himself, a man so upright, enlightened and autocratic that he was known by everyone as 'King Richard'.

He arrived in Birmingham in 1798, the year of the Irish rebellion, of William Wordsworth and Samuel Taylor Coleridge's *Lyrical Ballads* and Horatio Nelson's victory at the Battle of the Nile. He carried with him a letter of introduction to the pioneer industrialist Matthew Boulton, James Watt's partner, and was welcomed by none other than Charles Lloyd, the Quaker co-founder of Lloyds Bank. With the leaders of the new, industrial Birmingham behind him, he set up in business in a former inn in Bull Street.

Cadbury was a fearsome figure, a convert to total abstinence, sharing with his descendants the distinctive Cadbury drive and slightly unworldly determination to succeed. He quickly built up a domineering position over the town, which then boasted a population of 74,000 – tripling in half a century – as chairman of the Board of Commissioners, the forerunner of the town council, and as Overseer of the Poor. This was not just the Birmingham of Boulton and Watt, of the first sparks of the Industrial Revolution, a burgeoning town of steam and coal that was pioneering a whole new way of manufacturing. It was a town that did not care what religion a man practised as long as he worked hard. Richard Cadbury was himself steam-driven. Whether he was measuring cloth or improving the benighted industrial poor, Cadbury did it with steely energy.

It is often said that the reason the Quakers came to dominate the chocolate market in Britain was because of the clear link between cocoa beans and slave plantations. They wanted to show there was a better way. It is certainly true that, since Quakers were denied entry to the universities or the armed forces, they tended to go into business. Their strict Puritanism often made them successful: you knew Puritans very rarely had their hands in the till. The chocolate pioneer and Quaker Joseph Storrs Fry was the wealthiest industrialist of the age. But in the case of the Cadbury family, chocolate was not the objective at all. It was only when Richard's younger son John was in business in the 1820s, as a tea dealer and coffee-roaster, that he tiptoed tentatively into the business of selling cocoa.

The very first Cadbury's chocolate advertisement dates from this time. There it was in *Aris's Birmingham Gazette*: 'John Cadbury is desirous of introducing to particular notice Cocoa Nibs, prepared by himself, an article affording a most nutritious beverage for breakfast.'[1] It was absolutely disgusting, but – in the weird way the English see these things – that seemed to prove it was good for you.

Even so, this was chocolate bought from local merchants. It was only in 1831, the year of the Birmingham riots, that he took over a warehouse in a winding back street known as Crooked Lane and began making cocoa and chocolate himself. John Cadbury was a great showman, with a lifesize cut-out model of a Chinaman in traditional costume behind the counter, presiding over the business of weighing out the tea.

John Cadbury was also his father's son in his determination to improve the world around him. He never sat in an upholstered chair. He encouraged his children to run a mile before breakfast. He was horrified to find that, having taken over his father's role as Overseer of the Poor, he was entitled to a slap-up dinner every week at public expense. He challenged the legality of the dinners and had them abolished, much to the horror of his colleagues. When cholera reached the Birmingham area in that same year, and nobody was willing to bury the only victim, John paid large sums to attract pallbearers – on condition they could smoke through the ceremony – and went along as a mourner himself.

He campaigned tirelessly against smoke pollution, to set up hospitals and savings banks, and to replace chimney boys with machines for sweeping chimneys, and he also fought a long and bitter battle against the local brewers. What should happen to all the barley, if you abolish brewing, asked his opponents? In response, John pioneered a new dessert dish called barley pudding. The burgeoning city of Birmingham knew him as 'Barley Pudding John Cadbury'. If the barley was eaten as a wholesome dessert, they it could not be drunk as alcohol, or so he reasoned. But with the best will in the world, it was not exactly an advertisement for abstinence. There must be some harmless way of taking the edge off the drudgery of life, surely? The answer was chocolate.

So if chocolate was only a sideline for the original Cadbury, it was becoming an increasingly important one for moral reasons. It was also the right sideline at the right time. During Richard Tapper Cadbury's lifetime, chocolate had emerged as a popular eighteenth-century drink, pur-veyed through the new chocolate and coffee houses in London's Pall Mall and further afield. By the time his son John was in business, Britain was getting through 143 raw tonnes of cocoa beans every year. A century later, it was 56,000 tonnes.

It was true that chocolate took its time to catch on. The original beans brought back to Castile by Christopher Columbus in 1492 had been thrown away as useless, but the conquistadors began to realize the magical properties of chocolate and to find ways of putting them to use. The great botanist Carl Linnaeus christened it 'the food of the gods', but there is no doubt that it was a bit problem-atic. The cocoa butter meant it was too rich to drink, so this somehow had to be removed or disguised. Chocolate in the 1820s was a hit or miss affair, a long way from the smooth brown comforter of the twentieth century, which left the old mixtures far behind. Only the Royal Navy car-ried on the old methods until 1968, keeping themselves warm on the bridge in all weathers with 'ky', a drink made with a slab of cocoa, butter fat and condensed milk, and so thick that the spoon would stand upright in it. There are those who claim that it won the Battle of the Atlantic in the Second World War.

But that is to leap too far ahead. Despite the unsophis-ticated nature of the product, John Cadbury jumped into selling chocolate with campaigning zeal, and was selling twenty-five different kinds by 1847, when he went into partnership with his brother Benjamin: Spanish Chocolate, French Eating Chocolate, Homeopathic Cocoa, soluble cocoa with added starch to absorb the rich cocoa butter to make it drinkable. Most of the marketing until the 1860s referred to how much chocolate could improve the health. Anything that tasted quite that bad simply had to.

Even then, Cadbury Brothers – as it then was – was interested in Camelot, in utopian experiment, model missions, model schools, model cottages and allotments for workers who were, like the Cadburys themselves, 'abstainers from drinking and smoking customs'.[2] There was even a special edition Model Parish tea, coffee and cocoa to help pay for the experiments. Their new factory in Bridge Street had all the hallmarks of an enlightened Camelot, with special machines to prevent air pollution, with a factory filled with girls of 'good moral character' from 9 a.m. to 7 p.m. six days a week. Once a week, the factory closed for a half holiday; twice a week there was an evening school on the premises. It was implacably idealistic, uncompromising in its moral determination, a Camelot among Birmingham's struggling commercial energy. 'Teetotalism is the rule,' wrote Walter White in *Chambers's Edinburgh Journal* after a visit. 'Instances of misconduct are rare, and when reproof is called for, it is administered by an appeal to the better feelings in preference to an angry demonstration . . . Factories conducted on such a system must be at once schools of morality and industry.'[3]

Barley Pudding Cadbury himself was as upright and as certain as his father and obsessed with purity in all things – the purity of his workers, his motives, his factories and also of his products. He was beginning the campaign that would dominate Cadbury's marketing for the next half century, against the adulteration of food, and it was a difficult business when all chocolate included additives such as potato starch, arrowroot, sago, treacle and refined sugar. Not for fifteen years would Cadbury be able to put pure cocoa on the market, but that was a detail that was not allowed to obscure the campaign.

In 1854, at the height of the Crimean War, Cadbury Brothers reached its peak with a royal warrant from Queen

Victoria and a brand-new office in London's Fenchurch Street. But the chocolate business is always a fickle one and, within two years, John's second wife Candia Barrow had died, his own health had collapsed and his business was beginning to struggle. Just twelve of his girls 'of good moral character' were left on the payroll and the company was on the verge of collapse.

His sons Richard and George were in their final years at school and were looking forward to life away from Birmingham, Richard to travel and paint and George as a Himalayan tea-planter. But it was not to be for either of them. In 1861, their father retired exhausted and Richard, twenty-five, and George, twenty-one, took over the struggling business, with little more than the inherited stores of steely determination and moral certainty of their forefathers. They invested the small sums of money their mother had left them, abandoned their dreams and plugged away, working until way into the night, week in, week out, almost certainly continuing the family tradition of using very uncomfortable chairs.

The slow recovery of Cadbury's was testament to their immense energy and their commitment to chocolate, as opposed to the tea and coffee their father had specialized in. They launched their new Breakfast Cocoa in 1862, Pearl Cocoa in 1863, Mexican Chocolate in 1864 and a whole range of health-inducing products such as Iceland Moss, a mixture of cocoa and dried gelatinous lichen, supposed to be seriously good for those who drank it. Samples were rushed round to the homes of London doctors. The first Cadbury advertisements began appearing on London buses and Richard Cadbury started to paint the chocolate tins, the first of a whole gallery of lids with little girls with kittens on their laps and flowers in their hair. The shape of the company that would eventually give birth to the Flake and the Creme Egg was beginning to settle in recognizable ways.

However, the real breakthrough was George Cadbury's journey to Holland in 1866 to buy a machine to squeeze out the cocoa butter in such a way that they could make chocolate drinkable without any extra starch at all. Without a word of Dutch, George negotiated for the equipment, brought it home and launched the first pure chocolate Cocoa Essence. Cocoa Essence did without the usual potato starch, sago flour and treacle. Its launch allowed the Cadburys to wade back into the emerging political debate about the adulteration of food, much to the rage of their Quaker chocolate rivals.

Their relationship with Rowntree in York and Fry in Bristol was supposed to be one of fraternal Christian respect. All three companies believed that price competition was unchristian and met regularly to agree what to charge, secretly and illegally. But the Cadbury campaign against adulteration seemed to Rowntree and Fry to be underhand and malevolent.

When George Cadbury gave evidence before a parliamentary committee investigating food adulteration he insisted that the word 'cocoa' should be reserved for unmixed cocoa beans, while 'chocolate' could be used for any mixtures of cocoa and other substances. To be fair to George, it was a heartfelt campaign. In 1891, he even abandoned his popular chocolate powder because it was adulterated, but it was a moral stance that also had an element of self-interest in it. The campaign also subtly promoted Cocoa Essence, and Rowntree and Fry were enraged. A statement by the Cadburys' rivals Dunn and Hewitt said:

What is far more significant is that Messrs Cadbury, in order to push a specialty of their own, have not

hesitated to cast a stigma upon all cocoa manufacturers in the country by their misleading statements:
'caution: when cocoa thickens in the cup it proves the
addition of starch', knowing full well that by the term
'starch' is conveyed to the general public only the substance used by laundresses, which as far as we know
is never used in the manufacture of cocoa.[4]

This extraordinary ability to combine moral rigidity
with corporate self-interest was to be a feature of George's
period in charge of his family firm. Previous generations
were too focused on the struggle to survive, but George's
moral certainty was so definite that the ripples seem to
have carried on right down to the present day, as if the
moral dilemmas that any company must face – and especially chocolate manufacturers – were magically open to
solution. But none of his descendants could quite conjure
up the same extraordinary self-interested conviction.

The other Cadbury inheritance also seems to have been a
propensity for longevity, despite – or perhaps because of –
all that mortification of the flesh. Old Barley Pudding John
Cadbury finally died in 1889 at the age of eighty-seven. The
Cadburys were always a long-lived family. Old Richard
Tapper Cadbury lived until he was ninety-two. But the early
death of both of John's wives pointed to the other side of
the longevity: every generation faced its own share of tragedy and early death, and this generation was no exception.

George's brother Henry joined the company in 1869
and took charge of selling their products in the west of
England. He succumbed to typhoid in 1875. George's
partner, his brother Richard, the artist behind the chocolate tins, took a trip up the Nile in 1899 and suffered
from a sore throat. The doctors told him it was hardly
serious and he carried on to Palestine, where he died of

diphtheria. He had just agreed with his brother that, when either of them died, their partnership would become a company. Richard's death triggered the agreement almost immediately, and that same year, Cadbury Brothers Ltd was born with share capital of £950,000. George Cadbury was anointed as chairman and, for the next generation, he moulded the company into a fearsome and idealistic machine which was to make the name Cadbury synonymous with chocolate all over the empire.

Founding Camelot

Before he died, Richard Cadbury had been instrumental in the revolutionary shift to new premises outside Birmingham, to give the company enough space to expand. That became a general trend for manufacturers in the dawning twentieth century, but Cadbury was one of the first: half a century later, there were fears about 'ribbon development', but when Cadbury did it, this was an enlightened idea. Rowntree followed suit. Of the Quaker chocolate triumvirate, only Fry clung tenaciously to a tiny site at the heart of Bristol.

The Cadbury brothers bought 14.5 acres of land between the villages of Stirchley, King's Norton and Selly Oak, four miles outside the city, next to the railway and the canal. The plan was to call the new factory estate Bournbrook, after the River Bourn which ran through the site. Before going public, they changed the name to Bourneville because it sounded French and French chocolate was then acknowledged to be the best. No matter how idealistic they were about this project, or any other, the Cadburys always kept a weather eye on the basics of marketing.

The first factory at Bourneville included a kitchen for cooking lessons for staff, dressing rooms to change out of wet clothes, a cricket field and a small dining room for Richard and George, where they ate their daily small piece of mutton set aside for their frugal lunches. The immediate problem was to organize commuter trains to bring the staff out to Bourneville. There was no train early enough for the first shift, which meant a cold walk out from the city, starting at 4.30 a.m. Richard Cadbury also organized men with lanterns to escort the women on the late shift home at the end of the day.

The lack of a waiting room for the girls at the station on cold winter nights particularly worried Richard. He would stand outside and would blow a whistle when the train was signalled, so they could run straight from the changing room in the factory, right on to the train. Perhaps it was something to do with their austere Quaker upbringing, but Richard and George were particularly concerned about the warmth of their employees. They were both known for crawling around on their hands and knees on the factory floor to make sure the hot pipes were on.

But then Bourneville was more than just a factory; it was a kind of fairyland. It was intended also to be a pinnacle of enlightenment, a statement of what business could and should be, a treatise on manufacturing and social change, a castle from where the Cadburys would ride forth on their crusades. A kind of Chocolate Camelot. It was also a living embodiment of what George and Richard believed their duties were as employers. As George's son George Junior put it in 1926, 'we only have the right to use the labour of young people if we make sufficient provision for their proper development'.[5] Not just a factory, but an educational establishment.

It had always been a pre-condition of joining the company, for anyone under sixteen, that they should go to evening classes twice as week. Now this rose to eighteen, or twenty-one for apprentices. There were camping schools in the summer, even a school on a barge in 1917. As George became increasingly involved with the Liberal Party, the employment policies of his company were beginning to show signs of radical liberalism, where employment and education began to blur excitingly together.

This was thrilling for radicals, because Cadbury was an increasingly important company. By 1899, when Richard died, there were 2,685 employees at Bourneville. It was they who provided the canvas for the Cadbury family to experiment in new kinds of organization, set out by George's son Edward in his influential book *Experiments in Industrial Organisation* in 1912. The book was the opposite of Frederick Winslow Taylor's time and motion study in the USA. Taylor had no interest in the other needs and imagination of his workers, apart from their ability to put the widget in the right place quickly. Edward Cadbury did.

In 1896, they also hammered out what was to be a different vision of industrial life: a whole village built around the factory, providing for the health, education and social and cultural needs of those who lived there, built to a high environmental standard. The idea of planned settlements was in the ether. It was two years before Ebenezer Howard's ground-breaking book *Garden Cities of To-morrow*. Port Sunlight, Saltaire and other new town experiments seemed to contain the possibility of a new category of place, beyond industrialized cities or impoverished countryside, where people could have a healthy stake in their own futures. To make a start on the vision, the Cadbury brothers bought extra land around Bourneville and the Bourneville Village Trust was born.

Bourneville became the personal fiefdom of George Cadbury and, as his own interests changed, so did those of the trust. It began to reflect his growing concern about homelessness, testing out a range of new kinds of social housing, low-interest mortgages and new designs for clusters of homes, with gardens and fruit trees behind each cluster. The 1900 trust deed broadened the purpose to include an ambition of 'the amelioration of the conditions of the working class and labouring population . . . elsewhere in Great Britain'.[6] It was more than Camelot; it was a laboratory for a more enlightened future. It also worked. By the 1930s, the infant mortality of residents of Bourneville had dropped to two-thirds that of the neighbouring city of Birmingham.

The village took some time to turn into reality, and the housing came first. By 1922 there were 1,100 houses (now there are 7,500). The First World War delayed things, but by 1925 the classrooms were finished – though in fine weather the classes carried on outside. There was a gym, a drawing studio, a laboratory, a library and a music room. There were Bourneville pageants, carpentry classes, choral singing, male-voice choirs, operas, folk dancing and the Bourneville works music festival. The poet John Drinkwater wrote special masques. It was a cultured place, a new design for living which drew from the powerful alternative culture of the 1920s – a mixture of fresh air and Englishness. Yet the economic power behind it was not alternative at all.

Only the writer J.B. Priestley struck a mildly discordant note, in *English Journey*, pointing out that employees at the new Cadbury factory in Tasmania, Australia, in 1922 had asked if they could forgo the proposed concert hall and recreation ground and just be paid more instead. Priestley wondered whether the ideal should not be this high-minded paternalism, but to treat staff 'not as favoured employees but as citizens, freemen and women'.[7]

So it would prove, but this was not George Cadbury's view. He had developed his own absolute sense of moral certainty, despite the serious complexity of going into business when you were a Quaker. He was also every bit as implacable as the upright Cadburys of previous generations. He got up at 6 a.m. in winter (earlier in summer) and walked to work by 7 a.m., sometimes walking home again for lunch in Edgbaston, and working on until 9 p.m. On Sunday mornings he got up even earlier, at 5.30 a.m., to teach at the adult school – the forerunner of evening classes – and did so for half a century. There was a morning reading of the bible for staff, which carried on until 1912. Staff were given half a day's holiday for skating when the weather was icy. If they wanted to learn to ride a bicycle, they took it in turns to borrow George's. Before Richard died, he and George would often kneel in prayer in the office over some knotty business question.

George was surrounded by other right-thinking Quakers. All his fellow directors were Quakers and all of them were pacifists. This immediately provided a source of moral dilemma. When the Boer War broke out, with radical Liberals such as Cadbury implacably opposed, the War Office decided to give a box of chocolates to every serving soldier for Christmas 1900. There would be a message from Queen Victoria in every pack. It was a moral minefield, but George was surefooted, ethical and self-interested, all at the same time. How was he going to square it? He accepted the order, but took it at cost so that the company made no profit out of it. Simple.

Appalled by British atrocities in South Africa and the treatment of the Boers in concentration camps, George yearned for a national stage and was cajoled rather reluctantly into buying the Liberal-leaning newspaper the *Daily News* by the Chancellor of the Exchequer, David

Lloyd George. It provided another source of agonizing moral dilemmas for any lesser man. George was against gambling and alcohol, which should have formed part of the newspaper's content and advertising; what would he do? George's answer was to make sure the *Daily News* included no mention of horse-racing at all and carried no liquor advertisements. The family trust which he set up in 1912 to own the paper set out its philosophy in Quaker terms: that arbitration should take the place of war, and 'the spirit of the Sermon on the Mount . . . should take the place of imperialism'.[8] It was probably unprecedented in the history of the newspaper business.

With the Boer War safely consigned to history, another moral dilemma peered above the parapet: the failure of the Cadburys' public campaign against food adulteration. Worse, there was now the possibility of a whole new kind of chocolate emerging which was copiously adulterated with milk. You might have thought his moral stance on adulteration would have led him to shun it in the name of Cocoa Essence, but George Cadbury was more clear-sighted than that. The mere possibility of milk chocolate changed the rules entirely.

There were relatively unappetizing versions of Ur-milk chocolate in Switzerland, thanks to Henry Nestlé's blend of cocoa powder, milk and sugar, and Cadbury could see the possibilities. He had bought a recipe brought back from Jamaica by the antiquarian Sir Hans Sloane, one of the original founders of the British Museum. It was dry and rather gritty, but it had possibilities. From 1902, he began experimenting to find the right recipe, just as the American pioneer Milton Hershey was up to his gumboots in milk and chocolate in his experimental dairy on the outskirts of Chicago. The Cadbury breakthrough followed two years later.

George's nephew William Cadbury, who was then the most dominant figure in the company after his uncle, was against milk chocolate and wanted to stick to the tradition of pure chocolate, but George persuaded the board to create the capacity for twenty tonnes a week and Cadbury's Dairy Milk – very nearly called Cadbury's Dairy Maid – was launched in 1905. It was a massive success. Since 1913, it has been Cadbury's biggest chocolate brand, its distinctive purple silver foil a feature of childhoods and hot summer afternoons ever since.

By now it was clear that the adulteration campaign was over. Once milk chocolate was on the market, George Cadbury quietly jettisoned the rest of his adulteration creed and launched the palatable mixture Bourneville Cocoa in 1906. It immediately outsold Cocoa Essence and has been selling ever since.

But Cadbury's Daily Milk had other implications for the business. Milk chocolate is seven-eighths milk. Those were the days before refrigerated railway trucks and lorries, so milk went bad in transit. When Cadbury realized it was throwing away 60 per cent of the stuff that arrived in Bourneville, it was forced to find some other solution. It set up a condensing factory in dairy country at Knighton on the Shropshire border. In 1915, it opened another one in Gloucestershire.

Yet the moral dilemmas were also growing. In February 1912, Cadbury Brothers went public. Most of the shares went to the public and the staff, so the room for manoeuvre for the Quaker directors was already being constrained. The shareholders now owned the company, though the presence of the moral authority – not to mention the moral certainty – of George Cadbury provided the company with a dreamlike aura of otherworldly rigidity which has never really gone away. When Roald Dahl wrote his children's story *Charlie and the Chocolate Factory* in 1964, it took little imagination to work out one of the seeds of the idea, the secret fantasy world dedicated to sweets. Bourneville was never secret – quite the reverse – but it had that other-worldly element to it.

The question of where the ingredients to Cadbury's chocolate came from was becoming increasingly urgent, as we shall see, but a far more overwhelming dilemma was on the horizon, because the world was about to go insane. In August 1914, Germany invaded Belgium. War was greeted with intense excitement, patriotic fervour and moral outrage at the plight of the Belgians. But Cadbury was run by pacifists. What should they do?

Lord Kitchener wanted to attract an army of a million volunteers. What should the company's attitude be? Should it prevent its employees joining up? Should it defend its 706 different product lines – Cadbury's Dairy Milk, Milk Tray – or should it help the government by shifting its factories to helping the war effort? Should it take a stance against the war and risk the opprobrium of its chocolate-addicted customers, or should it keep its head down and do the minimum the government required of it?

It was a sticky problem. George Cadbury, now seventy-five and at the height of his controversial reputation as an arbiter of morality – a hero to the radicals, a villain to the Tory press – managed, as always, to tread a surefooted path which combined morality with sensible business. The company announced that it wanted every employee to do what they felt was right. By the end of the war, 218 employees had been killed in action, and ten times that number had joined up. The company also assisted the government with its production capacity – not to make weapons, but to feed the besieged British population. The Frampton factory in Gloucestershire was converted into making butter, condensed milk and milk powder. Some of it undoubtedly found its way into soldiers' rations, but it was the intention that counted. By the end of the war, Cadbury's product range had dwindled to 195.

The truth was that Cadbury did very well out of the First World War. It was the great age of milk chocolate, and it was a product that thrived on peripatetic lifestyles. Soldiers carried it to the trenches. Sailors carried it in the North Sea. Munitions workers treated themselves to it at the end of their shift. Other forms of personal bonhomie were illegal or frowned on by factory owners and politicians alike, but chocolate was different. You could keep it in your pocket or handbag and it cheered you up. It was almost an instant meal in itself. It took so little time to eat, you could almost inject it. Understanding this had made Cadbury the leading chocolate manufacturer in the country.

Fry took the fatal decision to concentrate on the cheap end of the market, cutting the quality of its popular Chocolate Cream because of sugar rationing, making it taste gritty, and by the end of the war, the company was not really in a position to carry on. Fry approached Cadbury's with an offer of merger in 1919, and for a while it seemed that Rowntree would join in too. Seebohm Rowntree certainly wanted to merge, but – at the last minute – his father Joseph vetoed the idea. He was keen to see his own experiments in industrial democracy go ahead. As it was, Cadbury and Fry merged themselves into the British Cocoa and Chocolate Company. It was one of the strangest mergers ever conducted: there were no cost savings. The two companies just carried on operating separately, and did so for another four decades.

George Cadbury himself was now the grand old man of chocolate and the only person at Bourneville who could remember his father's original factory at Bridge Street.

Yet his final decades saw the emergence of a real moral dilemma for which, finally, he had no solution. He presided over, and survived, one of the biggest libel actions of the era, which was raised because of the continuing running sore behind the Cadbury story: the links between chocolate and slavery.

The 'S' word

George Cadbury died on 24 October 1922. One of his final public appearances had been some months before for the visit of the king and queen to Bourneville, the ultimate accolade for a radical. His reputation was not unassailable. His Conservative opponents resented his ability to dictate policy through the columns of the *Daily News*; his Liberal rivals distrusted the way he sponsored the careers of those he approved on the party back benches. But his moral certainty was legendary. The difficulty for the generation that followed him, starting with his nephew William as chairman of the board, was not so much that they found the moral tightrope more difficult – though they did – but that chocolate itself was tarnished.

The business of growing cocoa had begun in slavery in the Caribbean and Latin America, and – despite the successful campaign against the slave trade by upright Cadbury forebears and the outlawing of slavery in the British Empire in 1833 – the remnants of the old evil remained. Those who did the actual work on the plantations were the children of slaves, earning pathetically little money. Often they owed money for life's essentials to their employer and could barely break free of the economic shackles that had replaced the literal ones.

It was one of George's typically deft moral moves that getting into cocoa production in 1897 would not only tackle the plight of the growers, but it would also help secure Cadbury's supply at the same time. In fact, the two plantations it bought in Trinidad turned out to be a side-line. The long-term Cadbury solution lay in Africa, and in the British colony of the Gold Coast in particular, where the cacoa plant had been introduced by a native local blacksmith called Tette Kwesi in 1891. The colonial government there had tackled native poverty by banning white settlers from owning land, and what quickly emerged was a burgeoning network of small farms, mainly black farmers growing their own little patch, which was to make the Gold Coast the source of half the world's cocoa output within four decades.

This was the perfect solution for Cadbury: small-scale farming by individual growers working for themselves – it was the very essence of Liberal radicalism. But this was also the height of the British Empire and cocoa – like coffee – was the quintessential imperial product, and there was bound to be a contrast between the Chocolate Camelot at Bourneville and the more robust methods used to cajole the cocoa growers. The company buyers soon found that there were problems with the quality. The complete crop of one small farm would weigh about 60lb, not too much to be carried on the head of the farmer all the way to the market in Accra. The buyers were soon complaining that only one in ten bags was viable, and they all had to be emptied out to make sure the quality on the top was the same as it was on the bottom. The implications of this kind of search for perfection for the poor growers must have been even more unnerving. Imagine picking up the remains of a rejected year's crop.

So Cadbury sent advisors out to work alongside the growers and got special permission to set up an experimental estate to test out new techniques. It also experimented, rather less ethically, with different payment methods. We only have a nervous hint in the company's official history in 1931 of what this entailed: 'It substituted payment in cash for the system of barter – which was only primitive when cotton goods were given, but became demoralising when gin was used as the medium of exchange.'[9]

It was a potentially brutal business, but it was not exactly slavery, and it was possible to see how the situation could improve. Cadbury organized a joint buying agency there with Fry and similar ones in Nigeria and in Ashanti with Rowntree, as the business of cocoa spread around West Africa. On the face of it, at least, the company was working to embed a system of cocoa production that encouraged independence and enterprise, the very opposite of slavery. The trouble for the future was that small farms were outside its direct control – that is what made them independent, after all – and it was difficult to see exactly what was going on there.

Meanwhile, the family's campaign against slavery was gathering force back home. The *Daily News* trumpeted its opposition to importing Chinese labour into the Transvaal gold mines of South Africa. It continued to trumpet this after the Liberal landslide in the general election of 1906. But its main focus of attention was the Belgian Congo, and the campaign by Edmund Dene Morel and the Congo Reform Association after the bloody revelations of a former British consul there, Roger Casement. William Cadbury personally supported Morel, who happened also to be Casement's closest friend, and financed the campaign. He did so from rage and conviction, but there were whispers in the Tory press – vigilant for any weapon they could use against the Liberal government's supporters – that all the noise about the Congo was a way to draw attention away from Cadbury's own little slavery problem.

Certainly, behind the corporate facade, William was getting increasingly worried about this, and who wouldn't be? Not all Cadbury's cocoa could come from the Gold Coast, after all, and a small but significant part of the annual purchase came from two Portuguese islands on the equatorial coast of Africa, São Tomé and Príncipe, and there the rumours of slavery were hard to discount. As early as 1902, he was sent a copy of a sale notice for a plantation on São Tomé, with figures quoted per head for the sale of the labourers. He went out there to investigate himself, but the association of local planters denied everything.

The worries mounted and, in the following years, William stitched together an alliance with Rowntree and Fry plus a German company – the Americans were not interested in investigating – and together they employed a Quaker researcher called Joseph Burtt, who spent six months on the islands in 1904, notebook in hand. His findings took years to write, but they were explosive. He found that there were indeed slaves working on the plantations. They had been captured in Angola and sent down in shackles to the islands, where they were forced to sign contracts written in Portuguese. It was true that, at the end of contracts, they were formally asked if they wanted to renew, but Burtt could find no examples of anyone saying no and going home. Children also appeared to have no right to leave at all.

As the news filtered out, the journalist Henry Nevinson wrote in *Harper's Magazine* in 1906 that: 'The slaves are herded . . . in gangs by the official agent. They are ranged up and, in accordance with the decree of 29 January 1903, they are asked if they go willingly as labourers to São Tomé. No attention of any kind is given to their answer.'[10]

When Burtt's report was finally passed to the British Foreign Office in 1907, it was horrified, but for rather different reasons. It implored Cadbury to keep the matter quiet and let it deal with the matter behind the scenes. Portugal was Britain's oldest ally and a key buttress in the complicated power struggles around Africa. The government was desperate not to cause an international outcry. Its policy was in fact to ignore the problem, accepting Portuguese assurances that slavery had been abolished.

But it was too late. A resolution by the Liverpool Chamber of Commerce condemned the conditions on the plantations there, and the campaign had begun with Cadbury's as the target. A gleeful opposition press believed they had found a weak spot in the Liberal government in general and in George Cadbury in particular. As a result, the outcry began to mount to get Cadbury to stop buying cocoa from the islands.

What was William Cadbury to do? This was not one of his uncle's clear moral dilemmas, which could be dodged by one clear bound. It was much more complicated. Abandoning the Portuguese islands would not seriously damage Cadbury's supply, but it could damage the slaves. On the other hand, the idea that Cadbury's could be supporting slavery was unthinkable. He was chairman of the Anti-Sweating League, for goodness' sake, and his uncle had sponsored the Sweating Industries Bill in Parliament. The best thing would be to sort out the problem, while carrying on buying. The British government said Cadbury's could do this, and the members of the Portuguese government agreed when William Cadbury took Burtt to meet them. That was the path he chose, but events do not always work out as they should. In February 1908, the king of Portugal was murdered, the Portuguese government fell and Cadbury reluctantly withdrew its contracts from the islands.

It was too late for the company's reputation. The Conservative press had scented blood, and six months later the *Standard*, the Conservative morning paper, published the words that were to cause all the trouble. It accused Cadbury's of total indifference 'to those same grimed African hands whose toil is so essential to the beneficent and lucrative operations of Bourneville'.[11]

William Cadbury sued. What else could he do? The trial took place on 29 November in 1909 at the Birmingham Assizes and it attracted the leading barristers in the business. The future attorney-general Rufus Isaacs and future Chancellor of the Exchequer Sir John Simon represented Cadbury. The great Edward Carson, the basis for Sir Robert Morton in Terence Rattigan's *The Winslow Boy* (1946), appeared for the *Standard*. Carson was an orator of genius but even he faced an uphill task. Nobody denied there was slavery on Princípe and São Tomé; that was not the issue. The question was whether Cadbury was actually 'indifferent' to the plight of the slaves – whether it continued buying there because it was in its business interests to do so – and that was much more difficult for the *Standard* to prove, as it would have to do as the defendant in a libel action.

Liberal morality was on the line. The public interest was intense. Even the Foreign Secretary, Sir Edward Grey, was called to give evidence. George Cadbury himself made a brief appearance in the witness box, as certain as ever, saying: 'One has to use common sense and sentiment. Sentiment told me I should give up buying at once. But common sense told me it would do no good.'[12]

His nephew William had a much tougher ordeal, a sweaty three-day cross-examination at the hands of the greatest advocate of the age, during which he had to admit that he had indeed tried to stop the journalist Nevinson from publishing his article condemning British cocoa importers.

'Had you no conscientious objection to going on buying cocoa products under these conditions?' thundered Carson.[13]

William, in his final day in the witness box, replied that he would 'have had very serious objections if we had not been doing our utmost to secure reform'.

The judge summed up strongly in favour of Cadbury, and the jury was out just fifty-five minutes before coming in and finding in Cadbury's favour – and then administering a slap in the face. They awarded the company one farthing damages for the libel. The judge stepped in and made the *Standard* pay the huge costs of the case.

Cadbury never bought on the Portuguese islands again, but those behind the rival anti-slavery campaign in the Congo also faced an uncertain future. Casement was hanged for treason after gun-running for the IRA. Morel was arrested in 1917 under the Defence of the Realm Act and abandoned the Liberal Party for the Independent Labour Party, as George Cadbury did himself in opposition to the First World War. Burtt was packed off to America by the Anti-Slavery Society to bring pressure to bear on the American chocolate manufacturers. By 1914, five years later, as many as 14,000 of the impoverished workers on the islands had gone home. But, as we shall see, the worries about slavery never entirely went away.

The Aero effect

George Cadbury had eleven children and by the time he died, the youngest of these were coming home from the First World War to play a part in the company. The first cracks in the united family response to war were apparent. Bertie Cadbury had shot down zeppelins, after all, which was not pacifism by most definitions. But one of the most interesting members of the new generation was Paul, the son of George Cadbury's brother Barrow, who had taken part in the First World War in the Friends Ambulance Unit, and went on to turn the Quaker ambulances into a major international force in the Second World War. It was Paul who played such a dynamic role in the explosion of marketing between the wars that saw Cadbury's dominance in its own country entrenched.

This was the age of ribbon development, arterial roads, semi-detached houses and a whole new kind of industrial expansion – manufacturing motor cars, toothpaste, breakfast cereals – in new factories on the outskirts of cities. Cadbury was in fact the very heart of this new economy, beyond the coal and smelting that had dominated the Industrial Revolution, and the great chimneys at the heart of the cities. It stood for a different kind of lifestyle: instant meals, instant treats, instant gratification, for people who had been bound by class and tradition for too long, and who now just needed to reach into their purse. The ethics at the heart of the company were well-known. People came to see the factory, the Chocolate Camelot, as a leisure activity. There were as many as fifty-five excursion trains to Bourneville in 1929 alone. It was a glimpse, not just of another kind of industrial organization and another kind of living space, but of another way of life. It meant pleasure, classlessness and, strange as it was for a company founded by Quakers, the very antithesis of Puritanism.

Paul managed to capture the very English mixture of high morality, hedonism and duty that lay behind the Cadbury's brand. After all, Cadbury's Dairy Milk was not just chocolate, it was nurturing life-giving milk as well. 'A glass and a half of milk' was the company's most successful slogan, coined under Paul Cadbury's creative leadership of the marketing side in 1928. It was adult and childish at the same time. The milk chocolate recipe was said to be well-guarded. Between the wars was a great period of rumours about industrial spies sent to find it, encouraged no doubt by the company itself.

This was also the period where the enthusiasm for planned towns such as Bourneville, New Earswick, Letchworth and Welwyn Garden City led to a renewed interest in the future shape of cities, and Paul was at the forefront. He chaired the research committee which wrote the influential 1941 *When We Build Again* (which looked at the future of housing) and took a close interest in the future of Birmingham city centre. He had the misfortune in 1965 to be described as 'the father of the inner ring road and the new Birmingham'.[14] Thankfully, the hideous new Birmingham of urban motorways and the Bull Ring has since been swept away.

But it was George's son Laurence who was most obviously climbing the greasy pole to the top of the family tree. He had also been a Quaker ambulance driver in the First World War and managed to combine this with a passion for collecting antique guns and cannon. It was also Laurence who had to deal with the competition.

Fry was out of the way and Rowntree was struggling. In 1930, Seebohm Rowntree asked Cadbury's for a merger. Edward, Paul, William and Laurence discussed the idea and rejected it, believing perhaps that they could simply buy the company cheaply if they waited. Sure enough, Rowntree was forced to cut back to a three-day week, but – just at their lowest point – a dynamic leader emerged, having married into the Rowntree family. George Harris was responsible for Smarties, Kit-Kat and Aero, the big brands in British chocolate in the late 1930s, and Rowntree's Kit-Kat was the first serious challenge to Cadbury's leadership. Aero kept the lawyers in work for years, when Cadbury objected to the claims that the chocolate bubbles meant the Aero could be digested twice as fast as ordinary chocolate. It was a belated revenge for the adulteration campaign.

Then there was Mars, which arrived in the UK in 1933, and set up in Slough – the quintessential 1930s town, and subject of John Betjeman's incantation for 'friendly bombs' to fall on it. Cadbury's had to respond.

Laurence bought automatic moulding machines from Denmark and automated the production lines beyond Edward's progress in that direction after the death of George Cadbury; George had always resisted automation because it might put people out of work. Laurence's objective was to make production more efficient so they could cut the price, and the price cut was dramatic. Cadbury's Dairy Milk went down from two shillings to just 8d in 1934. Two years later, Cadbury was selling 250 tonnes of the stuff every week.

The tall, donnish Laurence had inherited all the austerity and sense of duty of his forebears, and their moral determination, but not really their politics. Laurence was more of a Conservative than a Liberal or radical, and it was uncomfortable – back in 1930 – to suddenly find himself chairman of the Liberal *Daily News*. His first action was to buy the other Liberal daily, the loss-making *Daily Chronicle*, and to merge them together as the *News Chronicle*. It quickly rose to a circulation of 1.2 million and won a major place as a quality broadsheet, flying the flag for Liberalism just as its parliamentary representatives began to gather themselves together to fight back against the new Labour–Conservative dispensation. After the 'strange death of Liberal England', the *News Chronicle* kept a whiff of Liberalism alive.

It also took an immediate stand against appeasement. The thinking middle classes looked to it for news and entertainment, though not horse-racing. Laurence Cadbury respected the newspaper but never enjoyed the business. He struggled with the company chairman, Sir Walter Layton, who was also chair of the newspaper and had been – a delicate business this – his economics tutor at Cambridge. The newspaper became a drain on his energy, a dead-weight, a business which he owned but barely seemed to control.

By the time the Second World War broke out, Laurence was a pillar of the establishment, and a director of the Bank of England. It was to him that the family turned at the outbreak of war to deal with the accelerating moral dilemmas. The Cadbury family were no longer exactly pacifists, nor were they all even Quakers, but it was clear that they operated within a pacifist tradition. Yet there they were, one of the leading industrial forces in the country, and this was a war of national survival. They could hardly stand by and watch, any more than they had in the First World War, and this time the stakes were even higher.

Paul relaunched the Friends Ambulance Brigade and wrote angry letters to his relatives, urging them not to help the business of war. George Cadbury Junior wrote to Edward, chairman since William's retirement in 1937: 'I cannot feel on conscientious grounds that I should not respond to the nation's call.'[15]

Cadbury's response to war was even more complicated when it came to rationing. The sweets ration was just three ounces a week. Milk was being reserved for making butter and cheese. People still bought chocolate when they could, and there was a requirement for rations for the armed forces and for provisioning lifeboats, but there was certainly spare capacity at Bourneville. Other manufacturers moved on to the site and began making gas masks, which could be described to Quakers with a delicate conscience as 'defensive'. Other new arrivals went further, filling rockets and – although the Cadbury's magazine was quiet about it – making arms. To deal with this influx, the family set up a company called Bourneville Utilities to manage the site and put Laurence in charge.

Descriptions of Laurence Cadbury emphasize his business flair, but also his sense of duty. You find yourself wondering whether his life was entirely his own. He owned a national newspaper because it had been thrust upon him. He helped govern the Bank of England because it was his duty to do so. There seemed to be an element of reluctance about it, as there must have been when the Minister for Economic Warfare, Hugh Dalton, asked him to fly to Moscow within days of the Nazi invasion in 1941 to assess the Soviets' war needs. The visit involved exhausting negotiations about how the Soviets would pay for the equipment and supplies they needed, and Laurence finally flew home in a seaplane without seats, at one stage chased by a fearsome-looking Heinkel.

Laurence finally took over as chairman of the family firm in 1944, and from then on the pattern of his next fifteen years was set. He used to spend his Mondays and Tuesdays in Bourneville, Wednesdays at the *News Chronicle*, Thursdays at the Bank of England and then back to Bourneville on Fridays. He had a flat in Curzon Street in London's exclusive Mayfair, where he ate a strange mixture of grilled bacon sprinkled with Bisto before catching the No.9 bus for the Bank of England. Like his forebears, Laurence was effective and far-sighted, long-lived and suffered more than his fair share of tragedy. His eldest son was killed in a motorbike accident in France, his daughter Anthea was killed in a plane crash, and – decades later – his youngest son Jocelyn, a Conservative MP, shot himself in the grounds of his parents' house.

The *News Chronicle* was particularly burdensome to Laurence and, when Layton retired, he had to take over as chairman himself. Lord Beaverbrook offered Layton the money to buy him out, but his old tutor decided he was too old. There were plans to merge with the Labour *Daily Herald*, but the Transport and General Workers Union stymied the idea. It was never clear why Laurence failed to make the necessary and obvious changes to guarantee the paper's profitability. They carried on running two printing plants in London and Manchester, and it might have occurred to them that this was over-capacity. But, whatever the reason, by 1960 he decided enough was enough.

At 6 p.m. on 17 October, the staff were told to stop producing the paper for the following day. The *News Chronicle* had been sold secretly to the *Daily Mail*, which closed it down. In vain the parliamentary Liberal Party offered to form an alternative consortium. As many as 3,500 staff lost their jobs, the biggest mass redundancy London's Fleet Street had ever seen. There was an enormous public outcry, and Laurence was pilloried on TV, excoriated in Parliament and criticized for hanging on to the franchise for Tyne Tees TV. The *New Statesman* called it murder, horrified that a newspaper with a radical tradition – from the opposition to sweatshops in 1905 to the opposition to Suez in 1956 – should have been sold to a newspaper which had at one time supported Mussolini and Mosley.[16]

The meagre £1.5 million the paper fetched was used up entirely on redundancy payments to the staff: one week's pay for each year of service. 'The chocolate handshake', one of the journalists called it.[17]

One of the country's best-known writers, James Cameron, complained that:

> If the *News Chronicle* could not survive, with its extraordinary advantages of tradition, and loyalty, and talent, who can, outside the great chain-stores of the trade? . . . The newspaper with the most admirable free-thinking radical tradition withered on the bough precisely at the moment when the nation was ripe to appreciate these Liberal qualities . . . a potential warhorse ridden by grocers.[18]

Ironically, just as a Liberal daily newspaper seemed most like an anachronism, the political scene was shifting and the first Liberal revival was discernible under the leadership of Jo Grimond. But the loss of the *News Chronicle* was a major blow for civilized debate and the diversity of the media. It marked a key moment in the unravelling of old George Cadbury's radical certainty.

The age of Smash

In the early hours of the morning of 21 July 1969, at least in Britain, the population was so entranced with the Apollo space missions that they stayed up to watch the pictures of Neil Armstrong's first tentative steps on the moon. It was the great age of *Tomorrow's World*, of technological hope, and among the images which stayed with us was the astronaut's food. The famous meal of beef and vegetables in a translucent plastic pack, which would turn to soft mush when they added a little hot water, was heavily promoted as the future of food. All meals would soon come in pills, tubes or plastic bags, without fuss or effort, utilitarian and instantaneous.

Four decades on, it did not quite happen like that, and we have celebrity chefs, organic food, the rise of urban agriculture and the business of cookery shooting up the cultural and political agenda. But at the time, it was a vision that was also intriguing the Cadbury generation that followed Laurence. Ironically, one of the most famous Cadbury's advertisements – for their Smash instant mashed potato – would include robot spacemen laughing at potato peelers. It was a sign of the times (also a mistake: by the end, it was instant mash that got the laughs).

Throughout the 1960s, British industry was beginning to realize that the customers were changing. They wanted something different. They lived more complicated, busier, more indebted lives. Women wanted paid work. There was a dawning realization at Cadbury that the company was actually in the fast-food business, and it might be in a good position to capitalize on an emerging market where people organized their eating quickly. Or even just unwrapped a chocolate bar as they went along. It was an extension of the instant gratification business.

The chosen instrument of this shift was Laurence's son Adrian, a man shaped by a lifetime of cold baths, who led the diversification into Smash instant mashed potato and Marvel instant milk, as well as the packaged cake market, snapping up Typhoo tea and Kenco coffee, launching new canned meats and beginning a major foray into jam, with the research department churning out less memorable food adventures from instant tea to Stroodles. But if Cadbury was going to become a more general food company, then Adrian and his fellow directors could see all around them an emerging battleground to provide the huge volumes, and vast turnovers, the new food distribution systems and new supermarket chains were going to need to satisfy demand for instant gratification by food.

Adrian became chairman in 1965, at the age of just thirty-four, and he brought in the American management consultancy McKinsey to help him restructure the new company. It helped him persuade his colleagues to finally integrate Cadbury and Fry, which had been legally merged back in 1919, but kept as separate entities, and split the new company into a confectionary division and a food division.

He also took the fatal step of floating the British Cocoa and Chocolate Company, the official name for Cadbury since the Fry merger, on the stock market. The company name was changed to Cadbury Group Ltd. Now it was going to be the analysts, markets and traders which called the shots.

Cadbury was not alone edging its way towards the new food dispensation. There were powerful players stalking the stock market, and a flurry of mergers and takeovers in the food sector. Food companies could see the emerging power of the mega-supermarkets and needed to get bigger to retain some kind of negotiating power. In 1968, the Timothy Whites chain merged with Boots and the Victor Value supermarket merged with Tesco. The familiar British brands which had dominated the childhoods of those running British business were now part of a wider game, sheltering under the giant conglomerates such as Rank Hovis McDougall.

But Adrian Cadbury had another major problem, especially when it came to pleasing the brokers. Cadbury now dominated British chocolate, controlling more than a quarter of the market, with the aid of some lascivious television advertisements for Flake. It was hardly possible to grow the company in its home market, but they had barely a foothold across the Atlantic. This became the dominating theme for the company for the next generation, and so when – some months before Neil Armstrong walked on the moon with his meal of packaged beef in his tummy – Cadbury was offered the chance of a merger which could give it that American foothold, it jumped at the opportunity.

The approach came from Lord Watkinson, the chairman of the drinks company Schweppes, founded by Jean Jacob Schweppe – the partner in the invention of carbonated water – in London in 1792. Watkinson also needed a partner to storm the American market, but Schweppes was already a player in the USA. He had initially approached Rowntree, only to be swept aside by the interest of General Foods (actually Rowntree resisted the overtures and stayed independent until 1988 when it was snapped up by Nestlé).

The merger went through in January 1969, valuing the company at £222 million. Cadbury Schweppes was now bigger than its rival grocers Tate & Lyle and Brooke Bond, but still smaller that the British giants Rank Hovis McDougall, Unilever and Associated British Foods. The Cadbury–Fry family trusts were the main shareholders, owning a quarter of the new conglomerate (this dwindled to only 2 per cent by the end of the century). Lord Watkinson was installed as chairman with Adrian Cadbury as his deputy and joint managing director with the Schweppes chief James Barker. Barker disappeared off to Unigate dairies not long afterwards, and Watkinson retired, leaving Cadbury in charge.

All mergers are tough, especially for those who are not immediately profiting from the pay-offs and commission. There was a painful hangover from all the excitement. Cadbury had the bigger assets but Schweppes made more profit. The pressure was on, therefore, to bring the Cadbury half up to the same level of profitability as Schweppes. In those circumstances, then of course the Chocolate Camelot was going to have to melt a little. Bourneville bore the brunt of the job cuts: 450 went in 1970, with 2,000 more across the group in 1971 when profits began to fall. Another 700 jobs went at Bourneville to compensate for the rise in VAT in 1979. Adrian later said about the merger: 'There was a sense throughout the business that it was a major break with the past. We were no longer going to be masters of our own fate.'[19] How right he was: Watkinson issued every manager in Bourneville with a notice for their office which said: 'The name of the game is profit.'[20]

It was a tough period of high inflation, price controls and energy shortages. The chocolate side poured on, and 1971 saw the launch of the Creme Egg. The food side engaged in a flurry of purchases and takeovers. It bought McVities biscuits and then spun off its biscuits and cakes division to United Biscuits. It was easier to buy established brands and integrate them than to take the risk of launching too many of its own. In any case, the basic attention of the company was now focused on the USA, rather than the home market.

The truth was that Cadbury Schweppes was unwieldy as a company. Its attention was abroad. The drinks market and the chocolate market were not actually very similar. Some management philosophy was required to drive this kind of confection in the same direction. Adrian Cadbury rejected fashionable command-and-control, and argued that the future lay with decentralized companies. He said in 1981: 'Large companies will become more like federations of small enterprises, not because small is beautiful but because big is expensive and inflexible.'[21]

But that begged the big question: if they were better off run as small enterprises, why squeeze them into one massive conglomerate?

Back to chocolate again

Adrian Cadbury was a manager of some prescience. That was why John Major asked him to chair his commission on corporate governance – the one which recommended non-executive directors to provide moral oversight on company boards – and why he spent his retirement chairing the pioneering community bank, the Aston Reinvestment Trust. But it took nearly two decades for the full implications of Adrian's statement about decentralized companies to unravel.

He stepped down as chairman in 1982, the year his father died at the age of ninety-three, to be succeeded by his brother Dominic, a businessman in a more conventional mould. Dominic cut the number of production lines at Bourneville from seventy-eight to a more sensible thirty-three, reducing the number of employees by 40 per cent, and forced the pace on American expansion, gearing up the drinks division to compete with Coca-Cola and Pepsi. He organized a highly successful share issue in the USA in 1984 to fund the expansion. A decade later, Cadbury Schweppes finally engineered the chance to buy the key brands they needed – Dr Pepper and Seven Up, for £1.6 billion – which won them the coveted number-three position in the US soft drinks market. But what did that have to do with chocolate?

By then Cadbury Schweppes accounted for 4 per cent of the world's chocolate consumption. This put them again at number three, after Nestlé and Mars. But there seemed no obvious way to burst out of the number-three position in either the drinks or chocolate markets. Adrian's decentralization had also driven the two divisions apart. The confectionary division was based in Bourneville while the soft drinks division was based in the USA, and its chief came to Britain only twice a year for planning meetings at the company's headquarters in London's Berkeley Square.

By the end of the 1990s, it was becoming clear that the company was still a good deal too complex, and the merger-mania of the previous three decades had not always made sense. Cadbury sold off all its remaining interests in food. The attempt to launch the Cadbury name in the USA was finally recognized as an expensive failure, and it sold its rivals Hershey a licence to make its products there. In December 1998, Cadbury Schweppes sold all the drinks brands that were bottled and distributed outside the USA to Coca-Cola. It was, according to the *Financial Times*, 'the end of an attempt to conquer the world for British soft drinks'.[22]

But what about Camelot? Ironically, that was also the name of the company chosen to run the British National Lottery, and – despite the Cadbury antipathy to gambling, stretching back to its foundation – Cadbury Schweppes became one of five shareholders in Camelot, aware that Mars would move in if it didn't. More controversial was the use of Cadbury's retail database in distributing the first 10,000 coveted lottery terminals. What was most obvious about the Camelot dispute was that – despite the company's history – there was so little argument about it. Dominic Cadbury said: 'As chairman, I've only had two letters of criticism about the lottery and both were from members of my family.'[23]

Cadbury Schweppes was concentrating on its strengths, but the cupboard was still well-stocked with brands: Trebor and Butterkist on the confectionary side, Snapple ice teas and Mott's apple juices on the soft drinks side. In the last two decades of the twentieth century, it bought nearly fifty soft drinks brands to add to its global collection. The question was: did the drinks and confectionary businesses really have anything in common? Yes, there was the ambition to be the world's number-one non-cola drinks company, but where did that leave the chocolate?

Such questions hung in the air, articulated behind closed doors or in the occasional report by financial analysts, until suddenly the company was forced to confront them. The real driver of change was the former owner of Snapple, the American financier and corporate raider Nelson Peltz. He was well-known for buying stakes in companies that needed to change and battling for places on the board to force the changes through. When it emerged in 2007 that he had built up a 3 per cent stake in Cadbury Schweppes, the board began to get nervous. Something would have to change and quickly, or Peltz would do it himself.

The man in the hot seat was the American CEO Todd Stitzer, the company's former chief strategy officer, from New Jersey. A hotshot tennis player and a man given to long and impassioned voicemails to his underlings, Stitzer was the author of the strategy to grow the confectionary business by branching out into sweets that blurred a little with medicine. It was Stitzer who bought Adams, Trident, Halls and Dentyne, and by doing so guaranteed his position as successor to John Sutherland as CEO. Next he moved into sugar-free chewing gum, launched the Global Gum Center for Excellence in New Jersey and also launched a new kind of Brazilian chocolate called Chocki, liquid chocolate designed for hot climates. His new Cherry Vanilla Dr Pepper sold more than $100 million-worth in 2006. But all this obscured the truth about Cadbury: it was basically now an American company with very different objectives. It had been decades since the original values of the company had been much in evidence.

In 2003, Stitzer took over the company he had worked with for two decades with a baptism of fire. First there was an outbreak of salmonella at a plant in Herefordshire which the company hushed up for five months, even though thirteen people had been made ill. Next there was an accounting scandal in Nigeria, followed by another embarrassing product recall: the nut allergy warning was wrong on a line of Easter eggs. Even in 2008, Cadbury products were caught up in the contaminated milk scare in China.

But Stitzer was a fighter. It was the arrival of Nelson Peltz that forced his hand on the structure of the company. One way to hold off Peltz and his allies was to cut costs, and Stitzer closed forty-one factories around the world, at the same time as forcing the Cadbury Schweppes market share up again in the crucial US drinks market. But the rumour was that Peltz and other activist investors believed the company was worth less than the sum of its parts and it should be broken up and sold off. If Peltz was determined to force a break-up, then it made sense to the board to do it themselves, under their own terms.

So finally, in May 2007, Stitzer announced that Cadbury Schweppes would sell its drinks company brands to private equity partners. It meant the virtual end of Schweppes as a business name. The share price shot up by a third and then collapsed back down again two months later when it was clear that – in the emerging credit crunch – there were no buyers.

'We have to show our investors that we can work and chew gum at the same time,' said Stitzer, the chewing gum champion. By October, they had come up with the answer. A year later – despite the collapse of the world financial markets – Cadbury Schweppes was de-merged. The Dr Pepper Snapple Group became a separate company with sales of more than $5 billion, and Cadbury was alone again – a different animal to the conglomerate that went into the 1969 merger – but not so unlike the confectionary company which had emerged from the 1950s to begin a foray into instant foods.

As always, it was Chocolate Camelot itself – the factories in Bourneville – that faced the immediate fall-out. Up to 15 per cent of the confectionary workforce lost their jobs in a production shift to chocolate factories in Poland. De-merging is always a brave move and no less so in this case. Despite the wisdom of Adrian Cadbury's remark about decentralized power being more effective, the financial markets normally prefer mergers to de-mergers, and – since the company was now in hock to the financial markets – this risked making it a plaything. It also left Cadbury still number three in the world chocolate market, potentially exposed to a renewal of the old slavery scandal it believed it had escaped a century before.

The curse of cocoa

There is a little bus station in Sikasso in Mali where slave traders wait for boys. Often the boys have been offered work in Côte d'Ivoire, with the promise of free transport to get there and fat wages. The enterprising adolescents are driven on motorcycles across the border into Côte d'Ivoire, as their suspicions mount, before they are handed over to the cocoa farmers to work for them. From then on, home is often a mud hut without windows, with beatings if they try to leave.

Côte d'Ivoire now provides half of the cocoa for the world's chocolate market, and while Cadbury still concentrates its efforts on Ghana next door – the name given to the Gold Coast after independence – much of the chocolate produced in Ghana is high quality which is often traded on to make top-range products, rather than going into the industrial chocolate produced by Mars, Hershey or Cadbury. The distribution and price of cocoa is now governed primarily by the speculators in Wall Street and the City of London, and – although this had been the case for a generation or more – the turn of the century saw the slavery issue suddenly back on the agenda.

When a slave ship carrying forty-three children and heading for Côte d'Ivoire was stopped in 2001, Cadbury spoke out. Certainly, of the three major players in what has come to be known as Big Chocolate, Cadbury is the least tainted by slavery. As much as 70 per cent of its buying operations are largely in Ghana, even if Cadbury products sold in the USA are actually made by Hershey, which sources its chocolate elsewhere. Even in Ghana, the farmers get precious little of the price, probably about 0.5p per 90p 200g bar of chocolate, and Cadbury was also part of the European lobby of big manufacturers trying to reduce the cocoa content in chocolate, which would mean paying them proportionately even less.

As political pressure began to mount, the US State Department estimated that over 100,000 children were working on the cocoa farms in Côte d'Ivoire, and at least 10 per cent of them were victims of slave trafficking. To make matters worse, there was rising tension in Côte d'Ivoire between the indigenous farmers and those from neighbouring Burkina Faso. When there was a mutiny in the Côte d'Ivoire armed forces, the fighting was fuelled by the profits from cocoa. The mutiny caused panic buying and speculation on the world markets. In August 2002, the London trading company Armajaro suddenly bought 5 per cent of the world cocoa crop. Speculation reached fever pitch, with farmers and manufacturers caught in the middle.

It was at this point that two American politicians stepped in. Democrat Congressman Eliot Engel from New York and Senator Tom Harkin from Iowa drafted a law forcing the chocolate industry to introduce a labelling system to guarantee that its products were free from slavery. The chocolate lobbyists fought back and the law that was eventually passed made no mention of labels, but it insisted on a voluntary code whereby the chocolate companies would end their involvement in slavery by 2005.

Of the big three Big Chocolate companies, Cadbury was again by far the least exposed to this. Ghana was not a hotbed of slavery like Côte d'Ivoire, and nor were Indonesia, India and the Caribbean, where most of the rest of Cadbury cocoa comes from. But it still bought chocolate on the world market. There was also a perceived 'ethics gap' between the Cadbury tradition and the way chocolate companies were being portrayed. Stitzer dealt with this by buying the fastest-growing fair trade chocolate brand, Green & Black's. There were criticisms that this was a cynical move, but it was also a bold and imaginative one. Green & Black's was not just an ethical organic brand, it was a high-quality product, with 70 per cent cocoa content compared to 20 per cent for most chocolate on the market. Green & Black's had recently been launched in the USA as well.

Stitzer stepped up efforts to improve productivity in Ghana to justify the 10 per cent premium they were paying there. The Cadbury Cocoa Partnership became an ambitious £45 million project, involving agricultural advice, microcredit and the whole gamut of enlightened local economic renewal. Neither of the other Big Three members, Nestlé and Mars, has managed anything comparable. But of course the project's funds were not spent in Côte d'Ivoire because Cadbury was not buying there, even if Côte d'Ivoire chocolate might make its way into the bars with the Cadbury logo on.

So it was hardly surprising that the 2005 deadline came and went and apparently nothing had changed. Engel and Harkin granted an extension until 2008. The law had required that the industry should launch a new body, the International Cocoa Initiative, based in Geneva, to actually make things happen, and they had to do so by July 2007. By 2008, the initiative was still employing only one member of staff actually in Côte d'Ivoire.[24]

By then Cadbury was once more a chocolate company, with a few Australian drinks brands. Some of the old corporate traditions are still in place. It is still impossible to buy alcohol in Bourneville, in accordance with old George Cadbury's ideals. In fact, the people who live there fought and won a court battle in March 2007 with Britain's biggest supermarket chain, Tesco, to stop it selling alcohol locally.

But despite the great moral edifice built by George Cadbury, selling human joy in an instant but dramatically ethical way – selling and rebuilding society at the same time – the chocolate business contains one critical flaw. Chocolate remains the quintessential imperial product. It is grown in the poorest countries in the world and shipped to the richest, where it is processed, branded and marketed, and occasionally sold back to the original growers, if they can afford it. Any chocolate company has to face this dilemma and respond to it. It was clear that more was demanded of Cadbury and, in March 2009, it finally announced that all its chocolate would be fair trade. It was a big move and it marked a 25 per cent leap in the sales of fair trade products in the UK. It was also a huge success as the fair trade Dairy Milk began appearing in the shops in the summer. But it was to have terrible repercussions.

By going fair trade, Stitzer had rattled the cage of the business analysts on Wall Street, where any compromise with ethical standards is regarded as a sign of weakness and an opportunity for profit. The fatal decision to make Cadbury a public company, all those years ago, was coming back to haunt it. In September, the huge American food business Kraft offered $10 billion to buy the company. The bid was to be financed by closing factories, as

123

Kraft had already done to the Terry's factory in York, and relocating to Eastern Europe. One descendant of George Cadbury described them as a 'plastic cheese company' and Stitzer rejected the offer, urging shareholders to 'hold out' for something more sustainable.

By November, Cadbury's American partners Hershey were also considering a bid. So was the Swiss chocolate giant Nestlé. But the financial vultures were circling the company and, finally, at 2 a.m. on 19 January 2010, it was all over – and for £11.9 billion. The British government made warning noises, but the institutional shareholders simply rolled over. In any case, it was a government-owned bank, Royal Bank of Scotland, which was financing the deal. An historic British company had been handed over to a management that was widely agreed to be worse than Cadbury's own, Stitzer would get a pay-out of at least £7 million, and the armies of City lawyers, PR advisors and financiers made about £250 million in fees. The Camelot tradition was over and the Cadbury family was left condemning what they called 'asset-strippers'.

Cadbury chairman Roger Carr said: 'We have done nothing wrong. We don't own the company – the shareholders own the company and the board has a fiduciary duty when appropriate value has been paid.'[25] Chocolate Camelot is now a dreamlike memory that – for 'one brief shining moment' – seemed possible and achievable. But, from the moment that Cadbury submitted to self-interested corporate finance, perhaps it never was.

CHAPTER 4

MARKS & SPENCER (1884): BRAVE NEW WORLD

I used to say that, to do well at Marks & Spencer, you had to have first, a little above average intelligence, second, a lot of common sense, and third, a slight Manchester accent.

Henry Lewis, joint managing director of
Marks & Spencer, in the 1970s

Cleanliness is next to fordliness.

Aldous Huxley, *Brave New World*, 1932

It is hard to imagine that the village in *Fiddler on the Roof* – or one very like it – might give birth to a British retailing revolution. Perhaps it shouldn't be hard, because the outpouring of ambitious and desperate inhabitants of villages like that all over the world certainly led to business innovation. But retailing? There were no shops there, for goodness' sake. Either way, one of the great innovations that emerged from fiddler on the roof culture was the British retail revolution known as 'Marks & Spencer'.

It was the Jewish artist Marc Chagall who first drew the picture known as *The Fiddler on the Roof*, and the image was eventually translated into one of the most successful Broadway musicals ever staged. It is a sad picture as well, not so much because of what it portrays – a Jewish village somewhere in central Europe – but because of what was about to happen there. Chagall painted it on a wall panel for the Moscow State Yiddish Theatre in 1920 before he left Russia for France, and painted *The Green Violinist* for himself afterwards as a memory of it. There is something fleeting about the violinist, and he is downright elusive in the musical, standing literally on the roof to play the evocative music of the past. But then, he stands for the Yiddish culture which inspired Chagall throughout his life, and which was all but destroyed, first in the murderous pogroms at the end of the nineteenth century and then in the Nazi holocaust.

The musical opened in New York in 1964, in the days when radical liberal opinion still looked to the state of Israel as an enlightened experiment in building utopia, a whole new world. People remembered the song 'If I were a rich man', sung by the milkman Tevye at the heart of the story – not just because we might all sing something similar, but because in the mouth of Tevye it seems miserably impossible.

Both play and film were based on an 1894 book by the Yiddish humorist Sholem Aleichem called *Tevye and His Daughters*. Even the song 'If I were a rich man' was based on his 1899 monologue which runs 'if I were Rothschild'. It is hard to imagine that those struggling refugees from the pogroms would ever become anything of the kind, even if they reached London or New York. But people did, and among them was a young man called Michael Marks, born in the town of Slonim in the province of Grodno, the Russian-controlled sector of what is now Belarus, probably in 1863.

Michael was the youngest of five children. His father was involved in milling and tailoring. His mother died giving birth to him and he was brought up by his older sister. It was a settled life on land where the presence of impoverished Jewish communities was tolerated, whose distinctive language and tradition rang with the memory of centuries of persecution and wandering, and a distant hope of the Promised Land.

That tension, between looking backwards and looking forwards, played itself out in the lives of Michael Marks, his children and those like them. It was more powerful than business, more galvanizing than profit and more inspiring than simple retailing. But then Marks & Spencer, the great British retailer which still bears his name, was designed – at least by his son's generation – to be about very much more than those things. It was intended as an engine that could right the wrongs suffered by Marks, his family, their relatives and so many like them in central Europe at the close of the nineteenth century. It was to be an experiment in a new kind of government, a practical utopia, a new world for those who never reached the New World.

Two generations before the holocaust, the little world that Michael Marks was born into was about to be blown away by a hurricane, driven by sword-wielding Cossacks and murderous mobs, that forced them to leave their homes and carry on wandering in the wilderness. The bomb which launched this particular hurricane was the explosion that in 1881 killed the reforming Tsar Alexander II, the day after he had finalized plans for an elected Russian parliament. The tsar had survived the first bomb of the day, but unwisely insisted on going to visit the spot where it happened, only to fall victim to the second bomber. He bled to death watched by his two successors, who vowed that they would never tempt fate in the same tiptoe towards reform themselves.

One of the conspirators turned out to be Jewish, unleashing a wave of violence that saw 200 Jewish people beaten to death immediately, and all the pogroms and violent intimidation that followed, driving the mass migration of a whole people. Between 1880 and 1910, a third of all the Jewish people in the world were moving continents, squeezed into dirty, lice-infested, black-funnelled steamships, arriving in London Docks or Ellis Island in New York Harbour, often owning nothing more than what they were wearing.

Marks was seventeen or eighteen when the tsar was shot. We know nothing about precisely why he left shortly afterwards. All we have are some photographs of him in middle age, short and dark with a neatly trimmed beard and moustache, like an English gentleman. The Prince of Wales had one just like it. We also know that he had what has been referred to as a talent for friendship. People trusted him. More than that, he seems to have possessed a talent for sympathetic understanding of the people he was dealing with, even if he spoke little or nothing of their language. On such talents, retailing empires very occasionally grow.

But he was not alone. Between 1881 and 1914, about 150,000 Jewish refugees came to Britain, and almost two-thirds of them lived packed into two square miles in London's East End. Marks seems to have decided on England because his older brother Barnet had gone there first. But as Michael arrived in London in 1882, with enough money for the train to Stockton-on-Tees, he found that his brother had gone – or was going – to the Yukon in Canada to join in the gold rush. His brother also went into retailing and opened a successful shop in Dawson City. Something about the Marks family seems to have put retailing in their genes.

So there was Michael, without language, money or prospects, but with something else. There was clearly something about the family that drove them to sell, and here he had arrived in the right place at the right time. There was a retailing revolution under way to serve the growing middle classes in their new urban terraced homes, like *The Diary of a Nobody*'s fictional Mrs and Mrs Pooter in Upper Holloway, with a little yard at the back and maybe a housekeeper and maid. There was a wealth of cheap manufactured goods now on the market, filtering through to the upwardly mobile working classes, whose incomes were steadily improving throughout the 1880s.

Shopkeepers were in the middle of their own revolution. From being owner-managers who also produced their own goods, craftspeople who could turn a shoe or bake bread, they were becoming selectors and purveyors of what they thought they could sell. It was a shift exemplified by the rise of William Whiteley and his vast department store in west London, employing 6,000 staff. A generation before, anyone setting themselves up in a shop needed a skilled trade. Now what they needed, more than anything else, was a sense of the tastes and budget of their potential customers. With his sympathetic identification with people, this is just what Marks had. He may not have been quite William Whiteley – and a good thing too, as Whiteley was later shot dead in his office by a man claiming to be his illegitimate son – but he knew what people wanted.

It was 1884 before he acted, the year of the siege of Khartoum, of *Huckleberry Finn* and the Fabian Society. He decided to move to Leeds, a burgeoning Yorkshire city with a population of 300,000 clustered round the railway line to London. He particularly chose the district of the Leylands, with its strong Jewish population steeped in the clothing trade. Here he was going to stake his claim to the new world, and here – lo and behold – he encountered the help he needed.

The local wholesaler Isaac Dewhirst was wandering along Kirkgate one morning when he was approached by a man who said just 'barons'. Realizing this apparition spoke no English, he turned to his manager who spoke Yiddish and discovered that he was looking for Barran Clothiers, which was known to give work to refugees. It was a lucky coincidence. Dewhirst was fascinated by Marks and offered to lend him £5. Marks asked instead if he could take the money in the form of goods and pay off the cost in instalments. Dewhirst agreed, and Marks became an itinerant salesman in the Yorkshire Dales, selling buttons, wool, tablecloths, sacks and socks. It is a measure of the slightly unworldly company that Marks was about to found that the firm of I.J. Dewhirst and its successors are still supplying it to this day.

Marks was a damn good pedlar, but it was an exhausting business. It meant being outdoors in all weathers. It was bad for the lungs and constitution, and there was a bigger problem Marks had to overcome. He could barely converse with his customers. Instead, he invested in a stall in Leeds market, just a hundred yards from Dewhirst, and sold from there on Tuesdays and Saturdays. By the end of the year, he was so successful that he had opened stalls at markets on other days in Castleford and Wakefield. Soon he was shifting into the covered market hall, open all week.

Market halls were to the working classes what department stores were to the middle classes. They were all-weather affairs. You could buy nearly everything under one roof, and they were cheap. But once again, Marks had a language problem. He solved it by laying out all his goods on the table, rather than keeping the bulk of them under it, so that people could handle what they were about to buy, rather than ask questions about it. He also began what became the credo of his company. He avoided long haggling conversations with the customers by classifying everything according to price. Above the section for penny goods, he coined what became one of the most successful advertising slogans ever invented: 'Don't ask the price, it's a penny.'

This may not actually have been marketing genius. It was just a good way of avoiding having to talk to anyone, but it was so successful that Marks decided only to sell goods that cost a penny. This had another great advantage. It meant he could dispense with complex accounts and keep it all in his head, but it also provided him with a secondary headache – the main problem for his company for the rest of its existence. Where could he find high-quality, low-cost goods which he could turn over in enough quantities to make a profit? He needed a constant supply of high-quality, low-cost cups, teapots, lead soldiers, balls, pencils, envelopes, hammers and everything else. The same problem, in a different form, was shared by all his successors.

Two years later, he felt secure enough to get married to a girl called Hannah Cohen. His son Simon was born in 1888 and the Marks dynasty was born. Around this time, his northern retailing empire began to expand seriously. In 1887, only five years since the original loan from Dewhirst, he was in the covered market in Warrington, over the border in Lancashire. In 1890, he was in the market in Birkenhead, and opened five penny bazaars using the same slogan. The following year he moved home to Wigan, set up his warehouse there on the main line to London, and opened Marks' Original Penny Bazaar in the oldest market in Lancashire.

But the key year was 1894. He struggled to open a fully fledged shop in Cheetham Hill in Manchester, and he realized he needed a business partner, preferably someone who could do the money side of the business. He asked Dewhirst, who said he was too busy, but suggested his own cashier, Tom Spencer. Spencer paid £300 for a half share of the business and ensconced himself with the account books.

The two men became great friends. Spencer had exactly the right mix of skills and, in any case, you feel that Marks' talent for friendship would have got him through whoever his partner was. They were certainly a contrast. Where Marks was small and slight, Spencer was vast, with a huge walrus moustache. Where Marks took risks to expand, Spencer was a careful organizer and a thrifty accountant. Marks & Spencer was formed that year on 28 September 1894. There was just one ominous cloud on the horizon: Spencer ate and drank to excess, but – for the time being – who cared? So did many people, in England at least.

With his new partner's organizational flair and his own brilliant ability to feel his way into the minds of his customers – though he was certainly not a member of the English working classes himself – Marks was able to accelerate even faster. When Queen Victoria died in January 1901, Marks & Spencer had thirty-six branches, including stores in Cardiff, Bath and London, and a new warehouse and headquarters in Robert Street, Manchester. Within two years, this was too small, and they built another one in Derby Street with an electric lift and a dining hall. Ever since one of his assistants died of pneumonia after a chilly stretch in Birkenhead market, looking after his predominantly female staff was high on Marks' priority list, as it would be for his son.

Manchester was important for what came later. It was no ordinary city, but a deeply political one. It stood for something. The Hallé orchestra was there, the chemical industry was challenging traditional manufacturing, the *Manchester Guardian* was challenging the government. It was a Liberal city, in opposition to the Conservative, imperialist government in London, developing a new vision of British industry and society. It was still the heart of the cotton empire and was also the northern outpost of a highly educated, powerful, thinking Jewish community. In this city, Marks decided to bring up his children. It was a decision that made Marks & Spencer different from almost any other retailer.

Even so, Spencer's health was breaking down. The year they reorganized Marks & Spencer as a limited company, in 1903, it was worth £30,000, a hundred times Spencer's original investment. The two partners distributed a few shares to staff but kept the bulk of them themselves, and here they made their big mistake. They made no provision for their successors. Since Spencer was about to drop a bombshell, this was unexpectedly short-sighted. That same year, he announced that he was retiring, and moved to Lichfield to become a chicken farmer. Two years later, he was dead. He was only fifty-three.

This meant the arrival in the company of Spencer's executor, a handkerchief manufacturer and M&S supplier called Michael Chapman. It also meant considerable extra strain for Marks, who had to shoulder the responsibility of what was now a major business all by himself. On Christmas Eve 1907, Marks took his nineteen-year-old son Simon and Spencer's son Tom Junior out to lunch at the Victoria Hotel, Manchester. As they walked home afterwards, Marks collapsed in the street and died. He was only forty-four, but he left an estate worth £27,000. The young man driven out of Slonim like the fiddler on the roof had in fact become a rich man after all.

The rise of Simon Marks

As the dawn broke on the morning of New Year's Day, 1908, Marks & Spencer was an energetic and successful retailer with sixty branches, mainly in the north, a number in London – including under the railway arches at Brixton – and a row of eight shops merged into one in Leeds. But it was a retailer with a problem. Both the partners were dead. Simon Marks had only just left Manchester Grammar School to join the company, but he could hardly take over yet. The company histories insist that Tom Spencer Junior was not interested in progressing through the ranks. We have to take that with a pinch of salt, but he had inherited his father's penchant for drink and that was bound to hold him back.

The shares were owned in equal numbers by the two families, with no obvious way of redistributing them to make sure the company leadership was galvanized. The stage was set for one of two bitter boardroom battles in the Marks & Spencer history.

In practice, Chapman was now in charge of the company, and he exercised a powerful influence over young Tom Spencer, who was now also on the board. The Marks family moved to appoint a friend of theirs, Bernard Steel, to look after their interest on the board, and the ballooning company carried on accelerating, doubling turnover again in the seven years to the outbreak of the First World War, more than doubling the number of branches, and opening two new warehouses in London and Birmingham.

But the clouds were still on the horizon. The American retailer F.W. Woolworth, operating along similar lines to Marks & Spencer, had arrived in 1909 and seemed unstoppable. There were other competitors as well. One chain was owned by Michael Marks' older brother Ephraim, who had escaped from the Russian Army and joined his brother in England, and who was presumably refused permission to join the family concern. Another was the London Penny Bazaar Company, a copycat version of M&S, which Chapman bought for £15,000 in 1914.

Another cloud was the relationship between Chapman and Steel. Both men realized that, although they were supposed to be representing the founding families, the company was probably theirs for the taking if they could work together. They planned to increase the share capital to £100,000, knowing that neither the young Marks nor the young Spencer could afford to join in. But so many of the most flawless plans unravel on just this sticking point: the two men just could not get on, which is why Marks & Spencer did not become Chapman & Steel. They irritated each other, and – when Steel ran into trouble with cost overruns building the new store in Portsmouth – Chapman forced him out, leaving himself in sole charge. The only check on his authority was now the young Simon Marks, who became a director in 1911.

It was a period of experimentation. M&S published a children's magazine and launched an unsuccessful library of popular classics. On the other hand, brushes sold so fast that it made sense for the company to make them itself. Simon Marks was put in charge of buying a small brush company. That was less than successful and the company was sold back to the previous owners two years later.

Chapman was not happy about this. Both set-piece boardroom battles in the history of Marks & Spencer were about profligacy versus thrift, at least on the surface, and the business of the brush company became symbolic. Chapman was worried about spending too much; the young Marks wanted to drive ahead. The battle was waged in the boardroom.

Finally, in February 1913, there was open conflict. The secret about Simon Marks was that, even then, he could not bear not having his own way. In other areas of life, this might have marked him as seriously pathological, but not in retailing. The combination of Chapman and the young

Tom Spencer, who backed him on everything, was deeply frustrating for the young man. Marks suggested Alexander Isaacs as another director to even up the odds. Isaacs was a trustee of the Marks estate, and could be guaranteed to swing the boardroom votes back in the direction of the Marks family, or – to be precise – in Simon Marks' direction.

In the chair, Chapman asked for a show of hands on the proposal. It was defeated. Marks insisted that the shareholders voted and, since the bulk of the shares were divided equally between the two families, this was close, but Marks won. Chapman then ruled that new directors required a two-thirds majority and so the proposal was defeated again.

A furious Simon Marks stormed home to his mother and sisters and began to plot. There were a few other shares available, given to employees back in 1903 and, for the next few years, Marks assiduously bought up any that were available. Chapman responded by refusing to register their transfer. Marks countered by getting perpetual proxy votes for them instead. Chapman ruled that they were invalid. It was all very exhausting, but it became Simon Marks' whole life.

As the boardroom battle progressed, a far bigger battle was looming. The First World War broke out in August 1914. The Chancellor of the Exchequer David Lloyd George staved off a banking crisis at the start of the international tension in the summer, and this, plus the massive increase in expenditure in wartime, led to serious inflation. The U-boat war meant that some of those crucial M&S penny mainstays were becoming scarce and expensive.

The slogan had to go. It was no longer economic to sell everything for a penny, and the massive turnover that was at the heart of the M&S business model was under threat. The solution, at least according to Simon Marks, was to buy. Buying was now largely his responsibility and he began to place larger and larger orders, stockpiling what the company needed, for fear that it might become unavailable – certainly at the same price. The company began borrowing in 1916 and its overdraft had reached £75,000 two years later.

Chapman was horrified, but he could hardly act to prevent it while the boardroom battle was left unresolved. Meanwhile, Marks' plotting was coming to a head. He was frustrating Chapman by failing to turn up to the directors' meetings, rendering them inquorate and unable to take decisions. He and his mother, plus his schoolfriend Israel Sieff and Alexander Isaacs, combined to force the directors to call an extraordinary AGM to appoint new directors. The meeting took place on 22 November 1915, as preparations for battle were going on along the Western Front. The whole rigmarole was repeated. The Marks family put forward a resolution to appoint Sieff and Isaacs as directors, which the directors voted down. They then called for a shareholder vote, which was exactly the same again – a narrow Marks victory.

All eyes were on Chapman. Once more he ruled that the proxy votes were invalid and the resolution had therefore been defeated. The shareholders drifted away and the directors met again. This time, Chapman and young Tom Spencer passed a resolution to reduce the quorum to two, effectively leaving them in charge of the company, and electing William Norris – the company's first male employee – on to the board. Only when Norris was in his post did Chapman offer to put Marks' friend Sieff there too.

The legal issue was now clear. Were the proxy votes valid or not? If they were invalid, as Chapman said, then

Norris was a member of the board. If they were valid, on the other hand, then the two vacancies had already been filled by the shareholder vote by Sieff and Isaacs. It was time to go to court.

These were the days when justice was swift, and the various parties to the dispute gathered in London at the Court of Chancery the following month. There they heard Mr Justice Peterson rule against Chapman on all points. Norris, the shortest-lived director in the company's history, was not a director after all.

But Chapman was a serious man who believed he was fulfilling his duty to the Spencer estate. Expanding the company during the war was foolhardy, and close to profiteering. Running up debts for stock which might never be sold was insane. It was his duty, as he saw it – although he was not now in perfect health – to stay as chairman of the board to make sure that young Marks and his friends did not bankrupt the company. He appealed against the decision, but this was dismissed the following month. Four months later, the real issue was played out in the board. Chapman put forward a resolution that was designed to stop Marks in his tracks – that there should be no expansion in the war years. Marks put forward a counter-resolution naming himself as chair. Chapman and Spencer Junior refused to vote, realizing that they would lose, and left the meeting.

Even then the struggle carried on, and it was over the issue of paying directors more that Marks and Sieff delivered the *coup de grâce*, realizing that Chapman was in increasingly poor health. The final decision kept being delayed until July 1917, and Chapman died the following month, leaving Marks, at the age of twenty-eight, in undisputed charge of the company for which he had fought. A reward for tenacity and rage.

Marks was not a forgiving man, but he was presiding over a forgiving company. Old Tom Spencer's widow Agnes was drafted in to fill Chapman's place on the board, and Chapman's handkerchief company carried on supplying M&S for decades afterwards. Even Norris stayed employed, and his son did finally become a director. But young Tom Spencer was not so lucky. He died an alcoholic at the age of only thirty-five, an unfortunate victim of the first M&S boardroom clash. Was he really unambitious, or was he destroyed by the bitter struggle he was unwilling to take part in? We will never know.

Sieff's alliance

Simon Marks had now come into his destiny as chairman of the board, but he had also been called up for military service in the Royal Artillery and was posted to Preston. His first few board meetings as chairman were shifted to the Bull and Royal Hotel there, so that he could be present. His duties were temporarily handed over to his friend Sieff.

Israel Sieff was then, and always, the critical figure in Marks' life. They had their background as sons of Jewish refugees in common, but that was all. Marks was five foot six inches and aggressive; Sieff was everything that Marks was not – tall, calm, thoughtful, understanding and placatory. As a partnership they were dynamic, and from the moment Sieff joined the company as a full-time employee – finally in 1926 – they shared an office together for the rest of their lives, often carrying on talking far into the night. For much of that time, they also lived together, and – most important – they married each other's sisters. This is something of a pattern in successful British family companies.

In fact, it was Marks' sister Rebecca who originally drew them together. Sieff caught sight of her, got to know

139

her and ended up being invited home. There he and Simon discovered a mutual interest in cricket, followed by a mutual interest in business, Zionism and the right shape of society. There is a photograph of the two friends just after leaving school, both with hair carefully combed like model Englishmen, both with distinctive black moustaches, Sieff's curling up at the ends like that of the Kaiser. But from the start, there was no doubt who was in the driving seat. 'Simon was a monster,' said one former M&S director years later.[1] He had a ferocious temper and would not be crossed, but he recognized the calm intelligence of his friend and brother-in-law and the relationship worked.

Even before he found himself voted on to the board of Marks & Spencer alongside Simon Marks, Sieff had encountered the other inspirational figure in his life, who would become crucial to the design of the corporation they were both about to shape. He first met Chaim Weizmann in 1913, then a reader in biochemistry at Manchester University, and was completely bowled over. 'Magical, overwhelming, irrevocable,' Sieff later wrote.[2]

Weizmann was the iconoclastic Zionist who believed that the dream of a Jewish homeland was practical politics. Sieff's arrogant talk about fundraising irritated the sensitive prophet, and Sieff later admitted in his memoirs that, to start with, Weizmann did not like him much. Even so, the young man's commitment to the cause never wavered. He brought Simon Marks to meet him, and the two friends remained convinced Zionists for the rest of their lives. Their parents had been forced to escape from their villages like the fiddler on the roof; how could they not be inspired by utopian plans to end the wandering?

But Weizmann was also a biochemist and he believed in the new science which was to become so important both to the new state of Israel and to the growing M&S.

His scientific know-how brought him into contact with the government, and his relationship with the editor of the *Manchester Guardian*, C.P. Scott, brought him into increasingly influential circles. By 1917, with the Turks in full retreat and General Edmund Allenby heading for Jerusalem, there seemed to be a unique opportunity for that homeland to be somewhere near the original state of the biblical kingdom of Israel. The fact that other people were living there already was not an overwhelming obstacle to them: this would be a scientific and liberal utopia, after all.

After the Balfour Declaration, which set out just such a plan, Zionism suddenly became British foreign policy, and Sieff was sent out to help Weizmann and the Palestine Commission to work out how it might be possible. It was a difficult, dangerous and deeply influential period for Sieff. Simon Marks, still on national service, managed to get himself seconded to Weizmann's headquarters in London. The two friends were now at the heart of the practical business of founding a new nation and were thinking about how it could work. Like others of their generation, who reached the peak of their careers in the 1940s, utopia-building meant big, centralized, rational decision-taking. It meant science at the heart of policy and it meant training a new technological elite to make these systems work.

This was the generation that was inspired by the term 'social security', an example of just how much political language can be corroded. For Sieff, particularly, providing people with security was what life, politics and business were all about. Marks & Spencer would emerge in his hands as an experiment in providing security to staff and customers alike. It would also be an experiment in government.

When Marks and Sieff came back from the war and their Zionist training, the task of reshaping the company lay before them. The board was young and idealistic, and was soon joined by the *Guardian* journalist and prominent Zionist Harry Sacher, who married another Marks sister. They were close-knit and excited by new ideas, and it was often said that the board was practically in continuous session. Marks & Spencer was now heavily in debt. Its basic business model, everything for a penny, was unworkable. Other better-funded competitors were pressing on all sides. But Marks sensed an opportunity too.

This was, after all, the great age of retailing. Selfridges had opened in 1909, making London's Oxford Street the pre-eminent shopping destination in the country. It was a new age, described by J.B. Priestley in his *English Journey*, of dual carriageways, road transport networks, distribution systems and a whole new industrial revolution based on ribbon development and suburban expansion. Multiple retailers were on the march, bigger, lighter, more convenient, to the rage of those who detected a challenge to individualism. The writer G.K. Chesterton condemned them as 'not really shops at all, but branches of the accountancy profession'.

It was certainly a social revolution as great as anything in Marks' father's day. The middle and working classes were beginning to think like each other. Working-class women were venturing into the shops, rather than making their own clothes, and beginning to liberate themselves from traditional costumes. It was a new kind of integrated, classless society, perfect for experiment.

That was the background to Marks' first decision. The company would consolidate its stores and build more, buying the freeholds where it could to guarantee its own security. It would build new and massively. The 1923 Blackpool store had a front measuring fifty-eight feet. For a small man, Marks thought big.

His second decision emerged from his experience in the army. Chain stores were like armies on the march. They needed information sent to the centre. They needed intelligence, otherwise what you got was the blind slaughter of the Western Front. He knew that it was taking two months or more for sales reports to get from the stores to head office, and he needed information far more quickly if the company were going to get the right merchandise into the right places. 'How can I increase the value of this?' he asked, holding up a Woolworth's pencil, and was aware that he had no answer.

When a distant relative in New York invited him over and offered to introduce him to leading retailers in 1924, Marks jumped at the opportunity. He came back with ideas about bigger premises, new ideas in stock control and how to make the counter footage pay for the rent overheads, and was now dedicated to the American notion of 'super stores' with their pricing policy of a dollar for everything.

He later wrote: 'The policy we should follow was now clear. Nothing over five shillings, an extensive programme of enlarging and improving our shops, and the introduction of weekly stock checking lists which controlled the production and flow of goods from factory to shops.'[3] Simon Marks was bringing American-style shopping to Britain.

Profits had been increasing because of post-war inflation in Germany, which meant that Marks & Spencer could source its products there at a tiny cost. But the expansion would require more than just higher profits. Marks tapped the directors for preferential loans and then organized a new public share issue to finance the new stores, combined with a ferocious central control on spending. The 1926 share issue flopped. The National Strike was looming and it was not the moment, in Britain at least, for buying shares. Prudential Assurance, the underwriters, had to step in and buy most of them up, and they remain one of the biggest Marks & Spencer shareholders to this day.

The sourcing of products from Germany was an exception. M&S kept the Buy British policy forced on them by the U-boats, and it was to provide the moral core of the company for the next two generations. But it did raise another problem which had to be solved. There was far too little on the market which could be priced at five shillings, roughly equivalent to the dollar which was the basis of so much pricing in the USA. Buying from wholesalers in the traditional way was failing to provide what the company needed. The result was a major shift in retailing policy. It would buy direct from manufacturers.

That was the only way it could achieve Marks' vision of high-value, low-cost goods. It was not then or later a rational economic policy: economics would normally suggest lowering the value and marking up the price. But Marks had inherited some of his father's intuition. He sensed that the new classless Britain needed something like this and believed he could provide it using mass production, bringing economies of scale. These were the great days of Henry Ford and the production line, and this was at the heart of the M&S plan. But first of all it had to slay the monster of the wholesale system.

The man charged with dealing with this was the gentle, persuasive Sieff, who joined the company full-time on the day before the General Strike. The main obstacle, especially now that M&S was specializing in clothing, was the Wholesale Textile Association, set up specifically to stop retailers and manufacturers from having anything to do with each other. Sieff had some success, but the handful of small manufacturers who accepted orders insisted on arriving at the M&S headquarters by the back door in case they were seen. Sieff's weapon was the prospect of very large orders at a time of depression in the textile industry.

To that end, he set off to Leicester and knocked on the door of a textile company called Corah, whose famous brand name 'St Margaret' was taken from the statue of the shepherdess saint outside the factory. They refused to see him.

It was not until Sieff's fourth visit to Leicester that the chairman of Corah agreed to meet, only to inform him that he could never accept a direct order. On his way back to his chauffeur-driven car, Sieff was followed by the plant manager, who had overheard. In a brief conversation, they agreed that the orders would be placed using a secret number that only they would know about. It was inevitable that the secret would come to light and some months later the plant manager was sacked. Sieff went back to Leicester and successfully argued for his reinstatement. Marks would never have managed it.

Sieff's plan was to build close supportive relationships with these suppliers. To give them the know-how they needed and help them invest in the plant, and to guarantee the prices too. At the end of the century, the idea of blurring the distinction between managers inside the company and suppliers outside was coming into vogue among management consultants and it was always Marks & Spencer that they pointed to, with some awe, as the originator of the philosophy.

Under Sieff, it was primarily a moral idea, about providing security that would allow a long-term, trusting relationship to thrive. The Corah annual report four decades later stated:

We do not forget that it was through his [Sieff's] inspiration, perception and encouragement that the names of Marks & Spencer and Corah have become so closely associated so uniquely, in our trade and industry. In 1966, we are forty years on from the opening of the account in 1926. At heart and in fact our relationship has never stood so strong as it is today.[4]

The St Margaret brand had been registered on the very first day of the 1875 Trade Marks Registration Act, which made it the oldest brand name for knitted goods in the world. Marks was impressed. But M&S wanted its own trademark in the store, maybe some other saint. It was inevitable perhaps that Marks would chose his father's name. So for the next six decades, 'St Michael' was instantly recognizable on the company's gold and green bags, which was how an overwhelmingly Jewish company borrowed Christian nomenclature as its trademark.

Yet the mixture worked: security for staff and suppliers, high quality, low cost, no advertising or marketing, and big, light stores. In 1938, the second M&S Oxford Street store opened, the Pantheon at 178 Oxford Street, and it was clear that – quietly and without fanfare – a whole new institution had arrived. It was for the mass consumer market, but it was decked out like a luxury department store, with wood panelling and oak blocks. This was not functional: it was classless. Marks & Spencer was profiting from the new society which had the BBC beamed into every parlour, where the memory and prospect of national service had driven the classes together. And it was profitable: £1.7 million a year by the outbreak of the Second World War.

The ultimate accolade had been reached six years before, when Queen Mary visited the Marble Arch store, a sure sign of ubiquitous appeal. It was a nervous moment because Queen Mary had a reputation for making outrageous demands for gifts. Turning to his assistant and breathing a sigh of relief as she disappeared, Marks said: 'That wasn't bad for the son of a pedlar.'[5]

An experiment in government

It was a glittering evening of intellectual progressives at Sieff's house in Manchester in 1932. The guest of honour was Sir Oswald Mosley, the future fascist leader, then in his pre-fascist New Party days and still wrangling with Harold Nicolson about whether the British 'brownshirts' should be wearing grey flannels. Perhaps forgetting where he was for a moment, Mosley said that political progress required somebody to hate and described the Jews as 'the best hate plank'. It was his first recorded anti-Semitic remark.

'Of course, that doesn't apply to Jews like you, Israel,' he added quickly. Sieff rang the bell and told the butler: 'Sir Oswald is leaving.'

Sieff may have dismissed Mosley, but there was also something of the authoritarian spirit of the age about Marks & Spencer. Marks was desperate to avoid bureaucratic structures and axed them brutally, loathing anyone who threatened his own personal control. But there was something autocractic about Marks, however benevolent. He chose the lamps in the offices, personally inspected every new line, took all the decisions. He refused to let his property director Arthur Giffard attend meetings in case anyone asked him what he was doing.

Marks presided over the directors' dining room, where lunch was served at 12.30 p.m. every day by waiters in white gloves, and where nobody would speak until he did. He sacked his chief accountant in 1945 for daring to question one of his plans. One poor shop assistant he met was too frightened to speak when he asked her name.

He was, as always, perfectly balanced by Sieff's placatory skills. It was as if they had borrowed from the style of secret policemen, where Marks did the kneeing in the groin and Sieff offered the cigarette.

There was no doubt that it was a benevolent dictatorship. When Flora Solomon famously met Marks at a dinner and said: 'It's firms like Marks & Spencer that give the Jews a bad name,' he recruited her to set up a welfare department. There were pensions and healthcare. Nobody was allowed to skip lunch and eat at their desk. It was all about security for staff and suppliers alike. Six years later, by 1939, it was employing a small army of over 18,000 secure staff.

The reason Sieff was hosting a dinner for Mosley was that he had already started to get interested in social issues and political reform, fascinated – as his generation was – by the idea of central planning as the antidote to the kind of irrational waste they saw on the Western Front. When his friend Max Nicholson published an article called 'A National Plan for Britain' in the magazine *Week-End Review* in 1931, Sieff and his friends clustered round and formed one of the first think-tanks, dedicated to making the plan a reality.

Sieff was among the first chairs of Political and Economic Planning (PEP), which began that same year, and found himself in the company of people like the radical agronomist Leonard Elmhirst of the Dartington Trust, the romantic architect Clough Williams-Ellis, the author of the future 1945 Labour manifesto Michael Young, the zoologist Julian Huxley and his brother, the writer Aldous. Together they laid the intellectual foundation stones for some of the giant, centralized, classless post-war innovations, like the National Health Service. There was to be a limit on profits, planned imports and exports and a small cabinet of ten technocrats to decide everything. It was the model that eventually brought us the slogan, 'You can't stand in the way of progress.'

The Labour newspaper the *Daily Herald* called the proposals fascist. The *English Review* called them social-ist. Williams-Ellis rather let the side down by coining the slogan 'PEP – try it in your bath'.[6] Aldous Huxley drifted away after the early meetings, but his satirical novel about technocrats, *Brave New World*, came out shortly after-wards. It caricatured PEP's vision, with its classification of everyone into a utilitarian hierarchy, its goal of happiness before freedom, and its M&S-style worship of 'Our Ford'.

Sieff himself leapt into print with a series of articles on economic planning called 'A Policy for Prosperity'. 'The main purpose of building up a great business should not be merely to make money,' he wrote; it was the key to the M&S experiment, which mixed business, Zionism, tech-nocracy and utopian hope in equal measure.[7] It was no coincidence that Weizmann was a biochemist.

When the new Israeli state was founded in 1948, here was a chance to put all that utopian thinking into prac-tice, and – just as it had cancelled all its German contracts when Hitler was first elected, regardless of the cost – so now Marks & Spencer poured its resources into provid-ing technical information, sourcing food from the Jewish farmers, founding research institutes and much more. 'It is hardly possible for us as Jews of the Diaspora to prepare any programme or plans of action unless, in some way or other, we bring Israel into relation with our projects,' said Sieff.[8]

The Second World War was both a vindication and a test for the M&S ideal. The company seconded its experts to help with the government's utility clothing scheme, which was exempt from purchase tax. It massively increased its cafeterias, opening the biggest war restaurant in the country in Marylebone, London. It advised the Ministry of Food and it set up kitchens for the defeated soldiers from Dunkirk at the ports along the Kent coats. Especially in Coventry, where the Marks & Spencer store was destroyed, it helped feed the victims of the blitz.

Marks himself helped set up the Air Defence Cadet Corps, helped organize production in south-east England, and became an advisor to the Ministry of Petroleum Warfare, developing a flame-throwing tank, a machine for clearing fog from airfields and a cross-channel pipeline for D-Day.

Sieff had a mild breakdown, brought on by a disastrous affair that cost him £250,000 in an out-of-court settlement, and escaped to the USA in 1940, ostensibly to try to generate British exports there to earn desperately needed dollars. The truth was that he was also there as part of a plan to continue to control M&S from abroad if the Nazis invaded.

But then Marks & Spencer was never really a conventional business: it was a campaign, a lever to change the world, an experiment in practical utopia and centralized technocracy. 'If the needs of the people are to be satisfied in the necessary quantities, quickly and at reasonable prices, the methods and techniques learned in the war will have to be applied and even improved,' said Marks in 1945.[9] Shifting that wartime sense of mass production while catering for good quality for the whole population was the key to the company's phenomenal post-war success – and to its phenomenal crisis in the 1990s.

After Marks

Simon Marks remained the dictator until the end, and kept one explosion of temper until the last. On 8 December

1964, he visited the ladies' tailoring department with his nephew Michael Sieff and was not pleased with what he found. As he had done so often before, he threw the offending clothes on the floor and shouted: 'You are trying to ruin my business.'[10] He stormed out, collapsed with a heart attack and died immediately.

The year he died, annual profits had reached over £20 million a year. Marks & Spencer was a national institution. As much as 99 per cent of its products were made in the UK. It sold a quarter of all the men's pyjamas and underwear and children's socks in the nation, and a third of the bras, boys' underwear and children's dressing gowns. When Purchase Tax was introduced in the 1960s, it responded by lowering its prices to cover it. M&S had clawed its way into a unique position, almost a national institution alongside the BBC and NHS, tried and tested in wartime and the austerity years.

Marks had described his relationship with Sieff in terms of David and Jonathan.[11] Sieff wrote, 'While he was alive he dominated me. I always deferred to him. It never occurred to me to do anything else.'[12] Everybody did.

Sieff inherited the company and then stepped down to be replaced by his brother Edward, who survived an assassination attempt in 1973, shot through the nose by Carlos the Jackal. He had passed the baton on to the next generation the previous year. Marks' son Michael was a rebel, marrying five times and converting to the Greek Orthodox Church. He told his father he had no interest in the business: 'I'm sorry, I just can't get into Devon splits.'[13] So the succession went to Israel's son Marcus, a socialite, foodie and four-times married womanizer.

Marcus had begun his career at Marks & Spencer with a row about winter tomatoes. His manager marched him upstairs complaining that he was making a nuisance of himself, but Israel Sieff agreed: they did look mangy. After that, M&S flew in tomatoes from the Canary Islands in winter. It was Marcus who first bought broken Kit-Kat pieces from Rowntree and built it into such a successful sideline that Rowntree started to manufacture broken ones just for M&S.

It was also Marcus – if it was anyone – who was most responsible for the revolution in supermarket shopping that brought foreign, exotic-looking foods to the shelves from all over the world. He jetted around the globe, tried the food and brought it home. He sent his technologists to California to bring crispheart lettuces to grow in the UK. He developed packaged sandwiches for M&S' cafes. He introduced grapefruits to the UK and bought in Israeli avocadoes for the first time – one customer complained that they did not go well with custard.

When he tasted a frozen cake he thought was delicious, and tracked it down to a company called Sara Lee in Boston, he spent years trying to persuade it to make the cake under the St Michael brand name. When Sara Lee took over an old bakery in Yorkshire, it led to the launch of M&S frozen foods.

This was a whole new approach to food, obsessive about standardization and hygiene, using new polythene products to keep it fresh. Marcus Sieff had inherited his obsession with cleanliness – a key aspect of Huxley's *Brave New World* – from Simon Marks. Colds had to be reported. Kitchen staff in supplier companies could not use their own hankies. Smoking was banned in stores as early as 1960. Not since the refrigeration revolution in the 1920s, which allowed the produce from farms to be trucked into the cities, had such a shift taken place – and all through those same close relationships with suppliers that were soon to be ubiquitous throughout the supermarket industry.

It was revolutionary but it was also, to some extent, a poisoned chalice. It led to monopolistic relationships with growers, which were fine when there was trust on both sides, but could become corrosive among less trustworthy competitors. It also led to a new factory approach to farming. Marcus was on the Egg and Poultry Reorganisation commission in 1933 that led to the massive expansion of battery hens. Processed food suited a changing society – Marcus Sieff's chilled Chicken Kiev in 1976 led the way to TV meals – but it drove out skills, local links and much else besides. It led to flying in vegetables out of season, the destruction of British orchards, the impoverishment of UK farming and much more.

The technological revolution, as they put it in those days, was also being brought to bear on clothing, thanks to Weizmann and the biochemists. After the war, M&S was at the forefront of developing man-made fibres which dried quickly or needed no ironing, or were lighter and more casual; rayon, terylene and the other new textiles made up half of what it sold by 1965. By then there were over 200 people working in its scientific branch.

Again, it was more utopian than businesslike. Marcus also shared his uncle's deep suspicion of marketing and advertising. Marks & Spencer did nearly none of it. Marks had believed that good quality would sell itself, and made sure that it was making no more than 10 per cent profit on any line. Nor were M&S believers in the new arts of spin, either to customers or staff. 'You cannot get the good will of the people who work for you by changing words such as "canteen" to "dining room",' said Israel Sieff.[14] Marcus agreed. They also agreed that they could never beat the competition on price alone.[15]

It was true, but the world was changing. Marks & Spencer shares were now sold on the world markets. The financial analysts who so influenced their price wanted short-term profits, not long-term relationships. They wanted a different kind of progress, not this utopian elitism. Nor did they much like the slow blurring of the boundaries between M&S and government.

Simon Marks' war against bureaucracy had reached fever pitch in 1956 after he visited one store at night and found two girls bringing stock cards up to date. They were abolished, along with time clocks. Good relationships were the basis of efficiency, he said, though you have to wonder whether Marks hated bureaucracy so much because it undermined his personal control. The publicity suggested that, if the government did the same, it could cut nine pence from income tax. Once more, M&S was styling itself as an experiment in government. When the first non-family member took over as chairman from Marcus Sieff in 1984, he became known – as much as anything else – for his ability to help the government save money.

Sir Derek Rayner was gay, irritable and a chain-smoker. Marcus Sieff kissed the girls when he visited factories, but Rayner famously hid himself away in a flat in a Thai fishing village. His long-term partner would occasionally borrow the company chairman's Rolls-Royce to tour London's gay scene, but Rayner was a dour figure in public. 'Lord Sieff preached a message of good human relationships to a wide audience. I won't be so available to do that,' he said.[16]

He had investigated improving defence procurement for the Edward Heath government and cutting government waste for the Margaret Thatcher government. Rayner famously railroaded his monthly board meetings through in an hour and a quarter, and the suppliers were getting nervous. This was the new world of maximizing profits.

But for a while, M&S prospered. When it launched its chargecard in 1985, it was massively successful, reaching six million people in its first fifteen years because the brand was trusted. When Sir Richard Greenbury, Rayner's chief executive, took over as chairman in 1991, the golden age seemed to have arrived.

Greenbury had joined the company at the age of seventeen, and had been a protégé of Simon Marks, who called him 'Big Fella'. But Marks' old ideals were no longer working. Expanding overseas had never worked quite as it was intended, since Marks & Spencer opened its first continental store in the Boulevard Haussmann in Paris in 1975. When it opened a store in Cologne in 1996, the new German staff – famously surly – were flown over to London to watch M&S' finest in action. The media were told that the German staff were in tears, touched by the closeness of the relationship between customer and staff. But it was not quite enough. Marcus Sieff had been in charge of the expansion into Canada, rumoured to be because he had a girlfriend there. But the spare 1940s austerity style inherited from the days of Marks and Sieff did not go down well. One woman in Alberta complained that she had no wish to shop in a hospital ward.

Nor were the close links with Israel trendy and utopian now that the plight of ordinary Palestinians was so much better known, and Marks & Spencer were still buying around £240 million of products from there by 2000. Nor did the vast privileges enjoyed by the directors and members of the M&S families – the Sieffs, Sachers and Laskis and their private jets – sit quite happily with the war on waste and thrift at other levels of the company.

The company still instilled a powerful sense of belonging. Rayner and his successor spent their whole careers in it. They paid more to graduates to get them early, then crammed the whole loyalty system into them. 'They constantly wanted to turn you into the same kind of gingerbread man as everybody else,' said the future chair-man Stuart Rose.[17] But the company needed outside ideas, given that the outside world was changing: more image-obsessed, more fickle, less one-size-fits-all.

Then there were the long-term relationships with sup-pliers, and there were more than 800 of them in the 1980s. Cynics called it a 'vast system of outdoor relief for the British textile industry' but there is no doubt that it had secured their future for decades. But then when Rayner's old friend Sir Geoffrey Howe increased VAT in his first budget as chancellor of the exchequer in 1979, Rayner asked the suppliers to reduce their profit margins to keep the prices the same.

It was a fearful moment. Under Marks and Sieff, the company had always reduced their own profits to help suppliers. It was part of the partnership which they had laboriously created. Now it was the other way around, because the markets demanded it. Greenbury squeezed them again in 1991 and his successor Peter Salsbury did the same in 2000. Now it is a regular feature of pre-emptory negotiation between the handful of dominant supermarkets and their powerless suppliers, but the years of massive M&S profitability in the 1990s were torn in effect from their suppliers. It was no longer a relationship of trust but one of manipulation. It was the way monopo-lies had always treated supplicants.

Greenbury maintained the relationships, encourag-ing many of the suppliers – including Dewhirsts – to set up factories abroad. But he had been working to reduce the number of suppliers since 1980, engineering mergers and acquisitions, forcing out the small owners. Within a decade, there were ten big British clothing manufactur-ers left supplying two-thirds of M&S clothing. But they were being squeezed hard by the company, just as food suppliers would later be squeezed so hard by the big four supermarkets – and for the same reason: the company had developed a monopolistic hold over them.

Corah, the start of Israel Sieff's quest for long-term relationships, was among those which were now in trouble and losing money. It was taken over by the finance company Charterhall in 1989 and then broken up. The statue of St Margaret which had inspired Sieff and Marks stood by its vacant factory in Vaughan Way, Leicester, for some years, until it was bought by a local charity and moved into the nearby church. It was the symbolic end of the road for the closeness and trust shared with suppliers, but still not quite the end of the relationship.

The second schism

Despite all this, Greenbury and M&S appeared to be riding high. In 1998, it was the first retailer to reach Greenbury's objective: pre-tax profits of £1 billion, with 13 million customers a week. But something was wrong. Within a year, profits had dropped by nearly a quarter, the share price had slumped and Marks & Spencer was engaged in the second bitter boardroom battle in its history. Within three years, profits were down to £145 million, and the company was closing its European stores, including the one in Cologne.

One of the reasons was clearly that they had paid too much ($750 million) for the Brooks Brothers chain in the USA and Littlewoods in the UK, but it was also about the determined cost-cutting required to reach that magic billion. Money was lavished on the new stores, or the new out-of-town joint venture with Tesco in Cheshunt, but it was being sliced off staff and training. Profits on some lines had been pushed up to 14 per cent – well over Simon

Marks' maximum of 10 per cent – which had squeezed suppliers even further. It was the triumph of short-termism in a company which had been dedicated to long-term growth.

But it was also a new age. The days of mass production and economies of scale, which were at the heart of the original M&S utopian model of government, were over. People wanted changing rooms and clothes in extra-large sizes these days. They wanted to be trendy, to drift in and out of Gap, Next, Jigsaw, French Connection, River Island, Hennes from Sweden, Zara from Spain, and so on. Worse, the words 'quality value service', always on the cover of the annual report, had mysteriously disappeared. The St Michael's brand was also on its way out.

The customers were not very happy. One described her local M&S as like shopping in Moscow in the 1960s. The former *Harpers and Queen* editor Vicki Woods wrote in 1998: 'I nipped into the Newbury M&S . . . and found myself drifting round the clothing racks out of habit. There was nothing. Nothing. Aubergine blouses, skimpily cut in satin look viscose. Horrible little suits in cheap fabric, in funny colours like rusty brown.'[18]

The last family member on the board, David Sieff, urged it to go back to adding value, but nobody was listening. Nor was it possible in a world where the driving force was no longer customers but the financial markets, and they punished utopian thinking – or anything else that reduced short-term profits. Greenbury brushed off criticism. If we were getting it wrong, why are we making £1 billion a year, he asked? He never took criticism well, firing off intemperate letters, which became known as 'Rick-o-grams', to journalists and city analysts.[19]

The immediate problem was the succession. Greenbury had appointed four managing directors in 1994 and waited for them to fight it out. The most determined to succeed was the finance director Keith Oates, who had been recruited by Rayner – over the course of thirty-five interviews – to organize the financial services department. He was tall and dark and had a home in Monaco. Oates never liked Greenbury, but believed he would retire on his sixtieth birthday in 1996, leaving the field free for him to move in. When Greenbury announced he would carry on, Oates came to believe it was his duty to rid the company of him once and for all.

The stage was set for the second boardroom battle in the company's history, and the issue was ostensibly the same: Oates' plans for continental expansion versus Greenbury's more cautious cost-cutting. When the non-executive directors had decided secretly that Peter Salsbury would be made chief executive in 1999, they agreed among themselves that Oates would have to be handled carefully. They were right, but they were too late.

A few days after the announcement of disastrous results in November 1999, Greenbury set off to Goa on a business trip, to be followed by a week's holiday with his wife. The moment he was in the air, heading for Mumbai, a hand-delivered letter from Oates landed on the desks of all the directors, setting out the company's problems and naming himself as the man to tackle them. The Sunday papers had been squared and the weekend saw a flurry of criticisms of the company's direction. One analyst quoted in *The Sunday Times* said that: 'The whole bunch are a shower. Greenbury looks panicked, Salsbury is a wet blanket, and Oates has blown it.' The directors urgently summoned Rolls-Royce chairman Sir Ralph Robins to take charge of the company before Greenbury could get back. Greenbury realized he would have to return. He arrived, seething with rage, on Monday morning and drove to his flat where he met Stella Rimington – the former MI5 chief – and his other directors.

The 9 November board meeting was just hours away. The directors tracked down Oates, told him he had been fired, though – until minutes before the meeting – he was insisting he would still be there to carry on the fight. The tense meeting took just fifteen minutes and Salsbury was appointed chief executive, but the fall-out from the board-room battle lasted four years. Salsbury turned his back on his old mentor Greenbury, who resigned in June the following year. The problem was partly that M&S needed somebody to blame to convince the City that it was changing. Greenbury was the only one available to shoulder this role, but he naturally resented it.

There were swingeing job cuts and shouts of 'Marks and Sharks' at the TUC conference. It was also Salsbury who finally ended the long-term relationships with the British suppliers. Most went to the wall. William Baird, which had supplied clothing to M&S for thirty years, was given six months' notice. Its chief executive pleaded with Salsbury to delay the decision so that his merger with Coats Viyella could go through, but Salsbury refused and the merger failed. Sixteen factories closed and 4,500 textile workers lost their jobs. It was the end of the British textile industry.

M&S decided it could survive with just three British clothing suppliers, Coats Viyella, Courtaulds and a much reduced Dewhirsts, who were now relying on manufacturing mainly in Morocco, Sri Lanka and China and had largely become middlemen – exactly the opposite of Sieff's original intention of cutting out the wholesalers. Even the biggest, Coats Viyella, had shrunk from forty-five factories in 1990 to just fourteen (five of them part-owned). The company finally shocked the business world by making a pre-emptive announcement that it was no longer profitable to work with Marks & Spencer. The announcement was a deep embarrassment and sealed Salsbury's fate.

At the end of 1999, while Salsbury was carrying out his third restructuring, the rumours began that the retail wheeler-dealer Philip Green was planning a takeover, with a scheme to close the overseas businesses and put some style back into the clothing. He was forced to withdraw by a hostile press, but not before the M&S board had agreed to squeeze the suppliers again, promising the City to save £100 million from the supplier chain for no other reason than that it could.[20]

To lead the fightback, the board appointed the Belgian retailer Luc Vandevelde, a man who made his own olive oil. It was he who despatched Salsbury, after the Coats Viyella announcement, and poached the Kingfisher group high flyer Roger Holmes as chief executive. It was Holmes who brought in Next founder George Davies to launch his women's range 'Per Una'. Holmes and Davies together managed to force the share price upwards again in a desperate attempt to make M&S 'cool'.

But the real rescue story was to be allotted to someone else, a former M&S manager called Stuart Rose. He had been a friend of Green, and one of his guests at the famous toga party on his yacht *Lionheart* in the south of France. When Green renewed his bid, M&S were once more in serious trouble, especially given Green's recent success with British Home Stores. The banks Goldman Sachs and Merrill Lynch were backing him and putting up the funds and Green asked Rose if he would take on the food division if he won the ensuing battle.

Rose said no and was instead snapped up some hours later by Marks & Spencer as chief executive to lead the fight. When M&S dismissed his approach, Green was incandescent with rage. He drove round to its headquarters, grabbed Rose in the street and – depending on which reports you believe – either jabbed him repeatedly in the chest or grabbed him by his lapels. He vowed to win regardless, but Marks & Spencer still had 360,000 small private share-holders and 98 per cent of them voted against the bid.

Rose found the company was in a mess, describing five or six robber barons fighting each other and running separate businesses. He said later: 'There was no communication between the bridge and the engine room. It was like *The Cruel Sea* where Jack Hawkins is on the bridge shouting instructions to the engine room and all that comes down the tube is blood.'[21]

Rose is credited with turning the leviathan round, but in the financial downturn, M&S was one of the first to feel the pinch. There was no going back to the old command-and-control of Simon Marks and Israel Sieff, though Rose has insisted on keeping the jobs of both chairman and chief executive, in the old command-and-control style. In any case, the world had moved on. It was even more apparent that the days of economies of scale had gone. It was a new business universe of micro-production, local choice, customer fads and a massively segmented market.

M&S' new ethical branding is a hopeful sign, a modern reinterpretation of Sieff's maxim about business and price. The link Marks & Spencer made with Oxfam, providing vouchers to people who hand in second-hand M&S clothing, has been very profitable for both sides. But one condition of the deal was that the company stop buying goods from the occupied territories and labelling them as Israeli.

The food shops are still packed. M&S was also the first to phase out free carrier bags and to invest in renewable energy, though staff complained about the waste of flying up to the Scottish stores to show this off to the press. But the truth is that Marks' and Sieff's experiment in government is no longer viable in a world of financial markets and cool. It aimed to be universal, not trendy. John Lewis might be able to pull off the trick, but they are a co-operative, owned by the staff, who are paid considerably more, and they sell to just one niche in the class system. In a business world where innovation, except the most narrow profit-making kind, is punished by the global markets, the old Marks & Sparks is dead. It must follow its narrow band of competitors demanding further slices from its poor suppliers – 2 per cent discount on bills was the 2008 demand – or the markets punish them.

Simon Marks might have been a dictator, but he had a vision. It was one set in its own mid-twentieth-century time, technocratic, mildly authoritarian and designed in a mould of which Our Ford would have approved. The truth is that it will not – without massive financial upheaval – come again.

The final twist

There was an embarrassing footnote for M&S over the brutal business of the British textile industry. Samantha, wife of the Conservative Party leader David Cameron, was praised for wearing an off-the-peg polka dot dress at the party conference in October 2009. It transpired that all was not quite as it seemed. The dress had indeed been selling at M&S for £65 but it had actually gone out of stock. Mrs Cameron had asked Rose if he could find one, and Rose discovered that his company had actually ended its contract with the supplier, a small British designer called Amanda Marshall Ltd.

Not to be beaten, he asked Alison Mansell, who ran the company, to make another. They ran one up (it cost £150) and gave it to M&S. Rose sold it to Mrs Cameron with a 20 per cent discount. As journalists from the *Daily Mirror* and *The Times* began to probe more deeply into the story, M&S clothing chief Kate Bostock called Amanda Marshall Ltd and said: 'I want to know, plainly – are you going to the press? Because Stuart and I are very concerned.'[22] It was too late. The tale came out, just three weeks before Rose announced that he was stepping down as chief executive and handing over to Marc Bolland from the supermarket giant Morrisons.

It was the last twist of the long saga of Israel Sieff's grand plan for long-term relationships to provide the best of British industry. Alison Mansell said she had 'no plans' to work with M&S again, and has now been signed up by John Lewis, which appears to be playing a parallel role to M&S in its most successful days. Unlike some of the big New York retailers, there is no concerted action by British clothes stores to revive the textile and clothing industry here. You can't blame M&S by itself, of course, but the disappearance of an industry that dates back to the great wealth of English wool in the Middle Ages has ended with an even greater tragedy. There is almost no market for British sheep's wool, and most of it is now burned. There are imaginative schemes, like the Natural Fibre Company in Cornwall, that are finding new uses for it, but this criminal waste continues. Wool has largely been replaced in British products by the new fibres from petrochemicals that Marks and Sieff invested in all those years ago.

CHAPTER 5

ROVER (1896): THE DEATH OF THE GREAT CAR ECONOMY

I'm not sure George is wrong about automobiles. With all their speed forward they may be a step backward in civilisation. It may be that they won't add to the beauty of the world and the life of men's souls . . . They're going to alter war and they're going to alter peace. And I think men's minds are going to be changed in subtle ways because of automobiles.

> Eugene Morgan, a character in *The Magnificent Ambersons*, a film by Orson Welles, 1942

Transport made of man a new kind of waif: a being constantly absent from a destination he cannot reach on his own but must reach within the day.

> Ivan Illich, *Energy and Equity*, 1974

However fast the body travels, the soul travels at the speed of a camel.

> Middle Eastern proverb

'Nothing should be allowed to stand in the way of the great car economy,' said Margaret Thatcher in the 1970s. But something did. Rover was once at the heart of the biggest car-making enterprise in Britain. Its marques sought to define the national character. Yet, when Thatcher spoke, the great British car economy was already well past its peak.

Today Rover's remnants are scattered globally. Land Rover is owned by an Indian conglomerate, TATA. Minis are produced by German car maker BMW. A smattering of Rover's sleeping brands are controlled by, among others, China's Nanjing Automobile Corporation (NAC). The eminent car-maker has been variously sliced, traded and put into suspended animation. What came to pass?

Oil discoveries and the invention of the internal combustion engine in the nineteenth century are taken, typically, as the pre-conditions for the arrival of the car. However, Rover's actual parenthood was more prosaic, humble, and owed as much to another often overlooked and brutally extracted natural resource: rubber.

To say a car has a sewing machine for an engine is the worst kind of insult, but Rover's story actually begins with the manufacture of sewing machines. In 1863, the Coventry Sewing Machine Company was set up. Its owners realized quite rapidly, however, that to survive they would need to diversify and produce something else.

While on a tour of Paris, an agent of the company took an order for 400 Velocipedes, precursors of the modern bicycle, but France's war with Prussia intervened, forcing a renewed focus on the domestic British market. The Coventry Sewing Machine Company became the Coventry Machinists Company in 1869, with James Starley as the foreman. Initially, it made penny farthings and tricycles, transport devices mostly attracting only the brave, foolhardy and very resilient.

Various improvements followed, many introduced by Starley's nephew J.K. Starley, who joined with William Sutton in 1877 to form the company 'Starley and Sutton'.

The Rover name first appeared on a Starley tricycle in 1884. A year later, its factory made a Rover 'safety bicycle'. Its frame was triangulated, it had equal-sized front and back wheels, and a rear wheel driven by a chain with front cranks and pedals. The cycling press at the time (yes, there really was one) said it 'set the fashion to the world'. The basic design laid down the bicycle template still in use today. Coventry, once a small town, grew rapidly into the home of the cycle trade.

Most seemingly innocent steps of progress leave something crushed underfoot. It was true even of this wide-eyed innovation in personal transport. The bicycle's subsequent popularity was based on another innovation which also paved the way for the car. It, in turn, depended on a murderous trade from another continent. Rubber made possible the inflatable tyre, developed in 1890 by an Irish veterinary surgeon called John Dunlop. It turned the bicycle into something comfortable to ride. Harvested at gunpoint in the Belgian Congo under the infamous rule of Leopold II, rubber was the new gold.[1]

Having by then set up J.K. Starley & Co., which prospered, Starley himself became very rich when, in 1896, he formed the Rover Cycle Co. Ltd. Arguably the company had already been in existence for nearly twenty years, but this is the point at which it assumes the Rover name. The company made 11,000 cycles in its first year. At the turn of the century a cycling craze pedalled across the country. But the potential for various other powered forms of personal transport was becoming obvious.

As early as 1888, Starley tinkered, unsuccessfully, with the idea of an electric car. Motorcycles, however, became big business. The Imperial Rover Motor Cycle was introduced in 1902, with the substantial price tag of £55 (just over £3,000 today). By 1924 the company had made over

100,000 motorcycles and 400,000 cycles. But from the moment that Coventry's first production line car, a Rover, chugged from the factory in 1904, it was destined to be 'four wheels good, two wheels bad'. Just eight years later the evolved Rover Company claimed to offer a 'bigger selection of vehicles than any other firm in the world'.[2]

In spite of its proud boasts, for the first few decades of motoring, Rover remained a low-volume, specialist car-maker. It was clear, though, from very early on that Rover and the national interest, if not always synonymous, would be very closely aligned.

During the First World War, its factories were directed towards military ends. Motorcycles and cycles were made for both the British and Russian armies. Rover supplied government contracts for gas shells, mortars, bomb fuses and tank parts. Sunbeam cars and Maudslay lorries were made for the battlefront. It was the former wartime munitions factory at Tyseley in Birmingham that became the home of the Rover Eight, one of the company's most popular early models. It was a small car that helped forge Rover's lasting reputation for middle-class sturdiness.

And then, in 1930, a symbolic encounter between a Rover car and a continental express train would indicate quite clearly the likely direction of transport policy for decades to come.

In its time the Blue Train, or rather, Le Train Bleu, was as famous as the Orient Express. Formally known as the Calais–Méditerranée Express, it travelled back and forth from the French Riviera to Calais between the two world wars. It was exclusively first-class, the definition of glamour. Created to take the royal, aristocratic, rich and famous to 'season' on the Riviera, it inspired its own cul-tural wave. A ballet named after the train brought together Diaghilev, Picasso, Coco Chanel, Jean Cocteau and the

Ballets Russes. Less exotically, in 1928 Agatha Christie published *The Mystery of the Blue Train*.

After it began running in 1922, it became an obsession of car-makers and drivers to race and beat the train on its 750-mile night-time journey between St Raphael on the Mediterranean and Calais. Up until 1930, no one had succeeded.

Then, along came a Rover Light Six and a man called Dudley Noble. Starting out as a motorcycle test-rider, Noble went on to be a trials or 'rally' driver, and then one of the industry's early publicists. In January 1930, unabashedly pursuing media coverage, he led a team of three drivers who drove their car to the limit almost non-stop through the night to beat the Blue Train to its destination by twenty minutes.[3]

Even though the average speed of the Rover was only 38mph, it had conquered the glamour of the train. And, the international media ensured that the world knew about it. Now the car, not the train, represented speed and the fast life. It came to define modernity and social aspiration. It would take a few decades for the death knell of the train as the dominant mode of travel under assault from the car to be heard in Britain, but the slide had begun.

Although it seems hard to believe in a world where vehicle ownership is seen as almost a human right, there was nothing predetermined about the rise of the car to supremacy in industrialized societies. Famously, from the very earliest days of motoring, many people had deep reservations about the threat it posed. The triumph of individual, as opposed to collective, forms of transport was, like the cars themselves, carefully engineered. At times it was promoted with something close to fanaticism.

The year before Noble hurtled across France, chasing glory and an increase in Rover sales, over in the United

States, Charles F. Kettering, director of General Motors Research Laboratories, was encouraging the emergence of another 'great car economy'. He wrote an article in *Nation's Business* outlining his strategy called 'Keep the Consumer Dissatisfied'. He argued, wrote Michael Perelman, professor of economics at California State University, that the key to economic prosperity is the organized creation of dissatisfaction. Or, as Kettering himself put it: 'If everyone were satisfied, no one would want to buy the new thing.'[4]

Aggressive marketing, design and the creation of new fashions were deemed necessary to maintain turnover, and to keep the consumer buying new cars before their existing vehicle was worn out. But before they could do that there were other, more basic obstacles the industry had to overcome.

Nervousness about powered vehicles on the public highway went back at least to 1865, when the so-called Red Flag Act[5] obliged any mechanically powered vehicle to: have three drivers, go no faster than 4mph and be preceded by a man waving a red flag. Even in 1896, when the Act was withdrawn, the speed limit was increased to just 14mph. Pedestrians in possession of relatively frail human bodies were understandably suspicious of mixing with large, fast-moving objects.

As the car economy accelerated and vehicle numbers increased so did the roll-call of deaths and accidents on the roads. Although people were right to be worried, their concerns were often brusquely dismissed. John Moore-Brabazon was a Conservative Member of Parliament destined to become minister of transport. In 1932, he waved away complaints about the growing epidemic of people dying on the roads: 'Over 6,000 people commit suicide every year and nobody makes a fuss about that.'[6] His credentials for ministerial office in a great car economy were obviously above question.

We tend to think of concern about the impact of cars as being a very modern preoccupation, but an extraordinary, prescient passage of dialogue from *The Magnificent Ambersons*, Orson Welles' classic film made in 1942, shows otherwise. The film was made long before the road-building programme which re-engineered North America. Set in the first decades of the twentieth century in upper-middle-class society, Eugene Morgan is beginning to get involved in the manufacture of automobiles, but he is also romantically interested in George's mother. George dislikes the romantic interest as much as he does the arrival of the automobile. This is how the conversation unfolds:

> Maj. Amberson: So your devilish machines are going to ruin all your old friends, eh Gene? Do you really think they're going to change the face of the land?
>
> Eugene: They're already doing it, Major, and it can't be stopped. Automobiles . . .
>
> [He is cut off by George]
>
> George: Automobiles are a useless nuisance.
>
> Maj. Amberson: What did you say, George?
>
> George: I said automobiles are a useless nuisance. Never amount to anything but a nuisance and they had no business to be invented.
>
> Jack: Of course you forget that Mr Morgan makes them, also did his share in inventing them. If you weren't so thoughtless, he might think you were rather offensive.

Eugene: I'm not sure George is wrong about automobiles. With all their speed forward they may be a step backward in civilisation. It may be that they won't add to the beauty of the world and the life of men's souls. I'm not sure. But automobiles have come, and almost all outward things are going to be different because of what they bring. They're going to alter war and they're going to alter peace. And I think men's minds are going to be changed in subtle ways because of automobiles. It may be that George is right. It may be that in ten or twenty years from now, if we can see the inward change in men by that time, I shouldn't be able to defend the gasoline engine but would have to agree with George, that automobiles had no business to be invented.

Establishing a brand

To begin with, Rover competed with both Austin and Morris for the 'mass' car market but, from the mid-1920s, it began to create a niche by adding features and going upmarket. In spite of publicity coups such as the victory over the Blue Train, like many businesses Rover suffered in the early 1930s from the economic depression. To address its problems, in 1933 Rover came under a new managing director, Spencer Wilks. His strategy was to produce fewer, better models, pushing on into the 'prestige' vehicle market. Company policy would be to make a 'limited number of vehicles of the highest possible standard in comfort, refinement and performance'.

Adverts for Rover cars in the 1920s look as if they have been copied from a *Boy's Own* adventure comic. In one a Viking, the company motif, holds a spear in one hand, and the radiator grille of a Rover, doubling as a shield for combat, in the other. After Wilks' arrival, sophistication took over. From then on, advertisements could be mistaken for invitations to a society ball. The classic, simple curved outline of 1937's Rover 14, combined with an art-deco typeface, made for an advert that could easily sit on the mantelpiece as evidence of social arrival.

The new campaigns were aimed directly at an upwardly mobile middle class. In 1939, the company boasted that its Rover 16 model was 'the Rolls-Royce of light cars'. In a trend that would last for decades, Rover cars were repeatedly portrayed against the background of grand country houses, touring a genteel, very English countryside or adjacent to some other upper-middle-class pursuit such as sailing.

Certain adjectives worked overtime in the company's successful attempt to establish an image for its brand:

FIGURE 1: Rover's appeal in 1922

The 1937

ROVER 14

Quality of detail

The level of artistry in a Rover engine can proudly be read instantaneously by pressing a dashboard button.

One of Britain's Fine Cars

BUY A CAR MADE IN THE UNITED KINGDOM.   THE ROVER COMPANY LTD., COVENTRY.

FIGURE 2: All grown up and ready for the ball in 1937

tradition, refinement, quality, pride, performance and detail, but brought to the customer with a careful 'freedom from ostentation'. Altogether, the public was left in no doubt that this was 'One of Britain's Fine Cars'. It was a boldly affirmed message of superiority and self-confidence, veiled in understatement. A paradox that was meant to fit 'perfectly into the English scene'. It was meant, in effect, to define a type of Englishness, ensuring Rover's place in the public consciousness as an indispensable symbol of national pride. English roads without Rover cars were intended to seem as incongruous as a man attending his club without a club tie.

Then came the war. And Rover had a good war. Surprisingly good, in fact, because from May 1940 the company stopped making cars.

Britain, an island, had to import across dangerous seas whatever it could not make itself. As much as bullets and shells, the military depended on fuel. The drive to conserve resources at home was on. Petrol was allowed for 'essential travel' only. So-called 'inessential vehicles' were immobilized.[7] Private cars virtually disappeared from the streets. Something that was becoming an apparently indispensable part of life, at least for those who could afford it, had to be dispensed with.

A combination of rationing and cajoling about civic responsibility brought about the change. A perky public information poster urged: 'Use shanks' pony. Walk when you can and ease the burden which war puts on transport.' In the USA, messages were even more direct. In an attempt to encourage car-sharing, one poster read: 'If you drive alone, you ride with Hitler.' (Now that our current times face a potentially crippling combination of climate change

FIGURE 3: Wartime government poster

and the global peak and decline of oil production, we could learn a lot from this period of rapidly engineered change.)

In 1932, before Wilks took over the management of Rover, the vehicle-maker had been close to collapse. Its banker, Lloyds, was leaning on it hard. Rover made losses in a single year totalling around £250,000, a huge amount of money then. Things did turn around, to a certain degree.

Between 1933 and the outbreak of war, Rover produced its so-called 'new deal' cars – a reference to the name of the economic programme launched by President Franklin Roosevelt in the USA to combat the recession which followed the Wall Street Crash – and its output more than doubled. Even so, it never sold more than 11,000 cars in a year. Then came the 'shadow factories'.

Agitation from Winston Churchill, among others, about the threat of war returning to Europe led in 1936 to the creation of the Shadow Factory plan.[8] It was driven by the Air Ministry. The name was given because new factories to increase the production of aircraft engines were to be built 'in the shadow', or 'under the wing' of existing ones. Logically the government turned to the growing vehicle industry to help.

Morris Motors, based at Cowley in Oxford, was approached by the government about the possibility of making aero-engines. Initially, there were to be nine new factories. Rover was commissioned to build two of them. First there was Acocks Green in Birmingham, which started making parts in 1937. Two years later, Rover built a much bigger factory on farm land at Solihull to make engines for the Hercules bomber. The new factories would operate well within capacity to begin with, but if the international situation worsened the capacity was there to increase output rapidly.

In a move that was either incidental, or very far-sighted,

the Rover Company bought an extra parcel of land at Solihull that was nearly three times the size of the plot needed for the shadow factory. After the war, they would be glad that they did.

Back in Coventry, since the company's 1933 revival its new Meteor Works in Helen Street had become the heart of operations, the final point of assembly for all the cars. In peacetime it helped the city become a centre of economic activity, but – with chilling irony – during the war it was to become a magnet for almost unimaginable destruction.

The bombing of Coventry in 1940 became a symbol of modern warfare's capacity for industrial-scale annihilation. The Luftwaffe's deadly interest in the city was quite clear, as a communiqué from the German High Command explained: 'numerous engine works and aero accessory factories as well as other targets of military importance were attacked with bombs of heaviest calibre'.[9] The extensive damage to Rover's assembly plant was not incidental: the company was part of the target.

When one of our parents, June Simms, was a seven-year-old child she sat at the entrance to her family's crude, Anderson bomb shelter in the nearby town of Rugby. She listened to German planes pass overhead and watched the night sky turn orange as Coventry burned. Her father was an ARP, an Air Raid Precaution warden. Part of his job was to assess damage after a bombing raid. An amiable, friendly man, he was speechless on his return from Coventry and avoided ever discussing what he had seen.

From the early summer of 1940 until after the war, Rover's only service to cars would be providing spares and maintenance for vehicles considered part of the war effort. Its focus had become making engines for aircraft and tanks, vehicle bodies and aircraft wings.

By 1942, the company operated eighteen factories around the country. Six of them were government-owned 'shadow factories'. Total staff, including over 3,000 permanent company employees, numbered around 24,000. Even excluding the shadow factories, Rover's turnover during the war was over £20 million (approximately £520 million in current money).

One factory was not so much a shadow, as a creature that lurked beneath the ground. To build Drakelow, near Kidderminster, an extensive network of corridors was cut into a hillside. Designed to be invisible from the air, it was a secret 'feeder plant' for the factories at Acocks Green and Solihull, and covered fifty acres at its peak. Drakelow was not a moving production line like the factory of popular imagination, but something more industrially feral than that. In the artificially lit corridors, workers stood and sat at fixed stations, machining engine parts for hours that dragged on as long as the tunnels they toiled in.[10]

A chapter easily forgotten in Rover's history was its role in the development of the jet engine. From 1940, as an extension of being commissioned by the Air Ministry to take part in the shadow factory plan, Rover was engaged to develop Frank Whittle's gas turbine jet propulsion engine. A deal in 1942 later handed the work over to Rolls-Royce, whose name is still popularly associated with jet engines. Instead, Rover was given the contract for developing and manufacturing the engine for the Meteor tank (for several years the Meteor had been a popular Rover car marque). Britain's first jet fighter, the product of the early engine development, was also called the Gloster Meteor.

The story does not quite end there, however. After the war, a legacy of Rover's earlier work in the area was a team of twenty Rover engineers' secret development of the world's first gas turbine propelled car, called Jet 1. The innovation was ultimately unsuccessful for several reasons – the engines were too big and not fuel efficient, with one version, the Rover T3, scraping only thirteen miles per gallon. However, the gas turbine car was more than a mere footnote. From 1950, when Jet 1 managed 153mph in test runs, several further models were made, including the Rover–BRM car that was driven by Graham Hill in the 1963 Le Mans race.

Rover came out of the war bigger and bolder. Still making tank engines and with large potential capacity, it wanted to virtually double its pre-war output and make 20,000 cars per year. But, exhausted by the war, the country and the economy could not take it. The company had to wait.

Britain had entered the war as Europe's leading car producer, with Germany second, followed by France and Italy. But, several decades off, invisibly and unforeseeably, a hideous irony was stalking the Rover Company.

Between 1939 and 1945 the company competed with its future nemesis, BMW. The wartime loser would win, ultimately, on the battlefield of business. And, BMW would triumph in spite of its deep and shaming collusion with the Nazi regime. According to SS officer Karl Sommer, once head of the SS Economic and Administrative Main Office, the car-maker had been 'top of the list' of German companies who exploited slave labour.[11]

In many ways, the stage for the industry's coming decades was set before the war's end. The car industry would grow with a lot of help from its friends and, almost in spite of itself, with the appearance of success. But the dirty little secret of the 'great car economy' is that it was never really that great at all, and only grew due to a combination of state support, protection and subsidy.

Even as one of the world's economic superpowers, Britain

felt it necessary to develop its new industries behind a wall of economic protection.

Ever since 1915, something known as the 'McKenna tariff' had been in place. A tariff of 33.33 per cent was put on imported goods that were considered 'extensively used solely for the purpose of luxury'.[12] It was introduced as part of the early war effort, partly to save shipping space. This covered cars and their component parts. Although introduced under the stress of war, the tariff stayed in place afterwards and remained until 1956. In effect, it choked off imports, allowing Britain's car industry, in particular, to develop relatively unchallenged. To see how successful it was, you only have to look at the brief experiment with free trade in 1925. When the tariff was lifted, the share of imports in domestic sales shot up from 15 to 28 per cent.

In 1937, imports were less than 6 per cent of sales. Not only was the British market highly protected, but British manufacturers also had the benefit of 'imperial preference' in the international markets that were under British control. This meant that, at a time when Britain still vied with the USA for global dominance, a staggering 97 per cent of all cars sold by British makers were sold in protected markets.[13]

At home, the early growth of car ownership was mainly pushed by advertising and public relations, something that Rover was proving adept at. Then, as now, credit in the form of 'instalment purchasing' enabled people to buy the ultimate consumer item which, at face value, they could not afford. To keep the consumer hungry for upgrades and the latest model, sales were also pushed by continual product development and innovation.

However, in Britain, even after the worst of the pre-war slump, car ownership remained a realistic possibility only largely for the middle classes. The price of an average family car was comparable to the cost of a semi-detached house in some provincial towns.[14]

In the USA, things were already different. Henry Ford's mould-setting focus on mass producing a handful of low-cost models carried the car culture much further across economic and social divides. There was, though, always something paradoxical about Ford. While the company spread the franchise of car ownership to poorer social classes, its workers were aggressively disenfranchised from belonging to the unions that might improve their conditions in other ways. Ford initially brought its anti-union tactics to its British factories, and was checked only by the intervention of the politician Ernest Bevin. Fully Fordist production methods may not have crossed the Atlantic, but 'Taylorism' took root in Britain. Frederick Taylor's *The Principles of Scientific Management* led to the radical subdivision of labour into ever smaller tasks, carried out with standardized tools and at a pace decided by minutely controlled time-and-motion studies. It also heralded wages linked to performance. Although synonymous with a certain kind of economic efficiency, Taylorism was an assault on the role of the skilled craftsman in industry and was a big stride down the desolate road to alienated labour.

Although lagging behind the USA, Britain was the leading car-maker in Europe until 1956. By 1963 there would be one car for every seven people in Britain. Industrially resurgent Germany, armed for peaceful economic combat with the iconic Volkswagen Beetle, would not reach that level until a year later. Car-crazy Italy would not reach those levels of ownership until 1967. The USA, of course, left the rest standing, having crossed that threshold in 1924.

In the 1920s and early 1930s, car-makers such as Austin and Morris led the British push into the emerging mass production market. At one stage Morris Motors had over 40 per cent of the market.

Immediately after the war, it took time for the domestic car market to revive. For a while only certain professions, such as doctors, were allowed to buy cars. All production was wanted for the export market to boost foreign, and especially dollar, earnings. Delivery vehicles leaving Austin's factories were emblazoned with signs boasting 'Austins for Dollars'.

As early as 1945, a government committee warned that, when the anticipated post-war 'sellers' market' was over, the industry would face a big challenge. More capacity would be needed to compete internationally, together with greater standardization and fewer key models. Initially, though, British industry recovered faster than the rest of Europe. In the 1950s and 1960s, almost one-third of industrial growth was attributed to the motor vehicle sector. The notion of the 'great car economy' was, at least from an orthodox perspective, grounded in fact. During the five years from 1957, Britain had a one-quarter share of the world trade in cars. Five years after that, though, it had fallen to less than one-fifth. The slide had begun.

Unlike Morris and Austin, though, Rover took the decision simply not to compete in the mass market, targeting instead the socially ambitious middle classes with their 'Fine' cars.

In the period immediately after the war, the company also took one other turn. It introduced a car that would become a motoring icon. To begin with it was a workhorse, inspired by a little difficulty that Maurice Wilks, Rover's manager and Spencer's brother, was having on his farm. He had an old US army Jeep that needed replacing and noted that no British equivalent existed.

And so the Land Rover was born in 1948. Its utility

bodywork was initially wrapped around a saloon engine and given a 4x4 driving system. In spite of its rugged nature and purpose, ultimately in various incarnations it too would be driven as a badge of social and economic success. The Land Rover was so successful that by 1951 it was selling twice as many as all other Rover vehicles combined. Today, the Land Rover and its 4x4 cousins are the only continuingly successful true Rover marques. Its good fortune came from appealing to two markets simultaneously, on one hand fostering a taste for off-road 4x4s among a broader public, and on the other supplying armies, police forces and other government contracts around the world.

Land Rover's take-up by the farming and land-owning classes deepened the company's association with the establishment, and made Rover even more synonymous with a certain kind of British or, more properly, English identity. It was something, again, that the company deliberately cultivated in its marketing.

During the 1950s and 1960s, Rover introduced a range of models that built on this image. The words used to describe them in adverts were often 'dignified', 'elegant', 'luxurious and well-appointed'. The Rover P4, 130,000 of which were produced up until 1964, looked in appearance the quintessential car for bank managers.

These models might have been the height of dignity, but there was also something inescapably self-satisfied about them. They were a little pompous and rather too certain of themselves. In terms of styling, the P4's bodywork could have taken its inspiration from the kind of jelly moulds that turned out desserts for the bourgeois Sunday dinner tables of Britain at the time.

A little more powerful and bullish was the P5: 'Fine appearance – Traditional engineering'. Likewise, it was designed to carry, in appearance at least, the solid, dependable and well-heeled senior managers of the middle-class establishment – just rather quicker. But it went beyond that. These were serious prestige cars, used by prime ministers such as Harold Wilson. And they lasted. The model's popularity endured so long that, when Margaret Thatcher arrived to take office in No.10 Downing Street in 1979, she stepped out of a Rover P5, even though they had ceased production in 1973. The ultimate seal of approval in a class-conscious society was bestowed when the Queen chose Rovers for her own use.

Next came a stylistic departure, the instantly recognizable Rover 2000 saloon. With a bonnet sloping down to the thin, pinched lips of its radiator grille, the 2000 dropped dignity in favour of sporting edge. Awarded European Car of the Year on its introduction in 1963, enthusiasts describe the model as starting a new trend for 'executive' cars. This is a somewhat over-enthusiastic claim, perhaps typical of an industry that was soon to suffer for its relative disregard of a changing world. In fact, eight years earlier in France, Citroën had launched its stylish revolutionary, the DS model – all curves, chic and elegance. The Rover 2000 may have had a 'simulated wood steering wheel', but the Citroën DS had hydro-pneumatic self-levelling suspension, as well as good looks.

Nevertheless, helped by the introduction of fast, high-performance models, the 2000 was a car set to become as popular with bank robbers as it was with bank managers. Its early adoption as a police car, just as crime on television became a successful evening diversion, helped give a new flavour to the Rover brand. By the time that its production ended in 1977, it had become its best-selling road car, with over 325,000 made.

In spite of its own successes, Rover's fate was to be

inescapably hard-wired to that of the British car industry as a whole. A rolling wave of mergers meant that, from 1967 onwards, Rover would never again stand on its own four wheels. These were decades when, for many reasons, the industry lost ground internationally. In 1955, there were four cars produced per industry worker in Britain, rising to five and a half in 1976. Comparable figures for Germany were just under four, rising to nearly eight; and for the USA it was nearly twenty cars produced per worker, rising to twenty-six.[15] What went wrong? There was a conspiracy of factors, some which could have been controlled, and some which could not. But the story is more complex than the political posturing that demonized, strike-prone trade unions would have us believe.

Compared to its international competitors, the British industry evolved in a way that put obstacles in its own path. It was, as it were, auto-hamstrung. At first glance, the conclusion of historians appears paradoxical: their analysis is that the industry suffered from over-capacity, but too few economies of scale. How could that be? A large range of models were produced at a large number of different plants. This meant, however, that the industry lacked the economies of scale on a few key models to compete effectively in the export market. There was also a lack of investment in plants, over-manning, restrictive practices and comparatively low productivity.

What grabbed history's headlines, though, were strikes. The industry seemed to suffer a chronic and worsening problem with labour relations. These emerged due to structural problems, but also for reasons of what seemed to be cultural prejudice. Leonard Lord was the chairman and managing director of Austin. Later, he would, in effect, run the industry as head of the British Motor Corporation (BMC). After the war the government exhorted managers and workers to co-operate in the struggle to rebuild Britain from the shock of the long conflict. In response, Lord quipped in 1947, 'With whom are we going to co-operate – the shop stewards? The shop stewards are communists.' During the war, increasingly management functions had been given over to shop stewards. Lord was clearly bitter about the experience, but his attitude did not help.

Between 1948 and 1973, strikes in the car industry increased ten-fold and the number of working days lost went up by seven times. This was worse than in the USA, and much worse than in Germany. Why were things so bad in Britain?

Irritatingly, of course, there's no single, simple answer. The lack of cohesion has been attributed to a combination of: comparatively irregular employment, the use of piece rates when workers are rewarded by the number of tasks completed (a form of performance-related pay) and the domino effect created when initially high levels of stoppages lead to further contentious problems to do with the terms and conditions of pay and contracts. It was a mess compared to the very different form of labour relations used in Germany. There, top-level representation in the management of the company was given to workers, in return for certain commitments not to disrupt production. They called it 'co-determination' and it was much more effective at central bargaining. British unions, by contrast, had weaker internal structures and failed, relatively speaking, to enforce collective agreements.

However, ascribing the long-term decline of the industry to the feckless unions of Conservative political folklore would be as wrong as assuming that Margaret Thatcher, the future prime minister who touted her roots as a grocer's daughter, would logically protect the interests of Britain's small shops.

In fact, according to economic historians, 'the direct effect (on productivity) of working days lost due to labour disputes was marginal'.[16] Fluctuations in productivity varied little from the lower strike period of the 1950s to the more problematic period after the mid-1960s. Also, Britain was 'not exceptional' in having labour problems. The French and Italian industries also had high levels of strikes, as well as worse absenteeism and staff turnover rates. On the last two counts Britain was better than the rest of Europe.

Global competition

If all the British industry had to do was struggle with its own internal demons, the future might have been different. However, the global market developed aggressively. Having learnt from the British, among others, Japan leapt ahead as a car-maker. Its rise in the 1960s had an indirect effect when it focused an export drive on the USA. In response, the USA invested heavily in an integrated global network of production facilities. This increasingly international division of labour brought huge advantages to makers such as Ford. And, driven by the rhetoric of free trade and the desire to attract inward investment – whether or not that investment would undermine Britain's own indigenous industry – successive British governments went out of their way to help foreign multinationals such as Ford.

As a result, during the 1970s, car imports to Britain rose and Ford became powerful in the domestic market. In 1975, the nation was spending more on importing cars than it was earning from exporting them – the trade balance in cars had gone into the red. The writing was now on the wall for the British car industry as jobs, the value of sales and the numbers of cars produced fell away, parting company with the trajectory of the rest of the economy.[17]

According to one economic historian, by the early 1980s, Britain had become 'little more than an assembly centre' for foreign makers such as Ford. The government policy of ingratiating multinationals backfired for British industry. Many cars that were subsequently sold as 'British' were mostly so in name only. In 1973, for example, cars from Chrysler's British subsidiary were almost entirely made from parts produced locally in Britain. Just a decade later such 'local content' had fallen to less than one-third.

On top of all of this, cars built in Germany and Japan were proving more reliable. The British industry was being hollowed out from within and attacked from outside. It found it increasingly difficult to plan for the future. Internal shocks to do with industrial unrest then coincided with the fuel crisis. Edward Heath's Conservative government responded with a range of emergency restrictions that further hampered the car-makers.

One of which, of course, was Rover.

Mergermania

It started quietly enough and, unusually for what was to follow, with Rover taking over another vehicle-maker. However, it was soon to read with the complexity of an overwrought television soap opera.

Alvis handmade cars that were both luxurious and rather beautiful. In business since 1921, it was based in Rover's original hometown of Coventry. Although it appears as little more than a footnote in the company histories, Rover's engineers had big plans for Alvis when it took the company over in 1965. It developed a prototype 'supercar', codenamed the P6BR, that was stylistically far ahead of its time. It would have kept the Alvis name, but it was never produced, falling victim to the politics of merger.

Rover was set to become the toy in a long and badly handled game of pass the corporate parcel.

In 1967, Rover merged with the more prosaic Leyland Motor Corporation, principally a truck-maker based in Lancashire. This was just a prelude for a much bigger, emerging master plan, designed to create a consolidated British car industry, one that would be capable of responding to all the problems at home and abroad, and competing in a rapidly changing global market. But it was also a response to the fact that large parts of the industry were close to collapse.

Austin and Morris had merged in the previous decade to form the British Motor Corporation. But, by the mid-1960s, this was in difficulty and merged again with Jaguar Cars to make up British Motor Holdings (BMH).

Just one year after Leyland's merger with Rover, and two years after the formation of BMH, the Leyland Motor Corporation merged with the seriously shaky BMH to form a corporate leviathan – the British Leyland Motor Corporation. All the auto eggs were in one basket. With few exceptions, the 'great' British car economy was now distilled into a single company. Nose to tail it would make a long parade including: Alvis, Austin, Austin-Healey, Daimler, Jaguar, Land Rover, Leyland, MG, Morris, Riley, Triumph and Vanden Plas.

Almost immediately, merger politics affected Rover's plans for Alvis. Having another supercar as competition under the same corporate roof as Jaguar was deemed unacceptable by the British Leyland management. The P6BR would become one of the great cars that never were, infuriating Rover. Ironically, internal competition between merged car-makers was nothing new. In fact, previously this had been a deliberate corporate strategy. So-called 'badge engineering' was when virtually identical vehicles were sold under different brands, effectively in competition with each other. It happened when Austin and Morris were merged. The loss of the Alvis project robbed Rover of a potentially bold and distinctive new direction. Under the new system, Rover would be merged further with both Triumph and Jaguar – seen as mutually reinforcing marques for their market niche.

Instead of the merger delivering the industrial might to take on the world, it seemed only to magnify the various, already existing problems. A kind of identity crisis ensued. What type of car were people really buying? Leyland had no reputation as a car-maker, British Leyland Motor Corporation even less so.

In 1975, a hasty official report was commissioned on the corporation's future. Within months, Harold Wilson's Labour government accepted the findings of the inquiry under Sir Don Ryder. As a result, and faced with the real prospect of the whole industry otherwise collapsing and leaving hundreds of thousands of workers unemployed, the government took over. It became the majority shareholder in the resultant new company, British Leyland Ltd.

Turning Japanese

For a while things seemed to go well. Two years later, Rover again won the European Car of the Year with its new, big-engine 'bad boy' called the SD1, a hugely praised executive car. Demand outstripped supply initially, which was exacerbated by continuing industrial unrest. It sold well throughout its decade of production. The police liked them so much that they stockpiled the car, bringing them into commission for years after Rover had stopped making them.

A new relationship also grew with Japanese industry. Honda was a relatively new kid on the car-making block. Like Rover, it began life in the world of cycles and grew as a motorcycle-maker. But in 1962, it ventured into cars. Inexperienced, it began collaborating with Rover under the new, nationalized regime. For Rover, it was an opportunity to re-enter the small-car market. The logic for British Leyland was that Rover's carefully nurtured image was one of the few remaining undamaged brands in its pantheon. That, of course, could not last. You can sell a name, but people are not entirely credulous: they do notice if, when the name is called, a different face turns round to greet them.

Many small boys are obsessive about cars. They memorize huge amounts of details about different makes and then compete with each other over their knowledge. Card games like Top Trumps tapped into this psychological quirk with enormous success. More importantly, for many children, society became stratified on the basis of which cars their parents owned. It allowed a child to impose a kind of order on life and find a place in it. Consequently even children literally scoffed in the 1980s when the MG badge – symbol of one of the few things British that was still cool and sporty – was stuck on a Metro. A Metro? The naffest of naff shopping runabouts. It was then that some of us learnt the meaning of 'travesty'.

In 1984, the first product of the collaboration with Honda was produced. It was known internally as the 'Triumph Acclaim facelift' after how it started life, but it was sold as both a Rover 200 and a Honda Ballade. It may have made economic sense, but it meant a certain disloca-tion of identity. Playing fast and loose with car badges became increasingly common. Two years later, another

Rover/Honda came out, further diluting the brand. And, in the same year, 1986, British Leyland, suffering from a chronically bad reputation, was renamed the Rover Group. There was something slightly desperate about the move, a bit like renaming the accident-prone Windscale nuclear power plant Sellafield. The names of the former giants of British car-making were disappearing in final, steady succession: Morris in 1984 and Austin in 1987. But their much smaller, higher-class cousin, Rover, lived on. Identity, reputation and marketing potential still mattered. The new game was gradually to change direction away from the mass market and towards Rover's more upmarket niche.

However, now well into Thatcher's era of deregulated market economics, privatization was not far away. When its time came, in common with many of the privatizations of the 1980s, the general public did not get a good deal when its national family silver was sold.

By then, the Rover Group had become the 'remaining skeleton of the British volume car industry'.[18] In 1988, the Thatcher government sold the public share to British Aerospace (BAE) for £150 million, a price considered by many to be undervalued. But the government also provided a huge cash 'dowry' of £520 million together with tax concessions and other 'concealed payments'. In some ways, being owned by BAE echoed Rover's historical involvement with the war-time shadow-factory programme. As a major aircraft and weapons manufacturer, BAE may not have been a state company, but its interests were intimately enmeshed with, and influential over, British security and foreign policy.

Other deals they were involved with at the time, with countries considered key economic partners, would later land BAE in court facing charges of systematic bribery and corruption. These charges were considered so sensitive that official intervention prevented further investigations. The conditions of the sale of the Rover Group to BAE fed strong suspicions that 'political considerations were paramount in deciding Rover's fate'. Within the new structure, Rover itself was now little more than a 'small and peripheral division of a large British conglomerate'.[19]

Rover was caught in an ultimately corrosive paradox. Not quite the golden-egg-laying goose, it was still considered the key brand within the group that had genuine value. As a result, the Rover badge was forced to keep laying in other people's nests. Each time it did so, it seemed to move another mile down the road to the corporation's nadir. The collaboration with Honda continued. In 1990, on the tenth anniversary of the launch of the Metro, it was rebadged with a Rover logo. Adverts carried the strap-line: 'Metromorphosis – with Rover engineering'.

Or maybe German . . .

The British-owned car industry, with Rover representing one of its proudest vestiges, was rapidly approaching the end of the production line. The ultimately fatal move was the sale of Rover Group to its former competitor, German car-maker BMW, in 1994. Honda had increased its interest. The Single European Act meant involvement with the British car industry was convenient to gain wider market access within Europe. But Honda were reluctant to take on the whole Group, and BAE wanted to sell.

For reasons that were as much to do with culture and history as they were to do with economics, the sale of Rover to BMW was big news. It dominated headlines. A whole book was written about just the mechanics and intrigue surrounding this single takeover.[20] It touched so many nerves simultaneously. The country's image of itself as a manufacturing nation was at stake. There was a swirl of issues between Britain and Germany to do with relative superiority in terms of engineering skill, culture and economics. Greater uncertainty in a rapidly globalizing economy was heightened by new job insecurities. In spite of blustering reassurances at the time, many fears proved to be well founded.

The story of Rover's doomed acquisition by BMW was told by an academic and a business journalist, Chris Brady and Andrew Lorenz. Both confessed that their interpretation of events, as well as the events themselves, were driven as much by emotion as cool analysis and reason. So much, then, for 'rational economic man' as the principal architect of our times.

When approached about the company's future, Honda offered to increase its stake from 20 to 47.5 per cent. It was not enough. As Brady and Lorenz put it, the 'financially stretched' aerospace group wanted a 'total and immediate exit' from the car business. And, given what it had paid back in 1988, together with the government sweeteners, BAE did very nicely for itself and sold the Rover Group to BMW for £800 million.

In explaining to its long-term Japanese collaborators why it had taken the money, turned its backs on them and run, George Simpson, Rover's chairman, apologized meekly, in effect blaming capitalism: 'I tried to explain that I was very sorry, that Western business had to deal with issues such as shareholder value, that it was extremely difficult to evaluate things like a 15-year partnership and moral commitments.'[21] Rover, who once helped defeat the industrial strength of BMW-backed Nazi Germany, was now to become the plaything of its former enemy and recent competitor.

It made sense to BMW for precisely that reason. Not only were German car-makers facing increasing competition from the east, including Japan, but also, to a degree, from Rover. In a stroke BMW weakened the profile of one competitor in the European market, and took possession of another. It wanted to increase production to compete globally, but also reduce costs. Buyer and seller walked away from the deal looking pleased with themselves.

The buyer's grin would fade first, and fast. To its new German owner, Rover would soon become known as 'the English patient'.

A year later Rover, with its original management still largely in place, was the worst-performing car-maker in Europe. BMW realized it had bought a 'congenital loss maker'. Rover had been 'dressed' for sale by BAE to emphasize its potential, but as soon as the thread was pulled the clothes fell apart. 'So established had the legend of Rover's revival become that it began to be widely printed as fact,' summarized Brady and Lorenz. The authors pointed out that, 'Will Hutton's best-selling *The State We're In* bracketed Rover with Marks & Spencer as benchmarks of British business excellence. In hindsight it looks like he was right to bracket them together, albeit in the wrong category.'[22]

Rover kept losing money, around £650 million in 1998. Its share of the British market fell to an all-time low. Cheaper imports from other European makers such as Renault, Volkswagen and Fiat gained ground. The cars Rover was making were either the wrong size, wrong price or in need of redesign. Relative success in exports was undermined by the value of a strong pound. Land Rover, on the other hand, was doing rather well. But if it was taken out of the Rover equation, the normal car division looked in even worse health.

What appeared to be a deal with which BMW could brace itself to take on the world now seemed to be a ball and chain that could drag it to the bottom of the industrial sea.[23] Plans for the future of the Longbridge and Cowley plants were shown to workers and their families, but BMW knew it was time for an exit strategy. All the Rover Group had left at this stage were the only things that might have kept it afloat: a replacement for the famous Mini which had been in development for years but was taken by BMW, and the group's big earner, Land Rover.

Perhaps we'll keep it . . .

BMW accounts show that six years of Rover ownership lost them £2.85 billion.[24] In March 2000 BMW announced that, after unsuccessful attempts to sell Rover to Ford, General Motors, Volkswagen and Toyota, it was selling the profitable division, Land Rover, to the US car-maker Ford.

At the same time, a venture capitalist company called Alchemy Partners launched plans to take over other parts of the company to produce MG-badged sports cars. In April, a rival bid was launched by the Phoenix Consortium, headed by former Rover executive John Tower, but it lacked proper financial backing. Alchemy then withdrew.

Amid all the mayhem, ironically, Rover had one of its best ever months, selling 22,000 cars. Phoenix finally got funding from a US bank and on 9 May 2000 they bought Rover from BMW for a nominal £10, renaming it MG Rover. But this was, of course, minus the new Mini replacement and Land Rover.

Those tumultuous two months included parliamentary inquiries into possible ministerial misconduct, union calls for a boycott of BMW and mass public demonstrations.

Compared with what was to follow, those were the good times.

OK, look to the East

The next five years consisted of a search by the Phoenix management team to find an international collaborator. Looking to various eastward points of the compass, it tried Proton of Malaysia and China Brilliance, and worked with the massive Indian conglomerate, TATA, to import the City Rover small car. For the first three years nothing worked and MG Rover limped along.

In 2003, hopes were raised as talks began with the Shanghai Automotive Industry Corporation (SAIC). They went on, agonizingly, for two years, but also failed to come to fruition.

Almost conclusively, MG Rover went into administration on 8 April 2005. But still Rover did not die. The administrators sold on the company's remaining physical assets and the rights to many of its marques. The buyer was a long-established Chinese car-maker but completely unheard of in Britain – the Nanjing Automobile Corporation (NAC). The new owners made various, often repeated promises to revive the manufacturer. And, after several false starts, a small, limited-edition run of MG-badged sports cars went on sale to the public, made by a small workforce in a little corner of the vast old Longbridge factory. It was barely audible and a fading echo of what once had been.

'The speed and scale of the industry's decline is one of the most dramatic developments in Britain's post-war economic history,' wrote Roy Church in his brief history of the nation's motor industry.[25] Consistent in the development of corporations has been the almost unquestioned assumption that bigger is always better. Negotiating mergers and

acquisitions has been the swashbuckling pinnacle of count-
less executive careers. And, over the century of its life, there
were times when Rover was passed around like a package
in a frenzied child's birthday party game of pass-the-parcel.

A pity, then, that nobody knew the unpalatable truth of
such macho business manoeuvres. According to KPMG,
one of the world's biggest accountancy firms, more than
half of big international mergers actually destroy value,
rather than improve corporate fortunes. It found that fewer
than one in five mergers turned out for the better, and nearly
another third made no difference.[26] These findings were
published just as BMW prepared to sell Rover. The fact that
Rover was once an attractive asset ironically seems to have
set the odds against it. 'Neither nationalisation nor priva-
tisation prevented Britain from becoming the first major
car-producing country to relinquish a domestically owned
independent national champion,' concludes Church.

But, at the time of writing, and although now foreign
owned, there is one Rover brand still in serious production. Its circumstances and likely future tell us much about
the changed environment and new predicaments faced by
the global car industry. It's the tale of the English patient's
more vigorous, outward-bound brother, Land Rover, and
it's a story that reminds us how business and politics are
inextricably entwined.

Roving around

A 1963 Land Rover advertisement stated: 'In the beginning LAND-ROVERS were used by the world's armies
(26 of them), police forces (37 of them), border patrols,
big game hunters . . . titled persons, oil companies.' From
the start, the Land Rover had an unmistakable image.
Immediately successful at its launch, Land Rover almost

single-handedly created the market for gas-guzzling 4x4 cars in Britain.

The vehicle may have begun in 1948 as the solution to a problem down on the farm of Maurice Wilks, but it became Rover's most successful venture. In 1970, its upmarket sibling, the Range Rover, was introduced. The comfort of an executive saloon was built into the off-road self-confidence of the Land Rover and made, well, bigger. These measures fitted perfectly with Rover's marketing tradition. They were 'statement' cars, almost like stately homes on wheels.

But Rover sniffed a much bigger, aspirational group of potential customers for 4x4s. In 1990, it launched the Discovery, helping to create and massively expand the market for mid-range, family-oriented, so-called 'sports utility vehicles'. Although marketed as adventurous off-road cars, if they ever left the road it was most likely to enter the supermarket car park or to mount the kerb for the purpose of depositing children on the school run. It was in this way that such vehicles earned derogatory nicknames such as the 'Chelsea tractor', after the wealthy neighbourhood in London. They also spawned whole new groups protesting against them, such as the Alliance Against Urban 4x4s.

The problem with being a brand leader is that you tend to attract attention. Just ask other controversial international brands such as McDonalds, Nike, Starbucks and Walmart, who discovered as much to their cost.

In May 2005, fifteen activists from the environmental campaign group Greenpeace (on whose board sits one of the authors of this book) were arrested after breaching security at Land Rover's factory in Solihull. They disrupted production by handcuffing themselves to unfinished vehicles. The campaigners said that emissions from Range Rovers were 'climate wrecking', pointing out that the vehicles did fewer miles to the gallon than the Model T Ford.[27] The company retorted that Greenpeace's action was 'regrettable and damaging'. It harmed, it said, a 'leading British business', forgetting, momentarily, that as a result of the great corporate carve-up, it was actually owned at the time by the US Ford motor company.

Land Rover's problem was that quite a few facts were on the side of the campaigners. A long way from their rural off-road roots, the new Land Rover models were being marketed explicitly for their on-road and urban uses. Adverts promised, for example, 'awesome tarmac performance'.

In an age increasingly defined by attempts to stop global warming, promoting these highly fuel-inefficient cars to the general motoring public brought into question the company's responsibility. The popular Land Rover Discovery models pumped out over three times more climate-change-causing greenhouse gases than an efficient family car. A growing body of evidence was also beginning to show that these types of cars, 4x4s, were also much more dangerous to pedestrians and other road users.

Worst of all, their problem of excessive pollution was locked into the essence of what Land Rover was now marketing – a bullish off-road vehicle that had all the comfort of a family saloon car. Dr Peter Wells, Senior Research Fellow at the Centre for Automotive Industry Research at the Cardiff Business School, wrote:

> Poor fuel economy derives from . . . the consequence of trying to match off-road performance with the levels of comfort and convenience expected by those that are going to drive the vehicles in urban areas. The basic design of the Discovery and Range Rover results in vehicles that are heavier and therefore result in a higher fuel consumption and CO2 emissions.[28]

It is a problem so much at the heart of Land Rover's business model that it is hard to see how it might escape the reality of a new, more resource- and carbon-constrained world.

Of course, a strong case can be made that the company has little excuse, should have seen this coming and should have sought to redirect production long ago. Environmental concern about the impact of the car is not a new phenomenon. Lead in petrol, bypasses concreting over the countryside, noise, congestion: many aspects of the quality of life have been pushed aside to great complaint in making way for the car. But now the stakes have been raised by the issue of global warming, as the Greenpeace action demonstrated.

In the face of such overwhelming evidence that our collective environmental life-support systems are on a collision course with the car industry, the search for technological fixes has grown ever more desperate. New hopes abound that hydrogen fuel cells and biofuels will provide an answer, but each solution seems to create as many problems as it answers. Hydrogen cells still require vast amounts of energy to charge, whereas biofuels displace food crops, put pressure on rainforests and some can contribute more to climate change than fossil fuels.

Relying on efficiency gains from engineering also has a poor track record. Improvements over the last two to three decades have been far outstripped by the fact that we are driving further, with more cars, and heavier, higher-performance vehicles. In the USA, overall vehicle fuel economy was lower in the year 2000 than it was in 1980. According to the Union of Concerned Scientists: 'Two decades of fuel-saving technologies that could have helped curb CO_2 have instead gone into increasing vehicle weight and performance.'[29] In short, it has been said,

'Our environment does not respond to miles per gallon, it responds to gallons.'[30]

Of course, the demand for large fast cars does not just happen. Around 6 billion euros was spent on car advertising in the five biggest European markets in 2000. In the USA, advertising costs to keep cars moving through the showrooms were around $10 billion in 2003 and still rising.[31]

If nothing else, the Range Rover and Land Rover brands have been triumphs of marketing. It's an impressive feat, because being fuel-inefficient is far from the only controversy attracted by Land Rover.

As the 1963 advert above rather proudly pointed out, Land Rovers have, for decades, been standard issue for a large number of armies and police forces. Inevitably, due to the lack of effective international controls on the sale of military hardware to dubious governments, that means that Land Rovers have ended up being used as tools of repression in a range of places.

The intellectual, anti-apartheid activist and founder of the Black Consciousness movement in South Africa, Steve Biko made the last journey of his young life naked on the floor of a police Land Rover. He had been brutally beaten during police interrogation and was being taken twelve hours by road to Pretoria, where he would soon die of his injuries in detention. It was September 1977, at the height of apartheid repression.

Two months later, a United Nations Security Council Resolution (no.418) agreed a comprehensive ban on the sale of arms to South Africa, which was to include both military vehicles and spare parts. But a statement by the African National Congress (ANC) to the UN Special Committee Against Apartheid in December that year made it clear that the car industry was getting round the ban:

The motor car industry, as the Special Committee already knows, is directly involved in supplying the defence forces with transport and other equipment, as well as engines and components for tanks and military vehicles. They also supply the police force with vehicles and where local vehicles are not made they import them. For example, British Leyland Land Rover Kits are imported from the United Kingdom and then assembled in South Africa and supplied to the South African Police Force. These Land Rovers were used in the Soweto massacre last year and representations made to Her Majesty's Government have so far only produced the response from Prime Minister Callaghan that there is no machinery to restrict the export of this equipment. We have therefore failed so far in securing a ban on these exports which help the South African Police in its repression internally.[32]

A long international campaign would follow to isolate South Africa economically. Not only would Land Rover suffer for supporting the apartheid regime with its vehicles, but so would other big businesses such as the bank, Barclays, and cricketers who toured South Africa in defiance of the sporting ban.

But the problems highlighted by anti-apartheid campaigners would not go away. During the 1990s, the UK government exported substantial amounts of military hardware to Indonesia, including tanks, planes and military-use Land Rovers. The Indonesian government gave pledges to the UK that the equipment would not be used for internal repression or 'offensive' counter-insurgency measures. Then, in 2003, the state launched an offensive in Ache (the province later to fall victim to the great Indian Ocean tsunami of 26 December 2004), using UK-manufactured Hawk jets, Scorpion tanks and military Land Rovers.[33]

Then, three decades after the issue being raised in South Africa, Amnesty International and Oxfam International again brought the problem of 'lethal Land Rovers' to light.[34]

In May 2005, Land Rovers were used by Uzbek security forces in the town of Andijan to repress, fire on and kill hundreds of unarmed people who were demonstrating, including women and children. Yet, because the vehicles and their components are not listed as military or 'dual use' (i.e. civilian or military) the British government said that it could control neither their export nor re-export. The vehicles in question had been sold to Turkey which then 'gifted' them to the Uzbek government. Nevertheless, Oxfam and Amnesty said: 'it is clearly unacceptable that . . . a military Land Rover which has been used for serious violations of human rights, is not covered by current UK export controls'.[35]

Sometimes, though, sins are committed against the mind as much as against the body or the climate. Given Land Rover's history in South Africa, you might assume that all relations since the end of apartheid would be conducted with extreme caution and respect. Which just goes to show how dangerous it can be to make assumptions.

In December 2000, Land Rover produced a large advert for the Freelander vehicle. It was published in a range of glossy magazines in South Africa, including everything from *House and Garden* to *Men's Health*, *Complete Golfer* and the international edition of *Time* magazine. It did not appear in a range of magazines aimed at a largely black market.

Instantly, it caused uproar. This is why. The South African advertising agency TBWA Hunt Lascaris wanted to show the speed of the Freelander and the way that it can dominate the African landscape. It chose to do so by having the Freelander race along across a 'barren saltpan' between sky and earth past a standing Himba woman from Namibia. So far, so reasonably straightforward. But the agency felt it had to really emphasize its speed and how the world around the Freelander bends to its force. To achieve this effect, the Himba woman, who is naked from the waist up, has had her breasts digitally manipulated. They have been elongated and pulled sideways, absurdly, as if they are being sucked along by the Freelander's slipstream. To add to the scene, a cloud of dust kicked up by the car surrounds her legs. For final effect, she is made to give the car an admiring glance as it passes.

Years later, the advert that 'shocked South Africans because of its racism and sexism' was still being debated.[36] It was condemned by the South African Advertising Standards authority as 'a violation of human dignity that perpetuated gender and cultural inequality'. Diane Hubbard, of the Legal Assistance Centre in Windhoek, Namibia, commented that: 'It smacked of the same kind of exploitation that occurred during colonial times.' She asked, 'Would a white woman in a bathing costume have been given the same treatment?'[37] Tour operators complained that the advert would encourage people in 4x4s to drive recklessly over the Himba's remote ancestral grazing and burial grounds. Land Rover offered a defensive apology, withdrew the advert and dropped the advertising agency.

And yet, again, few lasting lessons seemed to be learnt.

In 2003, Land Rover launched a model called the Freelander Maasai. There's nothing random in the names car companies choose to give their vehicles. They are typically the result of careful and exhaustive marketing strategies, themselves built on the foundations of thorough market research and audience testing. Why choose Maasai? The Maasai are a semi-nomadic people who live in Kenya and northern Tanzania. Images of its warriors carrying distinctive shields, spears and throwing clubs, are widely reproduced. The desirable connotations of a noble wanderer passing through natural landscapes are not hard to see. Award citations for the Freelander Maasai advertising campaign go a little further.

They commend the elements of 'the exotic and excitement of the unknown'.[38] The image in the advert shows a group of Maasai standing in a line, tall to short, to suggest the shape of a Freelander. Shields are held so as to suggest the wheels. It's clever, but somehow, horribly wrong for Land Rover, a vehicle-maker pandering to the aspirations of the wealthy global middle classes, to appropriate the identity of Maasai tribespeople. The Maasai are pastoralists who, in cash terms at least, are among the poorest people on the planet.[39]

The notion that the average Maasai might ever actually afford to buy the car named after them, even if it was of any use, is laughable. Worse still, the car is typical, as we saw above, of a vehicle trend pushed by manufacturers for fuel-inefficient cars whose emissions contribute directly to global warming. The final insult is, of course, that pastoralists in Africa are on the frontline of climate change, their whole way of life under threat. Increasingly severe droughts linked to global warming particularly threaten the Maasai. Ironically, though, the development agency Oxfam suggests that the Maasai's acute survival skills, long ignored and considered irrelevant 'traditional' knowledge by successive governments, may hold the secret of survival for millions of others facing a drought-prone future.[40]

The future

Here, finally, is the great challenge for the future of the

car industry. It is far more fundamental than questions over national ownership which, in any case, have become increasingly meaningless due to economic globalization.

In 2008, Ford sold Land Rover along with Jaguar to the Indian industrial conglomerate TATA.[41] It was a year in which TATA's profile was rising internationally. In January 2008, it unveiled the 'Nano' car in Delhi, introducing the prospect of mass-market motoring to India. The 'world's cheapest car' was set to retail at £1,250 (100,000 rupees). TATA billed Nano as 'The Peoples' Car', but Dr Rajendra Pachauri, head of the Indian NGO TERI and chairman of the Nobel Prize-winning Intergovernmental Panel on Climate Change, was less optimistic: 'This is not the transport option for the country of a billion people, many of whom cannot afford to buy even a bus ticket.' The Nano, he said, was giving him 'nightmares'.[42] The Nano could not substitute for bicycles and would only add to the already chaotic traffic conditions in urban centres.

In 1950, there were an estimated 70 million cars, trucks and buses on the world's roads. Towards the end of the century that had risen to between 600 and 700 million. By 2025, the figure is expected to vastly exceed 1 billion. But the distribution of vehicle ownership is, and will continue to be, highly unequal around the world. In the middle of the 1990s, for every 1,000 people in the United States there were 750 motor vehicles. In China for the equivalent number of people there were eight vehicles, in India seven. Even by the year 2050, with the planned huge growth of car ownership in the majority, less industrialized world, rich countries with only 16 per cent of the world population will still account for 60 per cent of global motor vehicle emissions.[43] If it happens, we will all pay an even higher price than we do currently.

According to the World Health Organization (WHO),

'Deaths due to road traffic accidents will increase from 1.3 million in 2004 to 2.4 million in 2030,' mostly due to increased vehicle ownership in low- and middle-income countries.[44] As a result, traffic accidents are predicted to rise from ninth place in the rank of global leading causes of death in 2004 to fifth place by 2030. It is also worth pointing out that the four causes higher in the ranking are a mixture of respiratory and circulatory conditions, also linked to the pollution and sedentary lifestyles associated with car culture.[45]

However, one huge bump in the road lies ahead. A growing consensus suggests that global oil production is on the cusp of peaking, levelling off and beginning a long, slow decline. Each potential alternative fuel source brings with it, to date, a long list of other problems. This means that fantasies of rapid growth in global car ownership may remain just that. If so, car-makers around the world, in both rich and developing countries, will have to face the reality of converting to make goods more suited to a post-oil world.

In that case, Rover's long history may just bring it back to where it started out, with the bicycle.

In 2008, the *China Car Times* reported a story that first appeared in *Motor Trader*.[46] There were plans, apparently, by new MG owners Nanjing to use spare production capacity at the UK Longbridge works to make a modern version of the original Rover safety bicycle using Chinese designs. It would be a great example of reverse North–South technology transfer. Sadly, closer reading revealed that the story appeared on 1 April and the company spokesperson quoted was called 'April Furst'. It was a clever joke, an April Fool. But perhaps, like the best jokes, it contained a seed of truth and the last laugh would be on the pranksters.

CHAPTER 6

BP (1903): THE FIRST EXPLOITATION COMPANY

Oil is the trouble, of course. Detestable stuff!

Gertrude Bell, Baghdad, 1921

For the British oil was a long-distance industry which acquired from the beginning an association with national survival and diplomacy, and oil soon seemed part of the empire itself ... The companies seemed possessed of a special mystique, both to the producing and consuming countries. Their supranational expertise was beyond the ability of national governments. Their incomes were greater than those of most countries where they operated, their fleets of tankers had more tonnage than any navy, they owned and administered whole cities in the desert. In dealing with oil they were virtually self-sufficient, invulnerable to the laws of supply and demand, and to the vagaries of the stock markets, controlling all the functions of their business and selling oil from one subsidiary to another.

Anthony Sampson, *The Seven Sisters*, 1975

The meek shall inherit the earth, but not its mineral rights.

J. Paul Getty, oil baron

Cash, conflict and climate change

In their beginning was our end. Oil barrels transported by plodding horse and cart. Homes filled with sickly, sweet smoke from the kerosene used for heating and lighting. It takes an effort of imagination to visualize the world in which the oil industry emerged.

Yet, from this lumbering, dirty beginning, oil came to provide the modern world with the equivalent in energy of the work of 22 billion slaves.[1] The global economy is now said to be 'drunk on oil', just as a consensus is growing that a peak and decline in its global production is imminent.

From transport to agriculture and even your toothbrush, almost everything you use or touch during the day somehow or other depends on it. Talk of intoxication could not be more appropriate as the world now contemplates the serious effect of withdrawal. Climate change and the peak and long-term decline of oil production are challenging our hydrocarbon addiction. There is, of course, another more attractive reason why people talk of being drunk on the stuff. The way oil is measured by the 'barrel' stems from the earliest days of the industry, when it was collected in old whisky barrels.

The firm that was to become BP was a relatively late starter. By the time it got going, the industry in the USA had already undergone one lifecycle. America had nearly a half-share of global oil production, and one company, Standard Oil, controlled 85 per cent of that before it was broken up in a wave of anti-trust regulation in 1911. Some Russian oilfields, such as the one in Baku (in Azerbaijan), had already peaked by 1901 and were declining.

BP began as 'simply a personal initiative for profit'. It was the project of William Knox D'Arcy, a man who made a vast fortune from financing the Mount Morgan gold-mining company in Australia.[2] Any visitor who had the misfortune to stumble across Mount Morgan towards the end of the nineteenth century would see that it was a fortune built on the foundations of pollution, devastated landscape, disease, appalling working conditions and the dispossession of Aboriginal people.[3]

None of which, of course, disturbed the self-confident and satisfied demeanour of D'Arcy.

After leaving Australia and returning to England in 1889, D'Arcy remained chairman of the mining company's board. By 1900, he had a home in Grosvenor Square, a country mansion, wallpaper designed by the socialist craftsman and writer William Morris (wealthy clients were an irony that often stalked Morris' politics), a shooting retreat and, according even to BP's own historical account, 'led the self-indulgent life of a rich gentleman'.[4] Yes, D'Arcy was wealthy, but not, he thought, wealthy enough. He wanted more, and oil was the big new thing.

He heard about the potential for oil discoveries in Persia through a chain of establishment contacts. These led him to Britain's former Persian minister, who helped with local introductions. D'Arcy then sent Alfred Marriott, the young cousin of one of his financial advisors, to Persia to negotiate on his behalf. In 1901, within five weeks of Marriott arriving, D'Arcy had a deal to speculate for oil.

Many of the profound future faultlines in the geopolitics of oil were already visible in this original deal. First, D'Arcy overcame complaints and competition surrounding his negotiations by promising 'generous investment' in Persia, a promise which never materialized. Second, the deal was arranged only after he also provided a substantial slush fund to his Persian contact and fixer, General Antoine Kitagbi, to cover his own 'expenses' and to use for bribing officials.[5]

The 'First Exploitation Company'

On 28 May 1901, D'Arcy began several years of nervous,

211

hopeful expectation for his geological gamble to pay off. His close companions during the wait were his substantial but gradually ebbing wealth, and his own greed.

Mozaffar ad-Din Shah Qajar, the Shah of the Persian Empire, had given him 'a special and exclusive privilege to search for, obtain, exploit, develop, render suitable for trade, carry away and sell natural gas, petroleum, asphalt and ozokerite'.[6] (The latter is a type of naturally occurring mineral wax with a higher than normal boiling point which, when refined, was used in everything from cosmetics to candles.) More generous still, this 'privilege', which in the world of mining is called a 'concession', had been given for a period of sixty years and covered almost the whole of Persia, all except for a few northern provinces. In the event, it was to last until 1932.

The cost to wealthy William for these handsome terms was a £20,000 down-payment (between £2 million and £15 million in current values, depending on the method of calculation) and the same again worth of shares. Just 16 per cent of net profits were to go to the Persian government. The actual method for calculating this already low figure would prove to be a future source of friction.[7]

These were not the only seeds of later Middle Eastern upheaval to be planted in the name of oil in the early years of the twentieth century. In 1917, for example, during the First World War, Britain captured territory in Mesopotamia (see below), redrew some boundaries and created Iraq. When the British government then oversaw contracts to explore for and extract oil, not only were the terms once again favourable to the oil companies, but the concessions were to last until the year 2000.

From the outset, D'Arcy's terms did not receive general approval. Before he promised money to lever open the nation's natural wealth, Persia had been on the receiving end of numerous concessions bought by colonial powers. One after another, French, Belgian, Russian and Austrian deals, to develop everything from transport infrastructure to factories and public utilities, failed to bring benefits. Many Persians were understandably suspicious.

It was even worse at the local level. When George Reynolds, a self-taught geologist appointed by D'Arcy, arrived in Chiah Surkh to begin prospecting, he found that the local landowners, no respecters of the Shah or the remote elite of the government, had no idea that their mineral rights as local landowners, at least in the eyes of the company and government, were non-existent. They demanded what to them must have seemed quite legitimate additional payments. The Shah had, in any case, as yet received none of the promised initial payment from D'Arcy. This was to be delivered only when a company was formed to exploit a successful discovery. Shortly before the deadline to pay the Shah or see the deal expire, positive indications of oil finally led D'Arcy to form a business. It began life in 1903, and he gave it the remarkably honest title of the First Exploitation Company.

Anthony Sampson, chronicler of the oil industry at the peak of its monopolistic, global influence, describes Reynolds as among a tiny handful of the 'great pioneers of oil'. He was a 'tough loner', awkward, touchy and had a problem with authority.[8] Reynolds' team were mostly European and Canadian. The only Persian nationals were mercenaries hired to keep disgruntled local people away.

From the beginning, company workers were said to have an 'enclave mentality'. They lived in surroundings from which Persians themselves were excluded. That, and the involvement of the British government, meant that the 'activities of the company were frequently suspected by the Persians'.[9]

The problem of the company's attitude and management approach endured. In the early 1920s, by which time it had become known as the Anglo-Persian Oil Company (APOC), it attempted to squeeze more production from the Persian oilfields and pushed its refinery at Abadan too hard. This led to strikes over pay and conditions by the local and migrant workforce, and to a crippling fire that slashed production.

On this occasion, as on many others, the British government, courtesy of the British taxpayer, supported the company. Although the public held no shares in the company until 1922, by then the fate of the company had already become enmeshed in issues of conflict and national security for reasons rooted in a power struggle within the Royal Navy in the run-up to the First World War.

A wave of oil

D'Arcy's money had found oil. Now he had to find a market for it and that brought an unexpected obstacle. At the time, one of the most common uses for oil was to refine kerosene for heating homes and buildings. But Persian oil, it turned out, had a strong smell of sulphur that could not be removed by refining. Where could D'Arcy find a client for his smelly oil?

BP's great European competitor was founded by Marcus Samuel, the son of a trader who dealt in handcrafted shell gifts. He was aided by financial backing from the Rothschild banking family. He was zealous to compete with the mighty Standard Oil, and so developed the first ships considered safe enough to take the ocean shortcut from the east, passing through the relatively new Suez Canal.

The first ship in 1892 was called the *Murex* (a type of shell) and was followed by the *Conch* and the *Clam*. Well before D'Arcy came on the scene, Samuel lobbied Winston Churchill to persuade the navy to switch to fuel oil which, he argued, provided a military advantage, needing less storage space, and which delivered faster ships with better acceleration.

Naval interest in using fuel oil rather than coal had dimmed as Europe's imperial powers, Britain and Germany in particular, jockeyed for position in the first decade of the twentieth century. But that was set to change. The future of the navy played a huge role in the unconcealed imperial arms race with Germany. Churchill, who had become convinced by Samuel's arguments, said that oil gave 'more intense forms of war power'. The threat of German armament, and a joint lobby from Churchill and Admiral Sir John Fisher, triumphed over institutional resistance to change. In 1912 the naval hierarchies were won over to the new fuel source. However, the switch to oil was set to make British security reliant on guaranteeing foreign oil supplies. (Something that is true today because, since 2004, Britain is once again incapable of meeting its energy needs domestically following the decline of North Sea oil – a story we will come to later.)

Before then, the future of Anglo-Persian had been far from certain. It was small, lacked markets and faced bigger, more established competition. The other potential supplier of fuel oil to British ships was Royal Dutch Shell, the company with whom BP (as it would become known) would be locked in a strange combination of fighting and dancing for much of the century. Royal Dutch Shell, some twenty years earlier, had begun the lobby for the British Navy to turn to oil.

Anglo-Persian's managing director, Charles Greenway, adroitly used the security threat of Shell, as a 'foreign company', to push for state backing for his company. He lobbied the government for financial support in the same year, 1912, that the navy switched to oil. He played the card of 'strategic interests' and got his way. Churchill, in the Admiralty, decided he could not 'be sure of Shell'. An agreement was made guaranteeing that if oil-powered naval vessels were built, D'Arcy's company would meet around 40 per cent of the ships' fuel needs.

Rather than just striking a deal with Anglo-Persian, however, Churchill concluded that we 'must become the owners, or at any rate the controllers, at the source of at least a proportion of the supply of natural oil which we require'. The government subsequently bought 51 per cent of the company in 1913 and determined that it, and its directors, should remain British. Two directors with the right of veto were directly appointed by government.[10]

Revving ever louder at the heart of the brewing conflict with Germany was the increasingly popular internal combustion engine. The industries of all the key combatant countries were redirected from peacetime production to the manufacture of tanks, armoured personnel and military vehicles, and the new terror from the skies – the aeroplane. In Britain, one of the other eminent corporations, Rover, was just one of many to develop new factories and retool existing ones to supply the war. From having just 250 planes in 1915, by the end of the war British factories had made 55,000.

Switching the British fleet's fuel source proved a great success. Oil was easier to use and more efficient. It led to one of the war's most famous statements when Lord Curzon quipped that 'The allied cause had floated to victory on a wave of oil.' But it was a victory for the company too. Both it and the government had reason to be pleased with their relationship.

Britain gained further advantage when, instead of

capturing new oilfields for itself, in late 1918 it sabotaged oilfields in Romania that Germany, running desperately short of fuel, was relying upon. Hence, while oil literally fuelled the unimaginable destruction of the First World War, its lack of availability to Germany may have finally helped to bring the deadlocked conflict to an end.

By the end of the First World War, the company had supplied the military with 7 million barrels of fuel oil and the navy was buying 500,000 tonnes a year for its fleet. The war depended on the supply of oil, and Anglo-Persian may not have survived to become BP without the conflict. Supplying the navy was, even according to the official history, a 'crucial factor in the survival of the Company'.[11] Without it, Anglo-Persian could easily have been absorbed by Royal Dutch Shell before it was fully weaned as a major corporation.

Oil not only fuelled and spread the war over a greater area, and into the skies, it also introduced new targets with lasting significance for the modern world.

It was not a happy accident in 1917 that left Britain in control of Mesopotamian territory. It was design. The draw was, in fact, the area's oil-producing potential. Britain made the hostile capture and occupation of Baghdad a military objective, and blasted control of the city from the Turkish army. This was also an effective means of placing any potential supplies beyond the reach of the German military, on whose side Turkey fought. When Britain ran short of oil it had, up until then, needed to turn to the USA.

Britain's national interest soon became Anglo-Persian's profit. It took several years to negotiate, but by 1925 the company had nearly a 50 per cent stake in a joint venture whose concession covered most of what was by then Iraq, organized under the umbrella of the Turkish Petroleum

Company. Later, after the 1928 Red Line Agreement, pressure from the USA reduced the company's share in the concession by half, but still left it with the rights to a quarter of Iraq's oil, which was a quarter more than that enjoyed by the people of Iraq.

It is striking how place names recur in modern conflicts. Nearly a century on, the same names walk off the page like the solemn chant of a war report on the television news: Baghdad, Basra, Kirkuk . . . Not only was the war the making of Anglo-Persian, it also, half accidentally, provided its future public identity.

Up until the war, there were two dominant petrol distributors in the UK. One was the British subsidiary of Standard Oil, the other owned by the German Europäische Petroleum-Union. During the war the latter, along with many other German-owned businesses, was expropriated by the government. In 1914, it had a staff of 3,000 people and over one-third of the UK market. This gave Charles Greenway a unique opportunity to acquire a ready-made distribution company.

The German company that Greenway bought had been called British Petroleum to market itself to the British population. The purchase was one step towards his plan to build a fully self-contained corporation, 'engaged in every sector of the oil industry from the wellhead to the consumer'.[12] The company now had captive production and a guaranteed market with military protection and military clients.[13]

Greenway went on to be chairman of the company for thirteen years. Conservative and stuffy, he needed to be nothing else according to Anthony Sampson. Greenway was satirized in Upton Sinclair's novel *Oil* (1927) as the character, 'Old Spats and Monocle'. Deservedly, it would seem. Much later, in 1930, when Baron Greenway was seventy-four and in the more symbolic role of president, he said that BP's achievement as a growing company had not 'been equalled by any other concern in the history of the world'. It was a style of self-effacing humility that became typical of the company.

At that time, history did seem to be moving in the company's direction. BP's growth was shadowed by rising demand for the vehicles which needed its petrol products. As chapter 5 on Rover shows, the mass market for cars was exploding, largely metaphorically. Improvements in engine design were, in fact, dramatically improving the performance of cars, but in doing so, higher-octane, and literally more explosive, fuel was called for.

In 1931, the company was able to advertise that the petrol it was selling in the UK called 'BP Plus' (using the brand acquired in 1914 from the German company) contained 'a little something others haven't got'. Putting the chemical $(CH^3CH^2)^4Pb$ into their petrol must have seemed like a good idea at the time. BP cannot have envisaged that, decades later, campaigners would work tirelessly to have what was a toxic lead compound removed from petrol. Back then, the company was so proud that it even renamed the product 'BP Ethyl' to make the content, tetraethyl lead, more obvious.

However, within three years of Greenway's boast, the company was thrown into upheaval. Economic depression following the Wall Street crash of 1929 would see the company's profits cut in half. In response, the company's payments to its Persian hosts were slashed. In Tehran, the new shah Reza Shah Pahlavi responded by tearing up the company's production agreement.

Mistrust dating back to their earliest dealings haunted negotiations. A few years earlier the Persian government had discovered that it was being underpaid royalties as a result of some creative accounting by the company. Before that, it had been asked to agree to new terms that would have reduced its oil income to less than a third of its previous level.

Persia changed its name to Iran in 1935. Following suit, the company became Anglo-Iranian, although its future looked very shaky by then. But war had made the company and soon it was to save them again.

The second wave

In the two decades after the end of the First World War, the massively increased mechanization of conflict would make oil even more vital in the Second World War. The company's strategic importance was similarly raised as it became central to the logistics of the war effort. Sometimes its role was straightforward and sometimes less so.

It helped, for example, in the development of high-octane aircraft fuel. Technically difficult, it had to work out how to refine Iran's typically heavy crude oil. But, by the end of the war and after a major refit, the company's Iranian refinery at Abadan was producing 20,000 barrels a day. Even American planes were flying on the company's fuel. Production from small facilities in Britain also increased four-fold compared to pre-war levels.

Company staff worked closely with the Petroleum War Department. Some were seconded to the mundane tasks of making petrol cans and running storage depots, but others got to work on projects with intriguing canine code words. There was, for example, PLUTO – the 'pipeline under the ocean', a supply line to France designed to support the invasion in 1944, involving Marks & Spencer chair, Simon Marks. Then there was FIDO – 'Fog Investigation Dispersal Operations', which involved working out how to clear airfields.

Over the course of the war, the company saw forty-four of its tankers sunk, nearly half of the fleet, but profits soared too, from £7.4 million in 1939 to £23.4 million in 1945. To prevent war profiteering, however, the government introduced a special tax on excess profits that removed any surplus relative to 1939 levels.

Both official and company relations with Iran were, as ever, complex. The country declared itself neutral in the conflict, but its interests were entangled with the progress of war. Because domestic consumption in Britain plummeted due to the wartime fuel conservation measures, and shipping was a much more precarious activity, royalty payments from the company fell. To ease the important strategic relationship, the British government agreed to pay Iran compensation.

The British then went a considerable step further. In 1942, the Allies invaded Iran to pre-empt and ward off any similar invasion by Germany. Iraq had been reoccupied for the same reason in 1941.

One other key development during this period was the massive growth of petroleum production in Kuwait and Saudi Arabia in 1938. Also, in 1942, the Allies ended Italy's thirty-year rule of Libya. And, being on the winning side did, of course, help the company's prospects.

Anglo-Iranian successfully spread itself across a shattered Europe now busily rebuilding itself. Perhaps this is an historical example of what the author Naomi Klein refers to as the 'shock doctrine' in her 2007 book of that name: the process by which capitalist enterprise profits and grows from disasters. The company invested in refineries in France, Germany and Italy. The sale of its products grew from Switzerland to Greece, Scandinavia and New Zealand.

After the war, Saudi oil became strategically important in the implementation of the Marshall Plan to rebuild

Europe. But in 1948, the Red Line Agreement governing exploration in the Middle East, in place since 1927, began to break down. The companies that grouped together in the new, emerging regime became known as the 'Seven Sisters'. Close collusion between the major oil companies has been a consistent feature of their history. BP and Shell, for example, shared a joint petrol marketing operation in the UK between 1932 and 1976. But this was an unprecedentedly powerful group comprising Standard Oil, BP, Shell, Socony, Texaco, Socal and Gulf.

Then, just as power and control seemed to have settled into the cosy, shared laps of the Seven Sisters, trouble was brewing. In the years since the Red Line Agreement, the global economy had become dramatically more oil-addicted. Rather than the possession of oil being a geological curiosity that foreigners were welcome to sweat to extract, finding land marked with the tell-tale 'burning pillars' was like stumbling across a river bed scattered with gold.

Then, as now, Venezuela put the spark into the politics of oil. The original concessions enjoyed by the Sisters were negotiated to give outrageously one-sided benefits to the companies. But in 1948, the same year that the Red Line Agreement broke down, Venezuela set a precedent. The new split for companies benefiting from its natural resources was not going to be 16:84 in favour of the company, it was going to be 50:50. Faced with full-scale expropriation if they did not agree, the companies went along with it.

From the point of view of other producing countries, Venezuela's action delivered the 'threat of a good example'. The next year, Saudi Arabia wanted the same deal; Kuwait, which had been providing BP with oil since 1938 and Iraq since the decade before, soon followed.

'Sheer looting, not business'

This was when Anglo-Iranian – still puffed up with colonial arrogance – made a nearly fatal error. The Iranian government saw no reason why it should not also receive a 50:50 deal, but the company, under William Fraser, rebuffed it. Fraser was later described by government minister Kenneth Younger as a man of 'thoroughly second-rate intelligence and personality'. Fraser's insensitivity to the politics of the region had, he wrote, 'all the contempt of a Glasgow accountant for anything which cannot be shown on a balance sheet'. Britain's pretensions to continued imperial power, supported by its infamously serpentine diplomacy, were weakening. It was the beginning of decades of decolonization.

Trouble for Britain in the Middle East meant trouble for the company, too. It came in the form of the son of a rich Iranian land-owning family who became chairman of a government committee set up to assess oil policy. Mohammad Mossadegh was colourful, some thought bizarre, too openly emotional for British tastes and, as a result, he was seriously underestimated.[14] His committee concluded that BP's concession failed to protect Iran's interests. Saudi Arabia's 50:50 deal with Aramco gave a background of inescapable provocation, something Fraser failed either to understand or act upon.

General Haj Ali Razmara, Iran's prime minister at the time, had been negotiating new terms with Anglo-Iranian, but the so-called Supplemental Oil Agreement offered by the company fell short of what many nationalists wanted: something at least as good as the Saudi deal, or full repudiation of the concession.

Mossadegh publicly called for nationalization of the industry in February 1951. The following month, Razmara, who had been prime minister for less than a year, was assassinated. Within weeks, the parliament voted to expropriate the company's assets. And, after a brief, conciliatory attempt by the Shah to appoint a different prime minister, in April Mossadegh became prime minister himself. The speed of the turnaround in the company's fortunes was bewildering. But, more than that, it suggested that Britain's authority in the world could evaporate just as quickly.

Anthony Sampson points out the awkward predicament the Labour government found itself in. Britain had itself just nationalized a swathe of industries. Why shouldn't another sovereign nation do the same? How far would the country go in the name of one of its eminent corporations? In another echo of more recent geopolitical events, part of the problem had been bad intelligence. The government was dependent on the company, but under Fraser it did not see the problem coming. Even when it did, the flow of information about events was poor.

The belligerence of Fraser infected the foreign secretary, Herbert Morrison. Sabres were rattled and warships patrolled. But there were also voices of caution, such as that of Lord Mountbatten who oversaw the end of empire in India. A different strategy to military intervention emerged.

With the support of the other six Sisters, Anglo-Iranian managed to stage a boycott against Iranian oil. Of course, it also had Britain's imperial might behind it, too. Not every corporation can call directly on a state's military aircraft to scare away threats to its economic interests. On one occasion, the *Rose Mary*, a tanker sailing under Panama's flag, did take on oil from the Abadan refinery, but it was intercepted by planes from the RAF, forced into a British-controlled harbour in Aden and its cargo taken.

In circumstances that were later to repeat themselves, what saved the company was the lack of a unified regional stance towards the oil companies and the fact that there were so-called 'swing producers'. That is to say that if, for whatever reason, production by one important producer was cut off, there was another to turn to. The company poured money into expanding production in countries such as Kuwait. At a time of plenty of global capacity, Iran found that the world could turn its back on it with relative impunity.

Two years passed, Mossadegh was still in power, but international isolation was breeding internal instability. In the meantime, Anglo-Iranian had been renamed as the British Petroleum Company. Mossadegh wrote to the US president complaining that 'his country was being ruined by the political intrigue of the British government and BP'.[15] From the beginning of the crisis, the question of direct military intervention had been open for many in the British establishment, as had the idea of sponsoring a coup. But in the end, Britain preferred to get someone else to do its dirty work. While Mossadegh pleaded in one American ear, the British whispered in the other. Some in Britain found the whole business distasteful.

The government demurred from anything other than perpetuating the boycott, hoping that internal forces would correct the situation in its favour. Then a dark twist of historical unity intervened. In April 1953, Anthony Eden, the foreign secretary who refused to instigate a coup, fell ill. His position was taken over by the man that the company owed its very existence to, the Prime Minister Winston Churchill. His period of office, though brief, was long enough to approve a CIA-organized and -funded coup in Iran.

It was overseen by an American CIA operative with the exotic and unlikely name of Kermit Roosevelt, Jr, the grandson of Theodore Roosevelt. His parents were not to know, of course, that the age of television would later make his first name famous not for deeds of international subterfuge, but for a green hand puppet, shaped like a frog.

In over 1,700 pages of the official BP company history, the coup itself, on which turned the company's fortunes, is described in just two sentences.[16] One of them merely mentions that the events can be read about elsewhere. It is as if there is something tasteless, unnecessary, un-British even, in dwelling upon the ultimate, brutal means by which business objectives are met.

A different, earlier history of the company, published in 1959 and written more in the style of a *Boy's Own* adventure, is more direct. The title of a chapter describing the events – 'Honour is Served' – neatly summarizes the British view of the outcome. Mossadegh's assessment of what the company had done in Persia is there, too. Shortly before being deposed he said it was 'sheer looting, not business'.[17]

Seeking to rebuild relations with Iran in the aftermath, the British government again found the delicate diplomatic skills of BP's head, Sir William Fraser, in its way. Fraser wanted to be in charge of negotiations, but government cabinet member Harold Macmillan thought it would be a disaster, suggesting instead that Fraser be kicked upstairs. 'Why don't we make him a peer and be done with him?' said Macmillan.[18] The company was, in general, being treated more warily by the government.

The western powers' successful coup in Iran had wider ramifications. The CIA was thought to be so emboldened by its Iranian success that it gave it the confidence to undermine and overthrow many more foreign powers. Over coming decades, from Central America and the Caribbean, to Africa and Asia, governments that were not aligned with American interests would feel the CIA's breath, hot with Middle Eastern triumph, heavy on their necks. Often the hot breath shortly preceded a blade slipped between their ribs or their car mysteriously exploding.

Neither the British, nor the Americans of course, were to get things entirely their own way. On the contrary, the foundations of division and mistrust had been laid strongly enough to last for generations. During the coup, the Shah had fled the country, returning only when western cash and agents had removed the prime minister he hated. For this, he would remain tainted in the eyes of many in the region and, ultimately, be consigned to die in exile after being deposed.

BP faced repercussions too. Even bluff Sir William Fraser saw that, in the face of local resentment, BP would not be able to keep exclusive rights over Iranian oil. Britain could no longer engineer the appropriate regional security to continue its operations without American support. The result, though, was also to make BP broaden the horizons of its own corporate ambitions. Seeing assets that it considered its own suddenly appropriated was a shock. Diversifying supply would now become its key goal. The brutal economics of oil would be brought to more parts of the world to shore up BP's corporate security.

Some problems were still decades away, but another was just around the corner. It would be judged by history as the last serious attempt by Britain to express itself as a genuine colonial power. The judgement passed would be one of failure and humiliation. It involved the chief artery of the global oil industry, the Suez Canal.

'You had it, Madam'

For Britain, the Suez Canal crisis would be a perfect example of emergent consequences. It was a reminder about why you should be careful about what you wish for, in case it comes to pass.

In the midst of Iran's turmoil, a pan-Arab revolutionary rose, Gamal Abdel Nasser. In 1952, Nasser was part of a revolt that deposed Egypt's constitutional monarchy and established a republic. Before long, he would become the country's president. Nasser understood that Egypt's lack of actual oil reserves was heavily compensated for by the strategic importance of the Suez Canal, which lay in Egyptian territory. For Britain, the canal was symbolic.

The canal had been an economic and military artery to the British Empire's eastern colonies for decades. To the chagrin of the British, it had been built by a private French company. However, Britain had gained a large, minority stake in the canal six years after its 1869 opening, when Egypt's ruler was insolvent and sold his shares. Queen Victoria was given the good news by the prime minister, Benjamin Disraeli, in a short note that announced: 'You have it, Madam.'[19] By the 1950s, India was newly free of its colonial yoke, but the Suez Canal still carried an air of unrelinquished imperial identity. Even more, though, access to oil had replaced the administrative concerns of formal empire as a focus for Britain's interest in the region.

Two-thirds of Europe's oil came through the canal by 1955 and two-thirds of all the shipping passing through was carrying petroleum.[20] Empires and monarchs had fallen, but something new, valuable, dark and liquid was on the throne.

Nasser might have been a full-blown revolutionary, inspired by Mossadegh and with a vision of an Arab renaissance, but he was also mindful of what had happened to Mossadegh. Furthermore, he was an astute, populist politician and a diplomat. Britain had a major military presence in Suez, but as part of a regional political realignment it had agreed to a managed withdrawal. Nasser knew he had to stand up to the British enough to pursue his pan-Arab agenda and draw popular support, but not so much that it provoked a combined hostile response from Britain, France and the USA.

Working in his favour was the fact that both the old and new world powers he had to face were not of one mind. Even the chairman of the Suez Canal Company conceded that the Americans thought the current arrangement carried a musty, nineteenth-century odour that still drifted through the open shutters of a fading colonial period. Foreign control of the Suez Canal was a symbolic affront to Nasser's Egypt. The economics of the canal also echoed the unbalanced concessions of the oil companies. Shareholders in Britain enjoyed the lion's share of the earnings from the tolls paid to use the canal.

The original sin of the unbalanced Persian concession came back to haunt the British. When they argued that the canal was a vital part of their regional oil complex, Nasser pointed out that while it was now common practice for oil-producing countries to get half of the profits from their oil, Egypt got nothing like that from the tolls paid in the canal.

However, instead of better terms for the use of its sovereign land, Egypt was fobbed off with a World Bank loan to build a dam at Aswan. Even then, Cold War politics intervened. Nasser sought to capitalize on emerging superpower rivalries and bought arms from the Warsaw Pact countries. The result was an American backlash that saw the dam loan cancelled.

On 26 July 1956, Nasser gave a speech that referred repeatedly, and not in friendly terms, to the original French builder of the canal, Ferdinand de Lesseps. Like a trick lifted from an implausible spy novel, the name was the codeword for his army to take control of the canal. Syria also cut the oil pipeline that ran from Iraq to the Mediterranean. Ships would now have to travel thousands of miles further to reach Europe. In four months, BP's homebound supplies dropped by 140 million barrels.[21]

Britain and France were incandescent. They strained at the leash of their relationship with the USA for a military response, but America did not want a destabilizing war. There was a domestic election looming and President Dwight D. Eisenhower was running for re-election as an international peacemaker. Both Britain and France overlooked or misunderstood the circumstances and position of their key ally.

Britain's logistical skill in organizing a hostile response was soon to look as amateurish as its attempts at diplomatic sophistry. It was determined to use force to keep control of its regional oil interests, but found itself suddenly short of transport for its troops and tanks.

Moving house in the 1970s, you may well have relied on a Pickfords removal van. Friendly staff would let a family's children sit in the front in the van, as exciting to them as being allowed into a pilot's cabin. Tremendous fun for a child, perhaps, and the epitome of the rhythm of English suburban life. It should have rung a warning when, desperate to move tanks to the region to prepare for a hostile assault on a foreign country, the army had to ring up Pickfords and ask for help. If that was not bad enough, it also had to requisition tourist ocean liners at the height of the holiday season to move troops.[22]

An account of the Suez crisis by Hugh Thomas puts the rather desperate fumbling into context: 'Ever since Churchill converted the Navy to the use of oil, British politicians have seemed to have had a feeling about oil supplies comparable to the fear of castration.'[23]

There is an inverse political correctness in the scorn poured on conspiracy theories. But here was a text-book example, recorded in some detail for history. Together the British and French persuaded Israel to play a round of the great game. Israel was to begin a war of aggression by invading Sinai. The benefits to Israel were the strengthening of one of its borders and the chance to destabilize Egypt, considered an enemy and a hostile state. Then, playing innocent, Britain and France would intervene as 'peacemakers', separating the warring parties, and take control of the canal to protect vital infrastructure from a conflict that could overflow. It was a drama of supreme self-delusion of the type excelled at by empires in their dotage. To think either that this version of events would be accepted as true, or that it would be tolerated by the USA and the rest of the international community, was implausible. Of course, blinded by fear for their shrinking colonial *cojones*, they went ahead. The rest is a well-trodden history of national humiliation for Britain and the destruction of political careers.

The ripples from the stone dropped by Mossadegh in the great pond of oil that Britain considered its own continued to radiate outwards. The Hashemite king in Iraq owed his throne to the British who had installed him but, inspired by Nasser, members of the Iraqi army turned against him. A swathe of the royal family was executed in the 1958 revolution, and the prime minister, whose sentiments were also pro-western, was hanged. In place of the compromised monarchy, an unstable republic was created.

Iraq Petroleum was the composite company that had been born out of the Red Line Agreement. BP was a senior partner and it comprised most of the other oil majors in the region. The crucial exception, of course, was Iraq itself, which the companies had conspired to exclude from a share of ownership. In tune with the times, the new government now agitated for a better deal. In spite of the violent upheaval, the events 'passed all but unmentioned in the annual statement to shareholders'.[24] Sooner or later, the attitude of BP and its sister companies was bound to lead to a more organized reaction.

In 1959, BP 'unilaterally' cut the price of oil by 10 per cent and seriously upset the exporting countries which were seeking, and beginning to expect, improved terms. Following similar action by Standard Oil, it set in train moves that would lead to the formation of a producers' cartel that would stand up to the oil companies. The major producers were gathered together by Saudi Arabia and Venezuela in 1960. OPEC (the Organization of Petroleum Exporting Countries) was born.

Initially, its influence was limited because, compared to global demand, there was a glut of supply. But by 1970, things had changed. The USA was approaching its domestic production peak and decline, just as demand at home was rocketing. OPEC began to flex its muscles when Libya demanded an improvement on the 50:50 deal. If the companies refused, Libya said its oilfields would be nationalized. Once again there was a domino effect, with other producers following suit with similar claims. The companies had to agree. But ultimately giving ground did nothing to prevent a wave of nationalizations. From Saudi Arabia to Iraq and Iran the companies progressively lost direct control of their oil supplies.

Global reach

During the crisis years, BP dramatically increased its oil extraction from Kuwait, Qatar and Iraq. This, along with large cash reserves, meant that – in spite of a few lean years – the company was already making record profits again by 1954.

BP looked for oil in Malta, Papua New Guinea and Australia – turning full circle to the land whose mineral wealth had financed the birth of the company. It looked in Alaska, the Caribbean and the Rocky Mountains, with little success. It had more luck in Nigeria, where a joint exploration with Shell led to a discovery in 1956. It found oil, too, in the waters off Abu Dhabi. Alongside other majors such as Standard Oil, it discovered large reserves of high-quality crude oil that needed little refining beneath the sands of Libya.

The company's total production was booming. From 0.75 million barrels a day in 1954, by 1960 the figure had leapt to 1.5 million, and nearly 4 million a decade later.

BP's production – its 'upstream' side – grew so fast that it struggled to find a market for all that oil. Ironically, the answer to this challenge would create another seemingly intractable problem that is still with us today.

To diversify, BP moved into the petrochemical business. The seeds to this had been planted soon after the Second World War with the foundation in 1947 of British Petroleum Chemicals. By the 1960s, it had bought out Mobil's plastics division and was running a major chemicals plant at Grangemouth, along with a joint operation with controversial German chemical giant Bayer. In Britain, as a chemical company BP was second in size only to ICI. It was the birth of the age of plastic.

The living world is often described as the biosphere. Like a plastic cuckoo in nature's nest, a new technosphere made of substances that could not occur naturally started to grow. With the creation and rapid spread of hydrocarbon products reaching into every imaginable aspect of our lives, a slow shift of balance began. The result? Drains blocked with plastic bags, birds strangled by the lattice packaging that holds packs of beer together, oceans decorated with the floating indestructible plastic detritus of voracious consumer societies and more and more carbon released into the atmosphere.

As much as its use for transport, the less obvious products of the oil industry defined the second half of the twentieth century. Oil allowed humanity to defy gravity, literally in the case of kerosene to fuel passenger aircraft, and metaphorically in the way that petrochemicals underlie the fertilizers and pesticides that fed the hi-tech agricultural green revolution.

Things that we never knew we needed suddenly became necessities of life: the plastic bag, disposable pens, disposable cups, disposable razors, disposable everything. Of course, once thrown out, the waste from the new convenience-driven plastic society may have been out of sight, but it was filling ever larger landfill sites with rubbish, and the increased use of fossil fuels was causing long-term environmental changes.

Great historic shifts often seem to turn around seemingly prosaic pivots. On one level, the consumer society, with all its comforts, distractions and destructiveness, was called into being because of over-capacity and surplus oil production during just a couple of decades in the post-war period.

The science of global warming now tells us that climate change is the astonishingly expensive price that we have to pay for a little economic convenience. According to James Hansen of NASA's Goddard Institute, that price means we are on the brink of losing the climate in which civilization emerged – just to solve one mining industry's mundane problem of over-production.

Regional reaction

The path to an oil-fuelled consumer nirvana has never been smooth. For BP, the geopolitics of oil would lurch first one way and then another, like a badly loaded ship adrift in high seas.

From the escalation of regional tensions marked by the Israeli–Arab war of 1967 to the twin OPEC oil crises of the 1970s, oil continued to lubricate a succession of economic and political upheavals. Through these unpredictable waters, BP sailed its corporate ship, watchful for anything that might cause it to founder or, more specifically, lose money.

The 1967 war led to most major producers blocking shipments to anyone considered a 'friend of Israel', which included both the UK and the USA. The Suez Canal itself was made impassable by the scuttling of ships.

Getting supplies to Europe now meant much longer sea trips around the southern tip of South Africa, the euphemistically named Cape of Good Hope (given its notoriously perilous nature, Cape of Cross Your Fingers and Hope would have been more appropriate). It also meant a high demand for spare, available tankers.

BP was offered an initially expensive but ultimately good-value exclusive deal from a man whose name was to become synonymous with shipping and extreme wealth – Aristotle Onassis. It was offered his entire fleet for hire and was given just a few hours to accept on a take-it-or-leave-it basis. BP took the deal, making Onassis a lot of money, but allowing BP to keep meeting demand for its oil. In 1971, the recently self-installed Libyan leader, Muammar al-Gaddafi, unilaterally set new, higher terms for the price the company had to pay the country for its oil. Around the same time, British troops were withdrawn from the Gulf for the first time in decades.

Two years later, in 1973, OPEC representatives sat in conference rooms in Vienna negotiating new prices with the oil majors, while Egypt again waged war with Israel. BP had been prepared to accept a rise of 45 cents per barrel, but across the table the Gulf producers wanted $3. Against the backdrop of the conflict, within months the price of a barrel went from $3 to $11.75 and, for the first time, consumers in the West realized their state of hostile dependency on an acronym – OPEC. From then on, the term was just as likely to be heard in arguments in the pub as it was in the boardrooms of Europe's elite.

Queues at the petrol pumps, energy blackouts and unemployment: the fortunes of the oil companies' home countries were now being hit as hard as they were. The opposite was true of the oil producers: in just five years from 1972 to 1977, their annual income rose six-fold to $140 billion. The crisis would repeat itself with variations in 1979. And, long-term, unforeseen consequences would flow from the glut of petro-dollars in the global economy. They would leave whole countries virtually bankrupt and banking systems on the verge of collapse.

However, the conditions for successful exploration by BP were improved by a change in international law that allowed countries to exert sovereign rights over much expanded territorial waters. Then an unexpected windfall was set to rescue the fortunes of BP and soften the impact of losing direct control over much of the Middle East's natural resource base.

BP found oil much closer to home. It turned out that the North Sea harboured a lot more than fish and Norse sagas. Beneath its floor were large reservoirs of crude oil. Not as much as was to be found in Saudi Arabia, Iran and Iraq, but enough to produce ridiculous riches for a generation, and pay for the social and economic fall-out as inequality rose dramatically in a country in the grip of a political free-market experiment under the Conservative government of Margaret Thatcher.

To begin with, things had not looked so good. Like a worse echo of the long-frustrated search for oil that began its existence, BP had looked for oil in the UK for decades, finding little of significance. The discovery of large gas fields under the North Sea, an indication of what the geology harboured, was greeted with near euphoria. The bubble soon burst, however, when safety lapses – a recurring theme in the life of the company – led to the collapse of the Sea Gem exploration platform during a storm, resulting in mass fatalities.

The actual discovery of the Forties oilfield in the North Sea appears to have been triggered by an almost Monty Pythonesque fit of pique on the part of a company executive. BP had a new exploration platform called the Sea Quest under contract to another oil firm. It was drilling undersea in a place called McNutt's Half Dome. Harry Warman of BP thought this was a waste of time, and he also thought the location had a silly name, so the platform was relocated, and BP got lucky. The Forties field was found.

Oil was already produced on the British mainland, but in small amounts – just half a million barrels in the whole of 1959. When the pipe from BP's new Forties field was opened in November 1975, the company expected it to carry half a million barrels a day.[25]

It must have seemed liked the dawn of a new age. In reality, it was an industry set to live fast and die young. Just over two decades later, in 1999, UK oil production peaked and began to decline at the rate of around 7 per cent per year.[26]

Beyond petroleum, or stuck in it?

At the turn of the millennium, BP tried to become much more than just a company that made a great deal of money by helping to liquidate the planet's natural resources. It did what any self-conscious public figure concerned about the effects of ageing does – it went for a makeover.

It aimed high – at least it did if you believe the hyperbole of its advertising agency. In a short orgy of self-congratulation, Ogilvy Public Relations Worldwide describe how 'the newly rebranded, global BP sought to position itself as transcending the oil sector, delivering top line growth while remaining innovative, progressive, environmentally responsible and performance-driven'.[27] The initials 'BP' would no longer stand for British Petroleum, but 'Beyond Petroleum'.

Exactly how far beyond was left sufficiently vague. To drive home the new identity, no tooth-aching management cliché was left unturned. Brand champions wielded 'leadership communications, toolkits, chat room promotions, CEO satellite broadcasts, town hall meetings and celebrations'.[28] Everything was brought to bear to convince both BP's own staff and the outside world that here was a company truly looking to re-engineer itself for a changed world.

A decade later, however, the world would still be tapping its fingers, waiting for that new company to emerge.

It started well. BP was, according to the ads, variously 'looking to a greener future', going to 'think outside the barrel' (you can almost hear the mirth in the boardroom when that one came up) and 'develop a diversified portfolio'. Then, under the influence of chief executive John Browne and in the hunt for a genuine energy mix including a host of renewable energy sources, it said it would search 'from the earth to the sun, and everything in between'.

238

But, like a concrete roof on thin bamboo supports, the hype was not going to stay up for long. And, in fact, the commitment to change looked about as thin as the paper that the 'Beyond Petroleum' adverts were printed on.

In 2004, BP was directly responsible for 82 million tonnes of greenhouse gases (CO_2 equivalent) entering the atmosphere from its production cycle, and a further 1,376 million tonnes from the use of products it sold.[29] Together, this meant that 6 per cent of global greenhouse gas emissions from fossil fuel use could be traced back to this one company.

Using conventional accounting, the liquidation of our fossil-fuel inheritance is seen as a benefit to the economy. Natural commodities are treated as free income; no value is put on the depreciation of natural assets in the way in which a business, when doing its accounts, would have to account for depleted stock and depreciating assets. But the picture changes when a more comprehensive spreadsheet is used that subtracts environmental damage.

A rule of thumb used by the UK Treasury to estimate the damage caused by burning fossil fuels applied a cost of £20 per tonne of CO_2. An assessment of BP's performance in 2006, for example, when it announced an annual profit of £11 billion, would mean the subtraction of a carbon damage bill of £1.64 billion from its final profits for direct emissions, and a further £27.5 billion for the emissions created by its products. Together, this would produce a total environmental cost of just over £29 billion (not far short of all government revenue from fossil fuels), making the company effectively bankrupt.

The sensitivity of such figures might explain an extraordinary change in the way that BP calculated the scale of emissions linked to its business when new data were published in 2006.[30] Applying a new methodology to account for the emissions stemming from its direct operational emissions, and the products it sells, had the effect of more than halving the total.

Perhaps the sheer scale of related emissions was deemed incompatible with the company's aggressively marketed new green image. Yet its pattern of investments around the same time into research and development showed that the absolute focus on its core oil business was not set to change. In 2005, only around 5 per cent of its investment went into what it termed 'alternative energy' (a definition in which BP included some fossil fuel, gas-powered generation). On the other hand, over 70 per cent of its capital investment went towards finding even more oil and gas.[31]

A cursory reading of the information that the company made available to potential investors in 2006 showed that for BP the aim of its search beyond petroleum was, in fact, to find a lot more petroleum: 'Our main activities are the exploration and production of crude oil and natural gas; refining, marketing, supply and transportation; and the manufacture and marketing of petrochemicals.'[32] The year is important, because if there had indeed been any meaningful commitment of management and serious resources to changing corporate direction, it should have showed by then. Instead, rather than 'transcending the oil sector', and 'thinking outside the barrel', BP seemed to be languishing at its bottom, scraping.

So focused was the corporation's search to secure the carbon 'fix' needed to supply an oil-addicted economy, it seems that things like safety, the environment and other people's livelihoods were not allowed to stand in the way. Let's take a single month in summer 2006 as an example.

In July, BP was forced to pay a reported £3 million in compensation and legal costs to Colombian farmers left destitute by the building of a major oil pipeline through their land. Lawyers representing the farmers, Leigh Day & Co., accused BP of failing to compensate farmers for damage reaching back to 1995 and of gaining advantage from terror tactics employed by others to guard the pipeline. There was also a background to the story because BP had strong links in Colombia, for example in exploiting the Cusiana-Cupiagua oilfield. Oil revenues in Colombia funded the country's internal conflict and, in turn, companies had to pay to protect their commercial operations.[33]

Shortly after the embarrassment of being forced to pay compensation, in the same month BP faced more fines and legal repercussions after having to shut its huge Alaska Prudhoe Bay oilfield. A corroded pipe had led to a massive oil spill. The news caused world oil prices to hit another record high and the chief executive of BP America, Bob Malone, had to grovel. 'We regret that it is necessary to take this action and we apologize to the nation and the State of Alaska for the adverse impacts it will cause,' he said in a public statement.[34] What hurt BP especially was that, only the previous year, another safety failure led to a massive explosion at its Texas City refinery, killing fifteen workers and injuring more.[35]

Yet, in spite of the apparent remorse, a far worse safety failure was yet to come. In April 2010, BP experienced possibly its greatest public setback. An explosion on the Deepwater Horizon, an oil rig in the Gulf of Mexico forty miles from the Louisiana coast, caused one of the largest pollution events of recent times. For months, anywhere between 5,000 and 100,000 (estimates varied enormously) barrels of oil a day poured into the Gulf. In addition, eleven people working on the platform were killed. BP had leased the rig from another company, but whatever excuses it may have had, this built on a previous record of serious safety failures at plants. Within weeks of the disaster, BP's shares lost billions in value. A combination of meeting compensation claims, changed regulation, damage to reputation and immediate costs were estimated to produce at least £23 billion bill to the company.[36]

BP was not alone in its attempts to create a reality through advertising and a deliberate policy of reputation management that was at odds with real life. Where it led others followed, egregiously.

Another oil company, Shell, went so far that its creative efforts earned it a rebuke from the Advertising Standards Authority (ASA). The company's advertising concentrated on renewable energy to such a degree that a casual observer might think that Shell was, in fact, principally a renewable energy company. Its adverts invoked flower power, literally, as petals spewed from smoke stacks.

The ASA condemned Shell for creating the impression that all its carbon dioxide emissions were recycled to help grow plants in greenhouses, something which was true for only a fraction of 1 per cent of the emissions from its direct plant operations. Later, the ASA again ruled against a Shell advert which claimed that its exploitation of Canadian oil sands, one of the most polluting and least efficient forms of fossil fuel, was part of its 'sustainable' approach to meeting energy demands.

However, Shell's experience did not deter BP's doubly creative approach to advertising.

In 2008, BP's advertising again strongly focused on its commitment to a genuinely diversified energy supply, with slogans like 'the best way out of the energy fix is an energy mix'. This time, the claim drew the attention of the environmental group Greenpeace, which had obtained a copy of a presentation given by Tony Hayward, BP's new CEO who had replaced John Browne. It revealed, according to Greenpeace, that 'the company allocated 93% ($20bn) of its total investment fund for 2008 for the development and extraction of oil, gas and other fossil fuels. In contrast, solar power (a technology which analysts say is on the brink of a new technological breakthrough) was set to receive just 1.39% ($0.3bn).' The company's own greenhouse gas emissions at that stage were 'roughly equivalent' to the whole of Portugal. In response, the campaigners decided to award BP an 'Emerald Paintbrush' in honour of its 'greenwash'.[37]

By 2009, BP had not so much gone beyond petroleum as willingly fallen back into its sticky embrace. In a world more aware than ever of the problems of climate change, and the imminent peak and decline of global oil production, BP almost literally 'shut up shop' on its ambitions for alternative energy sources.

In June 2009, it closed the London HQ of BP Alternative Energy, its renewables operation. The division's boss, BP's most senior female executive, resigned. The company's rate of investment in renewables plummeted in the same year. BP pulled out of virtually all wind-power initiatives everywhere outside the USA (ironically given that the UK, BP's host nation, has the largest wind energy resources in Europe), closed solar plants in the USA and Spain, and cancelled plans for two power stations that were to be built with carbon capture and storage fitted.[38]

In September of the same year, the company celebrated a return to its core business, with the discovery of a large oilfield in the now badly polluted Gulf of Mexico.[39] Some old-fashioned oil controversy flared that month, too, after the early release from prison of a Libyan (who at the time of release was near to death with cancer) convicted of bombing a passenger aircraft. The suspicion was that this had in some way been linked to the promise of new oil concessions in Libya that would involve BP.

In the irony-free world of big business, BP's former boss, John Browne, called on the government to oblige banks under public control to invest in renewable energy.[40] For one of the banks which was at the heart of the financial collapse of 2007 and 2008, such a move would be equivalent to a radical religious conversion: the Royal Bank of Scotland formerly advertised itself as the 'Oil and Gas Bank' and was Europe's largest banking investor in the fossil fuel sector.

Yet BP's back-to-basics approach to its own industry is more than fraught. According to the *Financial Times*: 'An integrated oil company such as BP makes its living by extracting resources and bringing them to market. Both parts of that business are becoming more difficult.'[41]

It is faced with one problem which, it could be argued, is transitory (though equally it could be argued as a long-term issue). Demand is down in rich countries because of the financial crisis that began in 2007 and the ensuing recession. Where developing country markets are concerned there is little relief, as their doors do not swing open to the company so easily. So much, then, for the prospect of sales.

The other problem affecting BP's production side is not transitory at all. It is a geological inevitability. It just gets harder and harder to find oil and to get it out of the ground. As the *Financial Times* put it: 'Of the six countries suffering the steepest falls in oil output last year (2008), BP is active in three: the USA, the UK and Russia.'

Of finance and empire

BP's tale tells a story of the evolution of twentieth-century capitalism. It started out as money-making exercise. Everything in its path was bent to that primary purpose: conflict, international relations, the environment and communities. A century later, that primary purpose is intact and the world, including the gradual loss of an atmosphere that makes civilization possible, still bends to its will.

Of course, in between times, the internal culture of the company has reflected broader social changes. Sometimes it has been more patrician and caring to its staff, at others it has emulated the brutal, amoral austerity of Anglo-Saxon economics. Through it all, though, the single bottom line – to make money – has remained unaltered.

James Marriott, a long-term observer of the industry, argues that, fundamentally, major oil companies such as BP and Shell are banks.[42] They are about making and moving money around.

The oil industry is dominant in modern financial markets. Ironically, as awareness of climate change grows, more money floods into the shares of fossil fuel companies. That represents at least one significant difference from oil's early days when it had great difficulty getting access to the capital markets. Big finance in the second half of the nineteenth century was dug deeply into coal-mining. It took about half a century to get finance out of coal and into oil. Now oil is king and it is the upstart renewable energy companies that have struggled to attract finance.

So, how will we achieve the transfer of capital to develop a new energy source, especially as this time we have much less than fifty years in which to do it?

Marriott questions the extent to which a corporation such as BP either mirrors or forms the capital markets of its times. How does it determine successive phases of capitalism? To begin with, the company was an example of purely speculative capital investment to exploit another country's natural resource. In the 1950s and 1960s, it represented more 'welfare capital'. BP was half state-owned, and the corporation paid for the children of staff to go to school and university. It was a paternalistic model.

During the International Monetary Fund (IMF) crisis of the mid-1970s, the fate of the company got caught up in the broader shift towards financial deregulation. The Chancellor of the Exchequer Denis Healey was forced to go to the IMF for help. Terms set by the fund included a swathe of public-spending cuts and for the government to begin selling off its stake in BP. This the government did progressively, selling tranches right up to John Major's term as chancellor.

Today, we have a company with weak pension provision, the support once given to the families of workers is now gone and the once popular social clubs are largely forgotten.

The shift from speculative to welfare to finance-driven capitalism may interest corporate historians, but BP's importance goes much further. It lies in the deeper continuity of a corporation that, from its outset, has existed to make money by liquidating – in a few generations – an unrepeatable natural asset that took something approaching 200 million years to accumulate. That the consequence of doing so has been to potentially trigger catastrophic global warming is an inconvenient truth yet to make an impression on BP's core business model. Worse still, society has allowed corporations to operate in this way, directly undermining its own long-term interests.

For all the talk of a balanced energy portfolio that embraces renewables, 'expro' – the exploration and the production of oil – remains the heart and soul of the corporation, as revealed by its intention to expand the exploitation of tar sands, one of the dirtiest forms of oil reserves.

If society's challenge now is to phase out fossil fuels,

what will that mean for the future of BP and capitalism more generally? If, indeed, they have one in a world where environmental realities place impossible obstacles in the way of the ever-expanding capitalist process of money pushing the increasing production and consumption of commodities, in order to produce more money, a process which repeats and furthers itself in an endless upward spiral.

After money-making, the other great continuity has been a relationship between the oil corporation and the 'imperial' state. D'Arcy's view was that, given the uncertainties of early prospecting and the market, making money required concessions on massively preferential terms. In order to do that, he needed state backing.

From Persia to Nigeria (which in the 1930s was a British colony that gave BP and Shell a concession covering the whole country) to modern Iraq, the company pursued a basically imperial model. BP's Persian concession had been huge, around twice the size of France, and highly economically advantageous.

As a logical extension of the imperial model, the industry has also enjoyed an intimate connection with the military. The armed forces have been part of the production system and also one of its most important customers. It was a single military contract with the Royal Navy, after all, that brought BP into being, and war played a significant part in the company's growth. The British Army came to protect its production facilities in Persia from attack by angry local Bedouin people. Lieutenant Arnold Wilson, one of the soldiers on that mission, later became a resident director of the company. Today, the US military is the largest single-entity consumer of oil and, in times of crisis, large shares of oil production are earmarked for the prosecution of conflict.

'If, today, you were to make a list of the places around the world where BP extracts oil, and then make another list of the locations of senior company executives who find that they need armed security, you would find a remarkable correlation between the two,' says Marriott. Oil is an industry that conducts its business through armed security and exists by military means.

More than any of the other corporations in this book, the story of BP overlaps and underpins the most recent flowering of advanced industrialized society. But it also contains the seeds of its, and potentially our own, downfall. The extraordinary growth in humanity's material production, consumption and its sheer size over the last century would not have happened without oil. Now it is both running out and destroying the particular climate we have relied on. It is a paradox, yet, instead of adapting and changing course, BP is more committed than ever to its core business of extracting oil. In doing so, it can only, ultimately, put itself out of business. We can only hope that it does not do the same to the rest of us.

CHAPTER 7

BBC (1922): THE CARDINALS OF THE AIR

We must let listening-in drop into its proper place in our lives – not a very important place. Normal, reasonable lives of their own is what people want: a more direct exchange of life for labour, and some of the stability back again that our clever techniques have stolen away. If they had these things they wouldn't need to be compensated all the time with echoes of the lives of comedians, political journalists, experts in one thing and another, teachers, preachers and astrologers, or just with any noise in place of quiet.

Paul Bloomfield, former BBC producer, 1941

Why do we need this peepshow?

Winston Churchill, talking about television

The British Broadcasting Corporation. It is unlike other corporations in this book. The name rolls off the tongue with an involuntary hint of awe and reverence. It is, of course, the biggest broadcaster in the world, with its 24,000 staff, its batteries of radio channels and local stations, its armoury of TV channels worldwide (including BBC America, BBC Prime and the UKTV channels it runs jointly with Virgin). But it is its semi-religious aura of mission and its (under-fire but still formidable) reputation for impartiality and quality that set the whole institution apart. 'I'm not press, I'm the

BBC,' shouts Geraldine Chaplin in the Robert Altman film *Nashville* (1975). It's all very believable.

That is why it is so hard to grasp the idea that the BBC owed its very existence, partly at least, to something as fleeting as a stunt by a tabloid newspaper. The first tabloid newspaper, in fact: the *Daily Mail*. Tom Clarke, assistant to the *Mail*'s founder, Lord Northcliffe, had been a signals officer in the First World War, which had been over for little more than eighteen months. It was he who suggested that the *Mail* should sponsor a radio broadcast.

The first broadcasts had been taking place fitfully. These short musical items – even the train timetable read slowly over the crackling valves – had thrilled a handful of enthusiasts during the early months of 1920. The first licences had been issued by the Post Office the previous year. Now Northcliffe leaped at the idea that the newspaper would organize something truly professional, and as soon as possible.

To that end, on 15 June, the great soprano Dame Nellie Melba was transported to Chelmsford to sing into a microphone. She did and listeners as far as Newfoundland were able to listen (she never broadcast again once she discovered they could listen for free). They even cut a record at the foot of the Eiffel Tower. It caught the public imagination. Wireless, as it was called in those days, had arrived. It was barely a quarter of a century since inventor Guglielmo Marconi, who also made a base in Chelmsford, had taken out a patent for a transmitter and receiver capable of making a bell ring in a secret black box.

The first regular broadcasts were transmitted from January 1922 by the Marconi Company's radio station 2MT and, shortly afterwards, from Marconi House in London's Strand, the sound of 2LO – the forerunner of the BBC – first crackled through the ether to be picked up by the precise positioning of a cat's whisker. 2LO broadcast for one hour a day, repeated at teatime. Music was banned and, every seven minutes, there had to be a three-minute interval for official announcements. There never were any official announcements, but the early listeners welcomed the breaks – or so it was said – so they could pop next door or into the kitchen for a cup of tea. The terror of silence had not yet infused the early broadcasters.

From this small start emerged the leviathan – the best-known broadcaster on the planet, one of the biggest employers in Britain, known by those three telling letters; its ambition was boundless, its principles sacrosanct, its bureaucracy legendary, its determination to possess the hearts, minds and imaginations of its clientele absolutely formidable. What Marconi, Clarke, Northcliffe and the early pioneers created between them was to be an institution of unparalleled influence and almost sacred power, presided over by a burgeoning priesthood, ruled in their turn by a shifting inner cabal of cardinals and barons. In their hands, just as with medieval bishops, lay the psyches of the nation.

Over the decades, the BBC has been compared with medieval baronies and Soviet ministries. It is also a bulwark of public service broadcasting – a dam against a flash flood of commercial media whose dial on morals and programme quality is set only by the need to sell advertising. To different degrees it has been a little like all of these things, but most of all, it came to resemble the medieval Roman Catholic Church: an institution of vast influence over the nation, of curious privilege and mysterious allegiance, possibly to itself alone. It became a creature of obscure rituals and massive self-obsession, prepared to defend its apparent independence with ferocity. Like the medieval church, it sought to inspire, and did so most

powerfully among ordinary people. No wonder governments, decade by decade, have looked askance at this vast
influence on the minds of the people and – like medieval
monarchs – have plotted to somehow claw it back.

The apotheosis of John Reith

By the time 2LO was on the air, the British government was
already struggling with the question of how to organize a
better broadcasting system, while avoiding what it saw as
the chaos of American wireless which was even then the
driving force behind the Roaring Twenties. The last thing
the British wanted was anything too spontaneous or –
heaven forfend – jazz. The biggest six companies interested
in broadcasting formed a committee under the auspices of
the Post Office, which in those pre-privatization days was
a government department, and were charged with the task
of filling the one wavelength being made available. Two
days later, on 25 May 1922, the name British Broadcasting
Company had been agreed, its shares available only to
British manufacturing companies. It would be funded by a
five-shilling levy on wireless sets. This was the answer to the
choice, identified by the *Manchester Guardian*, 'between
monopoly and confusion'.[1] They chose monopoly.

The first BBC broadcast was a 6 p.m. news bulletin,
also from Marconi House, on 14 November. In line with
the government guidelines, no news was allowed that had
not already been published in the newspapers. It was read
twice, first quickly and then slowly with pauses, so people
could take notes. The third day included the first music,
with an evening of songs. Soon the BBC was squeezing
part of the Grenadier Guards Band into the tiny recording studio, hoisting the soloist up to the microphone by
means of a pile of books (he stepped backwards during the

broadcast and fell under the piano). Within six months, there were 50,000 listeners and the first complaint – the left-leaning *Daily Herald* said that the BBC was biased against Labour candidates in the local elections. It was an omen of things to come.

Among the founding company directors were former Attorney-General Rufus Isaacs, who had been implicated before the war in a Marconi insider trading scandal, and Sir William Bull, a director of the German engineering company Siemens, which was later to play a role in wartime slave labour. It was Bull who pointed a thirty-three-year-old Scottish engineer called John Reith in the direction of the advertisement for a managing director. Reith was six foot six, knew nothing about broadcasting at all, and possessed what appeared to outsiders as a direct line to God. 'I am properly grateful to God for His goodness in this matter,' he told his diary when he was appointed.[2] He was the fourth member of staff.

But Reith was far from the humourless Presbyterian that the corporation would later paint him to be, and the hierarchy has always been in two minds about his high-minded legacy. When one of the other three staff complained that the gruelling twelve-hour working days might lead to his breakdown, Reith replied: 'You might let me know when you're going to do it, then we can arrange to take it in turns.'[3] On the other hand, there was no doubt about his highly developed sense of mission which he so infused into the new company that it remains infused to this day. Reith believed he was creating an institution. The news was famously read at the microphone, on his instructions, by an announcer in evening dress, sometimes by Reith himself.

Reith became something of an embarrassment to the modern BBC, with its postmodern, relative values and its emphasis on 'yoof' programming, for what is now seen as his patronizing elitism and penchant for religion. In fact, the corporation remains what he made it, underpinned by Reith's initial conviction that radio should not be exploited for entertainment alone. It was Reith who envisaged the BBC as a moral force, and set about creating one, partly by stuffing the schedules with religion and partly by winning the support of Britain's sceptical religious leaders.

He began with Randall Davidson, the Archbishop of Canterbury, going to dinner with him to demonstrate the wireless in his own front room. When Davidson said he wished there had been a piano solo on that night, Reith phoned his office and ordered one on immediately. You could do that in those days.

It was part of Reith's strategy also to transform the ordinary company into something more magnificent. By the end of 1925, with the *Radio Times* already enjoying a circulation of 800,000, he set up his own committee of inquiry into the BBC's funding, packed it with fellow Scots, and recommended that it should become a state-owned 'corporation' with a royal charter. From 1 January 1927, the new Corporation opened for business. Reith was knighted and made its first director-general.

At first sight, although it enjoys the name, the BBC looks out of place in a book of eminent 'corporations'. It is, after all, a quasi-autonomous governmental body, as well as being a powerful player in the world of corporate media in its own right, owning its own commercial stations, websites, publishing houses and magazines. But it is also a corporation in the original sense, chartered for purpose just as companies were chartered for exploration and trade by Queen Elizabeth I in the sixteenth century. And then again, it was also something new – a gigantic social, non-profit enterprise, but a corporation none the less, the brainchild of a Conservative government but adopted with enthusiasm by Labour as a model for the London Passenger Transport Board and New Town Development Corporations. It was funded, then as now, by a levy or licence on owning the broadcasting equipment.

What is interesting about this structure and its peculiar funding regime (with no obvious link between income and productivity) is that it determined from the start everything that the BBC was to become. The shape of the new corporation meant two dilemmas for Reith and all those awesome figures who came after him. First, how to stay independent enough from the government to protect its own reputation, even though the governments decided on its level of funding and could – if they ever dared – take over completely. Second, how to justify its burgeoning claim on the pockets of the nation. Despite its growing power and influence over hearts and minds – and it needed to have an ever greater hold over the souls of the nation to justify its cost – both these dilemmas meant major compromises, decade by decade, with authority and with quality.

Behind these issues lay an even knottier one. The BBC was no free-floating international institution. Like the Red Cross, it belonged to one nation. If it had a commitment to truth, whose truth was it to be? And when objectivity meant not taking sides between good and evil, where was the morality that truth was being summoned to buttress?

The problem of independence emerged from the very beginning. The first solution – not to broadcast about anything of political, religious or moral controversy – broke down very rapidly. What would happen, for example, at a time of national crisis? And even before the company was transformed into a corporation, a national crisis did arise. The Trades Union Congress called a General Strike. Reith solved the problem as all his successors solved the problem

255

after him, sooner or later. To stay independent, to avoid being ordered about by ministers, there really was only one strategy available – and that was to do what they were told. Preferably before they were told.

Once the strike was underway in 1926, the Chancellor of the Exchequer Winston Churchill demanded that the BBC should be subsumed into his propaganda operation. The daily newspapers could not print. Only the BBC remained as an 'objective' source of news – but how objective could it be as a tool of the government? Reith cleverly helped maintain some level of independence by hitching his wagon to that of the more moderate Prime Minister Stanley Baldwin, and persuaded him to insert a short passage about it into his broadcast about 'longing and working and praying for peace'.[4] He also banned Labour speakers and any supporters of the strike from the microphone. With relief, nine days later, Reith was reading the news himself when the rumours emerged that the strike was over and the BBC had not succumbed to direct government control, at least formally.

He wrote afterwards, 'We do not believe that any other government . . . would have allowed the broadcasting authority under its control greater freedom than was enjoyed by the BBC during the crisis.'[5]

As in a medieval church, the BBC's inner priesthood came to believe that the defence of its independence was its predominant objective. Its right to inform and inspire as it saw fit, and to discharge the sacred duty of providing quality programmes, had to be unsullied by the dull compromises of politics. It was right, but this meant tiptoeing around politics. Indeed, it meant tiptoeing round everything. One early script by the poet and BBC employee Louis MacNeice even lost the sentence 'Henry VIII had vulgar tastes' on the grounds that people might mishear it as 'Edward VIII had vulgar tastes'.[6] When, in 2009, the BBC clung so much to the letter of its independence that it refused to air a humanitarian appeal for the victims of the war in Gaza, it was part of a long tradition of not quite seeing the wood for the trees.

It was no coincidence, therefore, that the BBC nailed its colours to the mast in the way that it did, and continues to do so. There would be flurries of exciting new projects and daring innovations and opinions, but otherwise, it would be enthusiastically, passionately, middle of the road. In fact, it was a key factor in its success with the public. People knew they would never be surprised, never shocked, never told anything that was too clever for them, never have an issue packaged for them with more than two sides, and they took the BBC to their hearts as a result, as their own beloved, predictable Auntie.

The most obvious drawback to this approach was in news. It was to be entirely factual, but too rigorous a culling of opinion and controversy meant that context and background also went out of the window. It is a problem that still besets BBC news – to fully understand the significance of something that has happened, you have to read the newspapers – but between the wars it could make issues completely opaque. BBC reporting of the Spanish Civil War, for example, was so 'pure' in its restriction to simple fact that the significance of the arrival of a German fleet in Spanish waters was lost. So was much of the Nazi rise to power: it was just too controversial to explain.

When television first began, it was so disconnected from context that commentators could not see the pictures that appeared on the screen, leading to the incident at the launching of the aircraft carrier *Ark Royal* when viewers were treated to a picture of the Queen Mother bending over, while the commentator exclaimed: 'There she is, that whole vast bulk of her.'[7]

Nor could producers deal with shades of opinion. Then, as now, the BBC was comfortable in controversy only if there were two neat opposing points of view. Mavericks, radicals and free-thinkers were all banned from the microphones, including any leading politicians at odds with their own parties. This latter category included Winston Churchill, who never forgave his treatment by the BBC and remembered it again at a crucial moment in the development of television.

But the problem of independence also led to another parallel with the medieval church. When medieval monarchs became jealous of its influence and privileges, they appointed archbishops they believed would bring churchmen to submission. In the twelfth century, Henry II appointed his friend Thomas Becket, only to find him so awed by his new responsibilities that his allegiance shifted. The same circular ritual soon took shape in the relations between prime ministers and the BBC, constantly sending trusted lieutenants to control the corporation, constantly frustrated that the self-important sense of sacred mission at the BBC was enough to subsume the most determined opponent. The ritual would reach a crescendo, the director-general or chairman would go, Becket would be murdered, only to find that his replacement was on the wrong side, and the whole rigmarole would begin again.

Finest hour

Reith himself was too smart an operator to be toppled. By the time he resigned in 1938, to be chairman of Imperial Airways, the BBC staff had multiplied itself a thousand times over since his appointment. As many as 98 per cent of the population could listen to the various regional broadcasts or the national programme (a thousand licences were being issued a day even at the height of the Depression) and the first television broadcasts had begun from Alexandra Palace in north London.

The machine that Reith had created was innovative and driven, with an internal culture capable of corroding the stoutest resistance. But it also had a labyrinthine structure of committees, which obscured where decisions were emerging from, and a bureaucracy more like a college of cardinals, as worldly as Jesuits, as determined as Opus Dei. Even Reith could describe his creation as 'soviet'. In the 1930s, the editor of the BBC magazine the *Listener* was not even allowed to know his own circulation figures. Decisions and policies were at the mercy of faceless committees of indefinable groups of elite abbots and archbishops.

'The BBC is capable of keeping a man in suspense for months, for years,' said BBC producer Paul Bloomfield in the late 1930s, reporting the words of a senior BBC official who gripped his arm in his first weeks in Broadcasting House. He said under his breath, 'Look here, for God's sake, you must remember that, in this place, walls have ears.'[8] Bloomfield was eventually sacked on the grounds that he was 'only 80 per cent BBC'.

It was a safe and reliable world, projecting Britain back to itself, shorn of controversy, complexity and vulgarity, yet adding its own BBC brand of reality. From somewhere inside the edifice, it had emerged – and been universally accepted by the BBC staff – that English should be spoken a certain way that bore no resemblance to the world outside. Or that people spoke in what one producer called 'sham colloquialism', the scripted 'well, er, um' which took the place of the real, spontaneous interviews the BBC dared not broadcast.[9]

But the first cracks were also appearing in the disappointing news service. The broadcaster Stephen King-Hall urged the BBC to employ an elite corps of foreign correspondents to provide the best news service it possibly could. Other forces were suggesting that this service be extended to the world, just as the motto said above the door to Broadcasting House: 'Nation shall speak peace unto nation'.

The chief news editor, a professor of imperial economic relations called John Coatman (a man said to have no political opinions except for 'a sentimental and almost religious attachment to the empire'), said that this was 'impossible policy, impossible finance and impossible technique'.[10] But the cardinals acted: Coatman was sidelined and the foreign correspondents began to emerge – though the basic problem of how to provide unbiased news with meaningful context has remained ever since. Ironically, it was news, and especially providing news to other countries, that was about to catapult the BBC into the gold-plated global reputation which it has never quite lost.

The Second World War was to turn the BBC from the cosy 'Auntie' to a pillar of national life, with its controversial broadcasts by J.B. Priestley, its dance music on the Forces Network and Tommy Handley's quick-fire humour on *It's That Man Again* (ITMA). The war forced television off the air (abruptly without explanation in the middle of a Mickey Mouse cartoon on the day Germany invaded Poland). It also forced the BBC to diversify into two national channels, the Home Service and a more entertaining Forces network – later the Light programme – designed to keep troops from listening to continental music stations. But it was the European Service, built up almost from scratch in the early months of the war, which was to provide the BBC with its formidable reputation for impartiality and moral purpose.

Broadcasting to the British Empire had been going on since 1932. There had even been an Arabic service for some years, independent enough to include in its first news programme the execution by the British of a Palestinian Arab for carrying a revolver. But as Europe fell under Nazi control, the European service – led by a pugnacious former *Daily Telegraph* sub-editor called Noel Newsome – emerged as a massive operation, broadcasting on three channels and in twenty different languages (including English) for a total of thirty-six hours a day, the biggest broadcasting operation in the world at the time.

Although nominally under the joint control of the BBC and the Foreign Office, and later the Political Warfare Executive (PWE), it was Newsome who shaped the daily line against Joseph Goebbels and dominated the voice of Britain in Europe, and then the voice of the Allies at Supreme Headquarters Allied Expeditionary Force (SHAEF) from Radio Luxembourg. Newsome pushed the limits of editorial control to the utmost, taking it upon himself to reject Hitler's peace offer to Britain over the radio in July 1940 without any reference to higher authority.[11]

The broadcasts were massively influential. By the end of the war, 15 million Germans were risking their lives to listen to the BBC. The BBC German Service's comedy soap opera, about the ordinary life of a Berlin charlady called Frau Wernicke, was a completely new style of programming for German listeners (it was the future West German leader Konrad Adenauer's favourite programme). After the Operation Torch landings in North Africa, troops were astonished to find Italian graffiti that said 'Viva il Colonella Stefans', a reference to Col. Harold Stevens (a nom de plume) and his daily broadcasts on the BBC Italian service.

Yet the BBC's contribution was so nearly nipped in the bud. Prime Minister Neville Chamberlain had played with the idea of closing the corporation or taking it over completely at the outbreak of war. The early months were not auspicious either. 'The BBC pours out into the air day by day an endless stream of trivialities and sillinesses, apparently labouring under the delusion that in any time of crisis the British public becomes just one colossal moron,' said *The Sunday Times*.[12] Even the Labour leader Clement Attlee agreed that it was depressing. Millions of people listened in to German propaganda broadcasts by Lord Haw-Haw from Berlin, ostensibly as light relief.

The crisis also led to the traditional conflict with the government. The Admiralty exercised a complete news blackout. Priestley's postscripts were deeply unpopular with ministers. BBC chiefs bowed to pressure for less radio sport from killjoy ministers hoping this would boost war production. Information minister Duff Cooper insisted on broadcasting a libellous attack (at least according to BBC lawyers) on P.G. Wodehouse, who had naively agreed to broadcast an amusing piece for the Germans from occupied France. Even Churchill was rumoured to have described the BBC as the 'enemy within the gates'.

Of course, it was a different news environment then. Naming merchant ships was strictly forbidden, and the location of air raids couldn't be published for thirty days. Then as now, there were strict rules about anything that could endanger military operations and, until 1940, the BBC was forced to read official press releases out in full. There were also regulations against publishing anything calculated to foment opposition to the war – which at one stage came close to being used to shut down the *Daily Mirror*. As the Nazis swept across Europe, the government even bowed to pressure from the French, who had been keeping their own population completely in the dark, and censored news about where the Germans had reached.

As the darkness deepened through 1941, the traditional dance began, and the BBC director-general Frederick Ogilvie and his committees became increasingly defensive. When Robert Foot, general manager of the Gas, Light and Coke Company, was appointed to join the BBC to investigate its finances, nobody greeted him at Broadcasting House. Nobody even came to his new office to see him. On the dot of 11 a.m. the phone rang. It was the long-departed Reith, urging him to sack Ogilvie. Sure enough, Ogilvie was forced out in January 1942 and replaced by Foot, who – as usually happened on these occasions – went native. At the beginning of this internecine struggle, while the BBC cardinals jockeyed for position, Broadcasting House had been blitzed and seven staff killed. The European Service was dispatched to the BBC's Maida Vale Studios in Delaware Road. It was cold, uncomfortable, without air-raid shelters and had only a glass roof to keep the bombs out. A string of vitriolic memos about it to BBC managers went unanswered.

In desperation, Newsome organized his own conspiracy over a quiet lunch with the junior information minister Harold Nicolson. This moved the European Service to Bush House, then the headquarters of the advertising agency J. Walter Thompson. It also took it outside the day-to-day control of the BBC. The senior Foreign Office mandarin Sir Ivone Kirkpatrick, the man who first questioned Rudolf Hess, was put in charge, nominally, at the BBC.[13] He regarded his role as defending the creativity of the European Service from BBC executives as well as government doyens of the Sealed Lips policy.

The idea that truth was a vital propaganda tool was shared by everyone at the BBC, and so was the idea that truth should be straight-talking and clear. The BBC was unnerved by some of the European Services' techniques and propaganda tools, including the V campaign – which encouraged listeners across occupied Europe to beep morse code Vs on train hooters or scribble it on blank walls (Goebbels was so nervous about the campaign that he adopted it himself, claiming that it stood for 'Viktoria' and hanging a giant V under the Eiffel Tower).

Newsome's critics inside the BBC would have preferred a sophisticated, tailored news system. The Sealed Lips critics outside would have preferred Goebbels-style bombast. Newsome said in his final broadcast from Radio Luxembourg: 'Our bitterest critics were those who objected to admissions that the Allies were far from perfect and had made mistakes and that our enemies were not all, to a man woman and child of them, villains beyond redemption.'[14]

Despite the controversy, the European Service forged an alternative approach to the basic BBC dilemma about news. It was truthful and as clear as was possible about its own Britishness, but it was also absolutely committed to a tremendous cause. Early in the war, Newsome wrote: 'I can well imagine that Goebbels would join his voice to those of our propagandists who urge us to avoid the moral approach, to eschew history, philosophy and religion in our broadcasts. For Goebbels knows that these are weapons against which these are mortal wounds and there is no defence.'[15]

When Churchill complained to Reith about the BBC's impartiality in 1926, he said you can't be impartial between the fire brigade and the fire. He may not have been right about the General Strike, but the principle was sound – especially when the BBC found itself being impartial about the bombing of civilians in Guernica. Unfortunately, this was not the way the mainstream BBC saw the way forward. Its executives never forgave Newsome for stealing the European Service from under their noses, and told him after the war that he would never broadcast again. His contribution is all but excised from the official BBC histories of the World Service. And foremost among his critics was the head of the BBC German Service, Hugh Carleton Greene, brother of the novelist Graham, and Greene represented the BBC's future.

From Reith to Greene

The war in Europe was at an end and there were a few scores to settle as the college of cardinals resumed its proper place and proper dignity, and the great bureaucracy eased itself back into action, dusting down its reputation for independence. In so doing, it disposed of the European Service, abandoning the wavelengths and the audiences that had built the BBC such a formidable reputation compared to the Voice of America and Radio Moscow. By the 1960s, Poland was broadcasting more to Western Europe than Britain.

Under Attlee's Labour government immediately after the war, broadcasts to the Soviet Union were stepped up, but nearly everything else was run down. Its Conservative successors ended broadcasts to Latin America and the Middle East. But then Britain was psychologically withdrawing from Europe, and the BBC was and is – if it is anything – a reflection and creator of prevailing opinion in Britain.

It was a peculiar period for everyone. The classlessness and idealism of the war sat awkwardly with the stodgy respectability of the 1950s establishment. The BBC bureaucracy expended great effort vetting the lyrics of popular songs, just as it is now drawing up lists of approved tracks to match the socio-economic profile of the listeners it wants. A retired brigadier moved into Broadcasting House to vet editorial appointments. Radio sank into a conservative stupor.

Television began to take radio's place as the vigorous younger sibling. BBC TV began again in 1946, starting with the same Mickey Mouse cartoon that had been so unexpectedly curtailed in 1939, while the corporation's new cultural radio channel, the Third Programme, started a few months later. By 1953, the BBC was televising the Coronation, after a huge lobbying programme and some sleight of hand. The BBC agreed not to attempt to show close-ups of the queen, and duly placed its cameras where this would seem impossible, knowing the camera operators would change their lenses on the day. As many as 88 per cent of the population tuned into the BBC to watch or listen, and afterwards the world had shifted. Never again would anybody dare exclude the BBC from a major occasion (Parliament was the exception, as always, for the time being).

The war had also shifted mainstream opinion against the BBC's monopoly. The Popular Television Association was launched to campaign against it, backed by people such as Rex Harrison, A.J.P. Taylor and W. Somerset Maugham. At this critical moment in the debate, the prime minister was once again Winston Churchill, who had been banned from the airwaves by Reith and was still smarting over his failure to take over the BBC during the General Strike.

Churchill and his Conservative Party had also conceived a suspicion that communists were infiltrating the BBC (having a former MI5 officer on the payroll was clearly no guarantee). He appointed the future war minister and another former brigadier, John Profumo, as head of the party's broadcasting unit to monitor the bias in the BBC – another repeated theme in the BBC's bizarrely circular history.

Politicians were only just waking up to the extraordinary potential, constructive and destructive, of broadcasting in the political process. By convention, the BBC made no mention of the 1950 general election in its coverage, and the first party political broadcast happened only in 1951. Even then the elderly Liberal Viscount Samuel inadvertently gave the signal that he had finished and cut himself off in mid-flow. With awareness of the power of the broadcaster came suspicion, and a little jealousy.

It was Reith himself who accidentally buried the BBC's monopoly by making a speech describing commercial television as 'like dog racing, smallpox and bubonic plague'. That was enough for Churchill.[16] He made up his mind to provide the BBC with some competitors.

Yet the arrival of ITV provided an unexpected boost to the BBC. The BBC upstaged the launch in September 1955 by broadcasting the death of one of the leading romantic characters in *The Archers* radio soap on the same night. The next morning, everyone was talking about Grace Archer's incineration in a fire. That coup was not to last: the BBC's audience share crept down to 28 per cent – the new ITV companies had far more resources – but it forced the BBC cardinals to rethink what made their own channel different, and to go back to some of the original Reithian principles. They were soon unveiling plans for a second television channel, commissioning ambitious Shakespeare productions, launching experimental comedy such as *Hancock's Half Hour*, pioneering natural history programmes such as Peter Scott's *Zoo Quest* and new kinds of sports coverage such as *Grandstand*.

They also sought out the kind of brilliant insiders, lodged somewhere in the bureaucracy, who could lead the corporation in this new broadcast duopoly and make it work. They found one in the shape of Hugh Carleton Greene, who had risen through the committees to shake up the BBC's lacklustre news division. Taking over in 1960, he was to be the most influential director-general since Reith, the first insider to take on the role.

Greene was a former foreign correspondent in pre-war Berlin and a great beer connoisseur. His first years in the post included a scintillating catalogue of achievements. The launch of BBC2, the opening of a new purpose-built Television Centre (twice the size of St Paul's Cathedral) in Shepherd's Bush, the foundation of a new national pop radio station to take on the irritating pirate stations, and a settlement for a hefty hike in the licence fee to £4 a year all sent out the message that the BBC was heading places. Greene received a standing ovation from his leading managers ('What a lot of Russians you are,' he told them).

Greene's nine years at the top were regarded at the time as the moment when the BBC burst out of its stuffy Reithian straitjacket, though Reith himself was still alive and cheering from the sidelines (he died in 1971). In fact, Greene embedded Reith's ideas more deeply: that it was the BBC's role to provide the best possible broadcasting, covering areas such as the arts where its rivals would never go, launching a high-minded 'mission to explain'. The problem was that the very existence of ITV sharpened the horns of the dilemma which had prodded the BBC from the start. How could it justify its taxing of the nation through the licence fee?

The answer, unspoken as always, was that it had to win the hearts and minds, and passionate commitment, of its audience. It had to enter into people's heads. But this could not quite be spoken aloud. Something else was necessary, especially to justify the burgeoning budget as well. It was left to Greene to voice the classic exposition of the BBC position: 'Why should people be willing to pay an additional fee for an organization whose programmes they were not viewing?'[17]

For Greene, and those who followed, this meant that, in the pursuit of people's attention, the BBC must provide everything. There must be no aspect of broadcasting, no socio-economic grouping that the BBC did not cater for. It was, and remains, the endlessly repeated justification that drives and excuses the BBC for being the biggest broadcaster in the world. It explained the new television and radio channels, and the plans – agreed in 1966 – for local radio stations as well. But it is at least open to question: the whole justification for the BBC is that people do benefit from it, even if they do not necessarily tune in, because it raises standards and provides them with choice. That may be an elitist argument, but it is the one that prevails. There is no doubt that the proportion of the BBC output that we do not watch, yet still pay for, rises year by year, and each time it does so, the corporation employs Greene's justification.

Say what you like about Hugh Greene, his reign coincided with the high point of the BBC as a focus of national unity. For some years after his resignation, the nation would still sit down as a unit to watch *The Morecambe and Wise Show* on Christmas Day. And the BBC that remains an affectionate memory in so many people's psyches – from *Blue Peter* to *Civilisation* – was a product of Greene's colossal influence. But the world was changing and it was not to last.

Structural difficulties

The difficulty lay in this business of reaching out to everyone. It was an answer to the second paradox of the BBC's structure, which led to trouble with the first. Like medieval monarchs looking askance at the sheer influence over ordinary people enjoyed by the church – interpreting, cajoling, influencing from every pulpit in every community – the government was increasingly nervous of the BBC. It could not be seen to exert undue influence, still less take over but, equally, its sheer dependence on the corporation was almost beyond endurance.

Until the mid-1950s, politicians and broadcasters had been kept apart by the so-called fourteen-day rule, which banned broadcasting about anything that was going to be discussed by Parliament within the next two weeks. 'Break this law,' Michael Foot urged in *Tribune*, but – true to its usual policy – the BBC did not break it. What did break the law was one of the biggest political crises of the century: the Suez invasion of 1956. When Prime Minister Anthony Eden announced in a live broadcast that the bitterly controversial bombing of Egyptian airfields had begun, the BBC faced a demand for an immediate right of reply from Labour leader Hugh Gaitskell. It was a tough call. The director-general was away and Lord Cadogan, chairman of the governors, refused to decide and went to bed. Gaitskell insisted he be woken and, by the following morning, Cadogan had agreed. Gaitskell used the broadcast to demand that Eden should resign. It was broadcast throughout the Middle East just as British troops went into action.

Eden had already been enraged by the BBC's refusal to allow a broadcast backing his plans by the veteran Australian prime minister Sir Robert Menzies (in the end it gave in, of course). There were furious accusations of treachery against the BBC in the House of Commons. It was the shape of things to come and the political battle would accelerate the BBC's already circular ritual – directors-general and chairmen toppled by furious politicians, only to find their replacements as entangled in the BBC's own view of itself as before. As the ritual went round, the next victim of the circular history was Greene himself.

When the purity campaigner Mary Whitehouse began her thirty-year campaign, it was Greene she blamed most for the permissive society. There certainly were innovative, realistic and dangerous programmes commissioned in its time – *Z Cars* (1962), *Cathy Come Home* (1966), *Till Death Us Do Part* (1966). Most dangerous of all was the satirical show *That Was the Week That Was*, known as TW3. But the BBC's policy, as always, was to maintain independence at all costs – and that meant doing as you were told, preferably before you were told. Greene axed TW3 before the 1964 general election. He ended *Till Death Us Do Part* after only two years. He also refused to show *The War Game*, the powerful documentary about a nuclear attack on Rochester.

But none of this deflected the rage of Labour Prime Minister Harold Wilson, who wanted to emulate Roosevelt's broadcast 'fireside chats', without having some right of reply by his political opponents. As Profumo had done before, and Norman Tebbit was to do later, he set up his own unit to monitor BBC bias, and got the postmaster-general Tony Benn (in his previous incarnation as Anthony Wedgwood Benn) to draw up plans to force the BBC to accept advertising.

A new corrosive relationship between media and politicians had by then begun to emerge, forged at ITV's Independent Television News by the Labour MP turned television producer Aidan Crawley and a young BBC radio producer, the former Liberal candidate Robin Day. They began by refusing to send questions to politicians in advance, then grilling them in the studio. The BBC was soon following suit. The temperature was rising and especially for a mildly paranoid politician such as Wilson (although, as it later emerged, while Wilson might have been paranoid, 'dark forces' really were also out to get

271

him). Wilson convinced himself that even the BBC Radio 1 disc-jockeys were operating a covert campaign against him and took revenge by appointing his own man as chairman of the BBC governors – choosing the very last person the BBC would have wanted, the chairman of their rival Independent Television Authority, tireless Tory critic of the BBC and former radio doctor, Lord Hill. It was designed to force Greene out.

When he heard the news, the director-general leapt out of his chair. 'How can I work for a man for whom I have the utmost contempt?' he exclaimed.[18] He was persuaded not to resign immediately, but his days were numbered. Even so, Wilson was astonished that, when the chips were down – and they were down – Hill backed the BBC. The semi-sacred influence of the BBC's mission had stolen him away.

This pattern began to accelerate and to go round the whole circle almost every decade. Despite compromises with popular taste and middlebrow opinion (and some triumphant achievements as well), the BBC stance of impartiality would so annoy ministers – like the medieval church so annoyed Henry II – that they appointed a Becket equivalent to sort it out, only to find the man (it always was a man) going native in the comfy sense of high-minded mission at the BBC. That was what happened to Lord Hill, just as it had happened before to Robert Foot. It was to happen again in the 1980s, during Margaret Thatcher's showdown with the BBC, and again later.

The confrontation between the BBC and the Thatcher government began in 1980, when a young reporter called Jeremy Paxman filmed an IRA roadblock for the political flagship series *Panorama*, informing the security forces about it only the next day. The series editor was sacked, but it was the rumpus over coverage of the Falklands War that really led to such a ferocious examination of the BBC's awkward objective of impartiality.

'We cannot demonstrate that the British have lied to us, but the Argentineans clearly have,' said Peter Snow on *Newsnight* after the first days of action in the South Atlantic. The incident led directly to the most undignified clash between director-general Alasdair Milne and his chairman George Howard, an aristocratic shooting-friend of Home Secretary William Whitelaw, before the Tory backbench media committee. At the height of the hearing, an enthusiastic young Conservative MP shouted: 'You, sir, are a traitor.'

'Stuff you,' said Howard.

To replace Howard, Margaret Thatcher appointed her friend Stuart Young, an advocate of the BBC taking advertising and the brother of the cabinet minister Lord Young, but would you believe it – he went native too. Only a few months later, there he was appearing alongside Milne urging the latest inevitably huge increase in the licence fee. The confrontation therefore continued, culminating in two controversial documentaries which, between them, undermined the position of Milne himself. Neither was actually shown. The BBC governors vetoed the *Real Lives* documentary about two Sinn Fein councillors (one of them was Martin McGuinness) and Milne vetoed a Scottish documentary about the secret Zircon spy satellite. But that wasn't the end of the matter. In January 1987, Special Branch raided the offices of the team that made the Zircon film and took away three vanloads of documents.

Even if nothing incriminating was found, the raid would be almost as damaging: when Special Branch raid your offices, you look guilty. Stuart Young had by this stage died (he died of cancer after only three years in post) and Mrs Thatcher – having failed to persuade British Airways chief Lord King – had appointed a former managing director of Times Newspapers, Marmaduke Hussey, a war hero who had lost a leg at Anzio. Two days after the police raid, Hussey sacked Milne. He was replaced by the BBC's finance chief Michael Checkland, who promised that the corporation would be smaller by the end of his tenure. Checkland was more cautious and more accommodating than Milne, but even he was not immune to the circular history.

The BBC's cycle came round to a similar point again at the beginning of 2004, in the aftermath of the Iraq War, with the apparent suicide of the government scientist David Kelly, who had been named as a source for a BBC story about the government exaggerating Iraq's capability of using weapons of mass destruction. Lord Hutton's inquiry into the death was unexpectedly harsh for the BBC, which had been prepared to ask a few tentative but vital questions about Tony Blair's hurtle to war. The BBC chairman Gavyn Davies resigned and director-general Greg Dyke offered his resignation as well. The governors were bitterly divided about whether to accept it, and Dyke admitted later that he had not expected them to. But he went too.

Dyke was popular with the BBC staff, having promised to 'cut the crap' from the John Birt years (1992–2000), and managed to reduce administration costs back to 15 per cent of the budget. There were soon demonstrations outside the BBC offices in his support. He has remained a bitter critic of Hutton ever since, even going so far as accusing the government of trying to kill BBC reporter Andrew Gilligan, whose story had caused the original trouble.

Dyke's successor was the former news chief Mark Thompson, who has so far survived a strange story about him biting a colleague in the news team on the arm, and has presided over another inevitable restructuring

– transforming the old board of governors into a trust and streamlining the old management committee into an executive board. He has also 'privatized' some of the off-shoots like BBC Technology and BBC Books to bring in some desperately needed income. All seems quiet, if a little strapped for cash, but there is no reason to suppose that the inevitable cycle has stopped rolling.

From Greene to Birt

Every historical rule has an exception, and the exception to the cycles of Beckets, appointed by frustrated occupants of the Palace of Westminster, was the bizarre revolution that took place at the BBC after the departure of Alasdair Milne. This was not a unique revolution either, but nobody could have accused Checkland's nemesis and successor, John Birt, of 'going native'. Milne's defenestration was followed by an extraordinary jockeying for power amid the remaining cardinals of the BBC, like intriguing churchmen at a renaissance court. The titanic, secret, backroom struggles between men such as Bill Cotton, Paul Fox and Birt, the tall, owl-like and supremely ambitious producer from London Weekend Television, led finally to Birt's appointment as deputy director-general. From that position, he organized an unprecedented upheaval at the corporation from which it has never quite recovered.

Birt was right in his basic analysis that outside the BBC the world, and the media world in particular, had changed. It was true that the days when whole swathes of the nation would gather around the television to watch *I, Claudius*, *Dad's Army* or *Monty Python's Flying Circus* had gone for good. The era when 18 million people stayed in and watched the last episode of *The Forsyte Saga* in

1969 would never come again (all these programmes were commissioned in Greene's period of office). Nor would the BBC ever again be the vast production warehouse it used to be, creating everything it ever showed. In fact, new legislation was forcing it to contract out at least a quarter of its output to independent producers.

Birt was also right to confront the perennial problem of the BBC's careful and contextless versions of news and current affairs. He saw clearly, as an outsider, how programme-makers preferred simplicity and good TV pictures to a genuine attempt to explain complex issues. It was a 'bias against understanding', he said.

Birt recognized, like other BBC grandees before him, the central paradox that the corporation must do what it was told by the government if it wanted to stay independent. He forged an effective partnership with the culture minister David Mellor, which outflanked Norman Tebbit and left him powerlessly spluttering that the BBC was an 'insufferable, smug, sanctimonious, naive, guilt-ridden, wet, pink orthodoxy'.[19] Wartime usually brought an inevitable confrontation with ministers, but not during the first Gulf War in 1991. Birt even took the French resistance comedy 'Allo 'Allo off the air in case it disturbed people. He won a unique tribute from a wartime prime minister, in this case John Major.

The problem was that Birt was gripped by a phenomenally complicated management consultant-style solution, which meant that every programme would become a self-managing business unit. Each one would buy in services from other departments in the BBC or from outside. Just as Eastern Europe was waking up to similarly stringent free-market reforms, set out by similarly stringent western management consultants – just as the same reforms were being tested on the NHS for the first time – the BBC was having to become what might be described by some as 'efficient'.

But efficiency was not the obvious result. The difficulty about such internal market reforms is that, unless the massive organization is similarly decentralized, the whole business becomes astonishingly complex. Internal markets in massive centralized monoliths, which cling to their hierarchical structures, are a recipe for confusion. It was soon clear that some of these new programme 'units' were having to negotiate and sign contracts dealing with eleven different suppliers.

Paper clips, it was revealed, would be provided centrally, but for other supplies, a vast new bureaucracy of accountants, statisticians and management trainers were soon moving in. After the so-called Big Bang of 'producer choice', April Fool's Day 1992, a series of glossy brochures also began appearing to persuade in-house producers to use in-house facilities. One of these was sent to all 2,000 employees of news and current affairs about their own department. 'If I ever forget what time my own programme is transmitted, this will be very useful,' one producer told the *Daily Telegraph*.[20] World Service staff, who had been provided with basic bed and breakfast if they had to work through the night at Bush House, suddenly found the charges had burgeoned so much that it was cheaper to check into the Waldorf Hotel across the road.

Birt was then appointed director-general, without an interview, and unexpectedly replaced Checkland. The Jesuitical air of secrecy and decisions taken elsewhere was hardly new, but this time the normally opaque BBC was fulminating with rage. It was the era of 'Birtspeak'. Examples of management jargon, torn out of reports and newsletters, appeared on the BBC staff noticeboards.

'We need to establish a less prescriptive corporate framework which offers business units greater flexibility within the parameters of common core corporate guidelines,' said one.[21] Translations were also provided. 'Liberating resources' meant sacking people, or so it was said. Not for nothing did George Orwell work on the Empire Service of the BBC before he wrote *Nineteen Eighty-Four* (1948).

Even Michael Grade, who had recently pushed BBC ratings back up to 40 per cent, and had moved to Channel 4, described his alma mater as 'a secretive and forbidding place to work'.[22] Officials searched the corporation for the whistleblower who had revealed that Birt had negotiated a secret agreement to be employed, not directly, but via his own company. It was hardly surprising, in the midst of this revolution – some of which was aimed at making current affairs less spectacular and more informative – that the BBC's audience share slumped back below 30 per cent in Birt's first full year as director-general.

Birt was followed by the populist Greg Dyke in 2000 with a mission to nurture the staff again and cut bureaucracy. But, as we have seen, the BBC's circular history was due for another rotation and Dyke was forced out by the governors over the bitter battle with the government over Iraq. The BBC under Mark Thompson is bigger in terms of budget (over £4 billion) and wider in terms of outlets, embracing the internet and various forms of digital interactivity (BBC Red Button, BBC iPlayer and so on). Despite the old aversion to advertising, it is also a massive hoover for available online advertising revenue and a huge global media business in its own right.

The old canard of Hugh Greene that the BBC's task was to meet every niche and every audience in order to justify its burgeoning financial demands was reinforced by John Birt's revolution and his conviction that what the BBC must offer was 'choice' – choice of time of day, format, media and style. The cycle therefore continues.

In the mind

Giving all due regard to Foot, Dyke, Thompson and all the other director-generals, the BBC has been the story of three dominant leaders – Reith, Greene and Birt. Each of them hailed new departures, new cultures and new ways forward. Each of them appeared to be a revolutionary figure at the time. In fact, all three pursued remarkably similar objectives, all of them in the high-minded missionary tradition set out at the start by Reith. Each of them was also caught on the horns of the same dilemmas: the BBC had to be above the mundane business of competing for money through audience share, yet it needed the passionate loyalty of as large an audience as possible to justify increasingly dramatic licence fees. The BBC had to be above the sordid business of politics, yet it had to be obedient enough to grasp what independence it could from the tentacles of government. These were more than paradoxes – they were and are uncomfortable contradictions.

The triumph of the BBC is that these basic values survive. Nation speaking peace unto nation, the gist of the motto carved above the doors of Broadcasting House, survives by the skin of its teeth through the World Service, endlessly cheesepared by successive governments. It survives also through BBC World, the global television service, the shoestring satellite channel launched too late – after CNN had stolen a march and grabbed the attention of the world during the first Gulf War.

But it still counts. When the last Soviet president Mikhail Gorbachev was put under house arrest during the coup of 1991, and was sealed off from the outside world, he was able to keep up with events by listening to the BBC on his transistor radio. When the Iron Curtain came down a few years earlier, many others were able to say the same. Yet the BBC was not the source of national pride that it ought to have been, even within the corporation. In fact, mainstream news at the BBC – a national service if ever there was one – has been slowly withdrawing from international coverage on the grounds that it can barely keep the attention of the audience.

This patronizing attitude to the audience has been a thread that weaves throughout the BBC's history, and not just in its decision to name the *Blue Peter* cat Socks in 2006, when the callers had paid to vote for it to be called Cookie. Watching local government election night any year, we are provided with expensive graphics, a full slate of national politicians, and even David Dimbleby's urbane charm reflecting on the likely implications at a general election. But look for details of what local government does, or the respective political battles inside each town, city and district, and you will be disappointed. Watching regional television news on a Saturday night, we are given the full gamut of car crashes and regional trials, but when we look for in-depth coverage of local issues and local politics, we have to buy the evening papers.

It isn't that such coverage is beneath the BBC, but – as in its attitude to foreign news – the college of cardinals have decided, without apparent debate, that hardly anyone is interested. It seems that what we need is more news about Westminster, read by somebody with a Yorkshire accent, and everyone will be happy – as long as nobody says anything on-air which part of the audience might not understand.

So although the values remain, sometimes it is now as mere husks of the values. Of course, mainstream BBC channels still resist advertising. This is a remarkable achievement in a world witnessing a headlong collision between western consumer lifestyles and planetary limits. In one area in particular, children's TV, advert-free programming plays a vital role in the psychological well-being of the next generation. Simply being free of advertising remains an important, culturally valuable contribution, a key condition which alone justifies the BBC's unique financing structure. Whether for the simple joy of watching a film from start to finish, uninterrupted by adverts, or to see a child grow up less conditioned by the lie of consumer culture that having more stuff makes you happy, in key ways the BBC becomes more, not less, relevant to the modern world. The alternatives look pretty dismal, from Fox News to Berlusconi. The great danger is that even this crucial element of the BBC's uniqueness is under threat. The advertisers come anyway, first in the names of sponsors of the great sporting fixtures – slavishly repeated – then in BBC magazines, then on its digital channels.

Yet, preserving core BBC values is central to justifying the continuing ambition of the corporation. In the early days, Reith used to remark that the BBC was ready to undertake any public service if required, even milk supply.[23] It was then, and is now, more of a rival government than either corporation or ministers would ever dare admit. It is ready and waiting for responsibility, and it believes in its popular mandate. It remains utterly committed to the usual old questions, the balance of public opinion, and the not-terribly-original challenge.

That is what objectivity means. Churchill's old accusation that it is impossible to be impartial between a firefighter and a fire, still muddies the water. One executive was told by a BBC manager at a recent seminar on objectivity, 'The BBC is not neutral in multiculturalism. It believes in it and it promotes it.' Yet, as we all know, there have been criticisms of some aspects of multiculturalism and the BBC will no doubt endorse those too, just as – three decades ago – in the first signature tune to *Start the Week*, it was able to include lyrics so racist that all reference to them has been suppressed.

So, cursed with a circular history, the BBC sails on – not quite regardless, but with apparent confidence – growing bigger every year, convinced of its cause, discounting opposition and criticism on the grounds that there is inevitably criticism in the other direction. But then the cause was a great one. Brilliant programmes were the result, but also some dreadful ones: mind-numbing panel games, hideous soaps – *United*, about a dull-witted football team, *The Newcomers* and the notorious *Eldorado*, which gobbled up its entire annual budget just building an expatriate village in Spain as the backdrop. Incisive political probing is the result – a bastion of democracy in itself – but then so was Jonathan Ross' three-year deal for £18 million (suspended briefly when he and the comedian Russell Brand made the equivalent of an obscene phone call on air to actor Andrew Sachs in 2008).

The scandalous payments to presenters and controllers are only one aspect of the strong sense among the cardinals that they are a race apart. Why do we need to be spoonfed by presenters on million-pound salaries? Why should the director-general earn £816,000 a year, four times as much as the prime minister? Why should there be forty-seven of these senior cardinals in the BBC bureaucracy, with their edifice of compliance check-lists? One BBC trainee was told on a recent training course, 'Congratulations, you are now part of the elite cadre of the top 2,000 BBC managers.'[24]

The short answer is that the chairman of Barclays,

Marcus Agius (basic salary: £750,000), chairs a committee which decides on the pay of executives, while the
presenters get as much as they can negotiate. We will never
know how much, because the BBC spent £200,000 on
legal action to keep those presenter salaries secret. The
long answer is that this is a secondary effect of the huge
scale of the BBC, its licence fee income of £3.6 billion a
year, its ambition and – like so many organizations that
are too big – its labyrinthine inward-looking obsession
with itself. This is also an effect of the BBC's exhausting
bureaucracy: compliance staff now inspect every programme – even recordings of church bells – to check for
inappropriate content.[25]

We need the BBC, or something like it – rather than commercial TV with government grants. But that means that,
rather than aping commercial TV and other commercial
platforms, for the money they receive, programmes and
other output have to be different and better, excelling in
their public service remit. There are brilliant programmes,
unique in broadcasting around the world, but for £3.6 billion, why should we have anything that is not great? Why
should we not build a civilization on the site of the BBC
beyond anything we have so far conceived of? Why should
we be content with the occasional costume drama, a concert here and there, and hours and yards of phone-ins and
game shows?

Still, it is easy to snipe. It is hard to imagine a more practical way of funding such an endeavour apart from the one
chosen right at the start by the Post Office. Whatever funding arrangements it chose would have had consequences,
and these lay behind the vices as well as the virtues of the
growing corporation. To convince the government to carry
on increasing the licence fee, the BBC had to appeal to the
people. And to do so over the heads of the government in

ever increasing area and volume, and with ever increasing passion.

In that conundrum lay the triumph and the tragedy of the BBC. To win the hearts and minds of its listeners it needed to engage and to influence, but to do more than just influence. It needed to do more than just attract a bigger audience as part of its campaign for a licence fee. It needed to hook in its audience permanently. Its sacred duty demanded it.

What was peculiar about this was that, throughout its history, the BBC has believed in its power to influence for the better. But it has never really believed – it could not believe – that it might also influence for the worse. When Alasdair Milne visited Mrs Thatcher for the first time, she reached into her red box and pulled out a report on the effect of television violence on children, making deprecating noises that maybe he would not agree with it. Milne flicked through and handed it back: 'You're right. I don't believe a word of it.' Nor did Hugh Greene ever agree to meet his increasingly prominent critic Mary Whitehouse. A pity: one would have liked it to have been the subject of a fly-on-the-wall documentary.

On the one hand, the BBC has been determinedly moral; on the other hand, it has been above morality. 'I don't care whether what is reflected in the mirror is bigotry and intolerance or accomplishment and inspiring achievement,' said Greene.[26] But of course Greene's ideal of reflecting society back at itself would do more than just reflect. Of course *Z Cars* changed the way the police talked to each other. Of course *EastEnders* has changed the temperature at which relationships are conducted between people. A whole generation has grown up thinking it perfectly normal to interact with each other on the basis of routine confrontation. This is how social norms are set. Of course

Newsnight has influenced the contempt in which people hold politicians.

When Chris Evans on Radio 1 corralled a caller to propose on air to his girlfriend, of course it affected the caller's life. When Angie from *EastEnders* attempted suicide in 1986, overdoses shot up 300 per cent around the country. There is an effect. But, most of all, the BBC changed us all by its need for its viewers and listeners not just to be entertained and informed, but to be obsessed, to fill in those embarrassing gaps in our relationships at home that used to be filled with awkward silences. It, too, has helped grow a culture in which the lives of celebrities, like cuckoos in the nests of our sense of ourselves, have hollowed out our own lives.

'If the home is to become a non-stop movie house, God help the home,' said Orson Welles in 1955.[27] It did, of course, and the result was a corrosion of family life, community cohesion, self-help and mental health, and the corruption of popular culture. During the television strike in Birmingham in the early 1980s, audience researchers found that 11 per cent were just watching the blank screen. This, and the sheer banality of so much of the BBC's output despite the licence fee, is probably a far more important issue than the multi-million-pound salaries paid to its presenters or the refusal of its staff to go on token 'honesty courses' after the various faking scandals in 2007.

The tragedy was that to justify its existence and its burgeoning budgets, and to avoid the painful cuts that failure to land a bigger licence fee would mean, the corporation deliberately set out to obsess the nation. It took away people's lives and gave back to them an approximate, virtual version, without heart or soul – a debilitating narcotic, with its subtle reinforcements of conformity. Of course, the BBC is not solely responsible for the corrosive effects of broadcasting, but in merely chasing the lead of commercial operators the BBC reneges on its unique advantage, opportunity and responsibility to be different. As television viewing declines, driven partly by its introduction of the BBC iPlayer (a wonderful innovation), it could be that – despite all the predictions to the contrary – we may be able to claw back a little of our own sense of ourselves from the cardinals of the air.

CHAPTER 8

VIRGIN (1970):
ONWARD VIRGIN CONSUMERS

What was the use of my having come from Oakland . . .
there is no there there.

Gertrude Stein, *Everybody's Autobiography*, 1937

Contrary to what some people may think, our constantly
expanding and eclectic empire is neither random nor
reckless.

Virgin.com official website

There is an unusual, leafy and watery corner of London,
between Paddington Station and the white Georgian and
brown Victorian mansions of Maida Vale, known as Little
Venice. Most visitors have no idea it is there, especially
now, behind the banality of the new Paddington Basin
development. Two generations ago, some of its original
atmosphere as an industrial water transport hub still clung
to the neighbourhood. Nancy Mitford lived there, opposite
the Regent's Canal. So did Lady Diana Cooper. But it was
also an area of cheap rented flats and decayed Edwardian
prostitution.

Then sometime in 1965, all that changed. The old
Victorian wall that divided the mansions from the water

was pulled down and it had a dramatic effect. Actors flocked to live there. Classics such as *Georgy Girl* (1966) were filmed there. Edward Fox and Alec Guinness wandered under the plane trees. Something amazing also began to happen to the canal. In the tributaries off Browning Basin, a whole fleet of gaily painted barges and canal boats – filled with a raffish crew of artists and impoverished bohemians – began to line the sides. One wall pulled down and an environmental revolution began. It seemed so simple. So easy.

Just nearby, in one of those same houseboats, a man who occasionally associates himself with part of the same simple environmental revolution was sitting on a barge with a battery of telephones, moulding what has become one of the most unusual and non-categorizable British business empires.

This was Richard Charles Nicholas Branson. He spent decades running his business from a barge called *Duende*, which he bought for £200 in 1972 when he moved out of his former girlfriend's narrower boat, *Alberta*. Now, nearly thirty years later, Branson is the 261st richest man in the world, and Virgin – a sprawling empire which goes from banks to spaceships – is a complicated mesh of interlocking enterprises controlled by a series of family trusts in the tax haven of the British Virgin Isles.

The story of Virgin is one of those very British tales of business development which is impossible to pigeon-hole, like the company, either as entrepreneurialism or flagrant hype. It is, in short, the very model of a modern British company. It revels in the red, white and blue. It adores tabloid headlines (most of the time) and it seduces prime ministers. It boasts a knighted business icon at its head. But one of the few things clear about it is that, with the offshore trusts and the business secrecy, it actually is not quite British. Perhaps, given the strange story of UK business in recent years, this in itself is enough to guarantee its Britishness. Business is paradoxical, and nowhere more than Virgin.

These days, if you type Virgin into the Google search engine, the legacy of that barge on the Regent's Canal is all too clear. The search prompts are nothing to do with sex, or the lack of it. Instead, the suggestions are all apparently wholesome and corporate (if such a combination exists). Scroll down the list and there is Virgin Media and Virgin Atlantic, followed by Virgin Trains, Virgin Travel and Holidays, Virgin Money, Virgin Credit Card, Virgin Active, and web mail. But that's just the surface. Scratch just one, Virgin Media, and another world of possibilities opens up: television, phone, music, broadband, games, shopping, news, movies . . . Oh yes, and then there's Virgin Drinks, offering up everything from cola to vodka.

Bright primary red is the corporate colour – connoting a childlike brashness, simplicity and fun, and a fresh attitude to business. Virgin captures, defines and promotes the essence of consumer society. To make absolutely sure this ambition comes across, there is even a site called Virgin Lifestyle with a section on 'You and your future'. Brash, personal, insubstantial and rather opaque, there is something about Virgin that defines a certain kind of British business brand – it exemplifies the age of the brand – in the late twentieth century. It demands closer examination.

Summers of love

Virgin is wholly identified with one personality alone, even more perhaps than any of the other companies in this book, although they all have had dominant figures at the helm. So it is hard, however we might want to, to look at the company separate from its presiding architect. Richard

Branson was born on 18 July 1950 in a nursing home in Blackheath, in south-east London, into a conventional middle-class family. His father was a barrister, his grandfather a judge, but it was his mother who seems to have been the driving force behind him. 'Ricky's going to be prime minister one day,' she used to tell people proudly.[1] She would send him out at the age of eleven, from their home in Shamley Green in Surrey, to cycle the fifty miles or so to Bournemouth and back.

He suffered from dyslexia and was expelled from a school on the Sussex coast for climbing into the headmaster's daughter's bedroom. Branson was always one for the ladies, but his biography tells the subsequent tale, which involved him writing a suicide note and giving it to a friend who would be unable to resist opening and reading it. So as he ran to his death on the cliffs, he knew that he would be pursued – and so he was. Pursued, caught and reinstated. It is rather a revealing story.

In 1967, he left Stowe School, a co-educational boarding school with a progressive reputation. His headmaster later predicted that he would be either a criminal or a millionaire. Branson quotes this admiringly, but you cannot help wondering if the prediction was quite as complimentary as he thought. It seems likely that the headmaster regarded the two categories as rather similar.

By then, a meeting with the writer Gavin Maxwell, a former Stowe pupil, set Branson on a rather different direction. With his friends, he launched a magazine called *Student*. These were the years of the student revolt, the rise of the counter-culture, of tuning in and dropping out, and all the other chilled-out versions of cool that Branson would come to embody for decades to come. There was no more exciting moment in the history of the world to be a student. There had to be a certain amount of sleight of hand about the magazine. It garnered the interviews and the advertising it managed to get by sheer chutzpah. There was a certain amount of 'Ted Heath on the line for you, Richard,' when outsiders were near the basement in London where they ran the operations.

Out of *Student* emerged a small advisory service for young people, though opinions differ about how much it was used. It seems to have sailed close to the wind when it came to the abortion laws – these were the days when David Steel's private member's bill had just made abortion legal in certain circumstances. But the law that Branson was actually arrested under was an obscure one designed to prevent quack solutions to venereal disease. At the end of 1969, he was charged under the 1889 Indecent Advertisements Act.

He was acquitted thanks to his barrister, the civil libertarian – and future creator of *Rumpole of the Bailey* – John Mortimer QC. 'The court case taught me that, although I was very young, wore jeans and had very little money behind me, I need not be afraid of being bullied by the police or the Establishment, particularly if I had a good barrister,' he wrote.[2] Branson is among the more litigious British business leaders, and this small victory in law was what gave him the taste. It is a maxim that has usually served him rather well.

By this time, *Student* had moved from its basement to 44 Albion Street in Paddington, which it leased in his parents' name. There were now about twenty semi-permanent members of staff, mainly living there, and going to great lengths to hide from the officials of the Church Commissioners, who owned the property and did not approve of businesses being run from there.

Student magazine was not strictly part of the Virgin empire, which was yet to be named, but it was Branson's first, slightly gauche, enterprise. It was created and run with a strange mixture of charm and ruthlessness. The promise of doing good and reaching a highly motivated student audience convinced a range of advertisers and contributors to support the magazine. It also convinced the Beatles' press officer to promise a special song from John Lennon as a promotional cover mount. But Lennon failed to deliver.

Lennon had retreated from the public after prosecution for cannabis use and because his girlfriend, Yoko Ono, had suffered a miscarriage. This was insufficient excuse for Branson. He considered a second brush with the law by suing for breach of contract. When the different parties finally met, a song was to be delivered. What Branson was actually given was the soundtrack of a baby's heartbeat that, after a while, stopped. Legal proceedings were ended. The last edition of Richard Branson's first enterprise announced the arrival of his second, Virgin Records, the mail-order record company.

Branson had been noticing two rather important things about his housemates. First, although he was personally tone deaf, they seemed to listen to a huge amount of music. Second, he could not help noticing the records they listened to were ridiculously expensive. These are the kind of insights that make or break entrepreneurs. Things irritate them. They imagine the world a little differently. Then, like Branson, they make some inquiries. It turned out that the minimum price agreement for records had been scrapped some time ago, without much actual effect on prices. Most records were bought in big, dull newsagents like John Menzies or WH Smith. Branson and his friends hit on the idea of a mail-order record shop.

There were huge difficulties. The main record companies refused to deal with them and they had to order through a very small shop in Ealing called Pop In. Most of the business still had to be done from a telephone box. They also had no name. The question of where 'Virgin' came from is unclear. Branson's autobiography says it was suggested by one of the girls on *Student*'s staff – he does not mention her name – but his controversial biographer Tom Bower says that it was suggested by his friend John Varnom.[3] Either way, it carried a whiff of hedonism, sex and the same kind of knowing innocence that characterized the Summer of Love. It was also very much better than 'Slipped Disc', the other name they were considering.

The famous red Virgin logo, scrawled like graffiti, carries the same undertones. It smacks of rage and revolt. Branson says it was written by the designer on the back of a napkin and used straight from there. Bower says that it was designed for £250 by Ray Kite, commissioned by Branson's cousin Simon Draper.[4] Maybe they are both true, but – as with so many things to do with the man and the company – it is hard to know.

Draper was visiting from South Africa and immediately became key to the success of Virgin. He was a perfect complement to Branson's business skills. He loved music and was fascinated by anything about the emerging music world. He had the background, the taste and the ability to make Virgin cool, and he went about doing so – obscure new releases from the USA, mildly subversive new tracks, anything which could give the company's youthful customers an edge.

It was at this point that Branson began his association with houseboats. The year 1970 saw the election of Edward Heath as prime minister. It saw Apollo 13 and the My Lai massacre in Vietnam. It also saw the grim apotheosis of the student revolt, with the Kent State University shootings in Ohio. The emergence of Virgin Mail Order has to be understood against this background, just as Virgin still does today. It was born out of the student counter-culture, and still somehow has its roots there, even though most of the biggest brands in the world are also now employing some of the power of student hedonism – shorn of its radicalism – to sell consumer products.

There was something wonderfully hip about the Regent's Canal at that time. There were still dead cats floating by in the great, grey-green, greasy waters, but there was a whiff of artistic revolt about the houseboats, a sense of loft-living without having to deal with all those stairs. Branson moved in. The pattern of Virgin's existence almost ever since was being set, as Branson began his habit of running his multiple businesses by phone from the canal. Virgin was then, and would be for the next few decades, almost perpetually in debt and sometimes on the verge of collapse. Often, the company's lurches from one new challenge to the next, before the last enterprise had quite bedded down, were as a result of the need for an urgent injection of cash as much as the desire to follow any kind of logical plan. Branson kept the show on the road by effortless charm but also occasionally by ruthless decisions.

By the end of 1970, the first of these lurches was approaching. The mail-order business was certainly turning over, but the profit margins were small and the cashflow was uncertain from one week to the next. Ordering the records after the cheques had arrived meant a long wait for customers. But ordering them before the orders had come in was a risky business, however impatient Branson and his friends were. Branson was thin-skinned and had something to prove. Many of the steps in Virgin's many steps are about Branson's need to prove his critics, or partners, or bankers – or anybody – absolutely wrong. Every billionaire has some inner need to keep on earning long past the point that they are comfortably off. This is Branson's.

Then came the postal strike of January 1971. What could you do if you were a mail-order business? Branson reckoned Virgin would be out of business within a week if nothing was done. It simply had to find a shop to sell its stock. His friend from Shamley Green, Nik Powell, wandered along Oxford Street and settled on an upstairs space at the Tottenham Court Road end. He even persuaded the shoe-shop owner downstairs that Virgin would provide him with endless customers for Doc Martens, though these did not seem to materialize.

Virgin was still in business and soon there was another shop in Liverpool and then more, and Branson was already thinking big. He was dreaming of his own recording studios and a country house to build them in. Virgin was barely breaking even, but this was the next vision. He found a country house with fifteen bedrooms in the Oxfordshire village of Shipton-on-Cherwell, and bought it, thanks to a loan from Coutts Bank, some money from his parents and assistance from his Auntie Joyce, who remortgaged her own home to provide it.

The country house provides some explanation of why Branson and his team found themselves, later that same year, buying records in Belgium, smuggling them into the country and selling them without paying tax on them. Records exported for sale outside the UK did not incur domestic sales tax. In a scam stumbled on by Branson himself the first time, Virgin took vanloads of records to Dover and had them stamped for export at the Customs office. They were therefore not subject to the purchase tax. Then, instead of actually exporting the records, they were taken back to London and sold via the mail-order service at cut prices, but still with a healthy profit.

Branson's own explanation was that the first trip was accidental, but still made an extra £5,000 in profit. He realized that three similar trips would pull them all out of debt. Whatever the origins, two Customs investigators called Mike Knox and Dick Brown were soon among the higgledy-piggledy mixture of staff, hangers-on, customers and accountants who wandered through their warehouse, marking the export records with an ultra-violet pen.

Branson was tipped off about the forthcoming raid and rushed the offending records round to the Oxford Street shop, not realizing that there would be a simultaneous raid there and in Liverpool. He was arrested, spent the night in the cells and then his mother arrived to take charge of negotiations with the Customs. She put up her own home as security for bail and, together, they made a deal with the investigators that kept Branson out of jail. He agreed to pay a total of £60,000 over three years.

Our own generation grew up with and breathed in the Virgin brand as something representing a cool iconoclasm in the business world. Virgin seemed to be almost anti-business. It retains some of that glamour even now. Simple tax fraud seems to tarnish the image a little but, for Branson and his friends, the contradiction was not so obvious. For Branson, Virgin has always been about us versus them. It is part of what made the brand work in the beginning, though it was to lose its lustre later.

In *Branson* (2000), the entrepreneur's very unofficial biographer Tom Bower sharpens his journalistic knife at this point to demonstrate that this example of Branson's business tactics was not exactly exceptional. Even so, it worked. By the time the Customs business was done and dusted, in Christmas 1972, Virgin had fourteen shops around the country. Branson's usual method was to insist on a three-month rent-free period, so that he could use the income from there to pay for the previous shop he had opened. Once again, he was staying one step ahead of insolvency, but creatively accelerating the business to provide him with the cashflow he needed to survive.

Virgin had a record business and a recording studio. Of course, the next stage was to think about product, and there was nothing quite so glamorous in those days as a record label. Virgin Records was born. Branson was and is nothing but optimistic, but even he could not have realized that he was within months of the kind of once-in-a-lifetime break that would provide the resources for everything else. When he and Draper planned the new company, they already knew whom they would sign – a former guitarist on the hit musical *Hair* called Mike Oldfield. His unique sound had already intrigued them when he played some of his work to them at the recording studios, and he had been singularly unlucky finding anything in the way of a contract.

Oldfield had been hawking his *Tubular Bells* around an uncomprehending music industry for months, so he was only too happy to represent the first signing for Virgin Records. It was soon clear that this combination of Oldfield's genius and Branson's talent for promotion was going to be a success. John Peel played the entire album on his radio show. The record began to sell and Oldfield was booked to perform at the Queen Elizabeth Hall. Branson had to cajole him into the performance with a promise of his new Bentley, a recent wedding present. 'I feel like I've been raped,' said Oldfield as he came off stage.

Tubular Bells eventually sold 13 million copies and Oldfield lived as a recluse for the next ten years. It was the best-selling album of 1973 and it gave Virgin the resources it needed to operate on a wider canvas, and provided unspecified sums which went into a series of offshore trusts. These, or rumours of these, would underpin the company at difficult periods for years to come.

What all the wealth of *Tubular Bells* didn't manage to do was to change the basic pattern. Virgin continued to expand from one project or investment to the next, each one more ambitious than the last, often before the previous one had provided the profit. In fact, it was often the acceleration which provided the finance to settle the bills of the one before. It wasn't long before the new company was seriously in need of another success.

Rotten and Vicious

Only three years separated *Tubular Bells* and the dawn of punk rock, which was destined to have an important significance for Branson at the time and for Virgin ever since.

The Sex Pistols were a potent mixture of violence and rebellion. The names of band-members Johnny Rotten and Sid Vicious have gone down in rock history for their uncompromising iconoclasm. Virgin turned them down in 1976, but Branson became obsessed with them. He knew that most record labels felt, at the very least, uneasy about maintaining them on their books. Their manager Malcolm McLaren played an unprecedented and successful game, turning most of the usual rules upside down, treating most record executives with contempt, especially the ones that had them under contract. But Branson knew that this kind of anti-establishment, in-your-face spirit was precisely what Virgin needed.

He made an offer to EMI to take the Pistols off its hands, which just happened to be before the famous swearing incident on daytime TV with presenter Bill Grundy. But the band slipped through Branson's hands again and signed with A&M. That contract ended when Sid Vicious was sick on the desk of Derek Green, A&M's managing director. Only Virgin was left in the running, and it was under the Virgin contract that the Pistols released their most notorious single 'God Save the Queen'.

Looking back on the Silver Jubilee year of 1977, with the benefit of three decades' hindsight, it all seems rather tame. But at the time, the line 'has made you a moron' – directed at the Queen herself – still had the power to shock. The BBC banned the record from the airwaves and pretended that it had not, in fact, reached number one in the charts.

Branson hired a Thames river boat, *The Elizabethan*, to launch the record. It sailed to a spot opposite the Houses of Parliament, shadowed by two police motor launches, and the band performed the song through amplifiers and loud-speakers. The reaction of the establishment suited Branson precisely. McLaren was arrested yelling 'fascist pigs!' One of the Virgin shop managers, who had the Pistols' album cover *Never Mind the Bollocks* with him, was also taken into custody for displaying indecent advertisements. John Mortimer defended on behalf of Branson again and secured the inevitable acquittal. Somehow, and in a subtle way, the world had changed.

This was not just about showmanship. Nor was it just about shocking people in order to make a splash. That kind of sensationalism had been practised for centuries. There was something more precise about it. It was as if, for the first time, a British business had realized the marketing power of that heady combination of hedonism and *épater le bourgeois* (shock the middle class). This was born in the 1960s student revolt, emerged into puberty with the discovery of the selling power of punk – and here Branson played a critical role – only to come of age in the 1990s, when nearly every brand manager for every corporation in the world was seeking a whiff of adolescent revolt, preferably with a hint of violence. The brand managers had found a perfect formula: in music they could provoke dissent that was ultimately easy to control, and highly profitable. Young people enjoyed a frisson of anti-establishment rebellion, while the new business establishment enjoyed the profits it generated.

The Chicago Bulls basketball superstar Dennis Rodman head-butted a referee during a match in 1996 and was swamped with offers of sponsorship. Nike and McDonald's joined the queue and the head-butt seemed set to earn him about $1 million. Twenty years after Virgin embraced the Sex Pistols, the idea that adolescent revolt was exactly what consumer brands needed was almost ubiquitous. For a generation or so now, we have watched while the politicians complain about the increasing brutality of the rising generation, while the same behaviour is moulded and encouraged by the corporations who ply those same politicians with money. It is a peculiar phenomenon, and Virgin was there at the beginning.

Not only that, Virgin has managed in many ways to continue that hint of carefully calculated irreverence about the brand ever since. The Virgin Lottery bid was going to be known as 'The People's Lottery'. Branson himself revelled in that anti-establishment bravado, with his untidy hair and his refusal to dress like every other po-faced businessman. He was determined to be a kind of People's Champion even while he was benefiting from the privatization of the rail network and deregulation of the airways. It was a careful balancing act and it worked because elements of it were actually true. That really was the way Virgin thought of itself, and it would continue to do so for some decades yet.

Also in the mixture there was something to do with the irreverence of sex, and that was less successful. The very name Virgin seemed to be rooted in sexual innuendo.

Virgin launches, right up until the present day, are famous for their ritual inclusion of barely dressed models, with Branson himself at the heart of them.

Of course, sex did still shock in the 1960s and 1970s. It was useful as a marketing device. It suggested superior open-mindedness and liberation. But by the end of the twentieth century, things looked a little different. Although artists, editors and TV producers still believed, almost obsessively, that sex remained a weapon in the battle against prudery, the truth was that the battle had long since been won. Nor were bohemians just impoverished artists in garrets; we were all bohemians now – and proved it with every bohemian item we put on our credit cards.

Sex worked for Virgin in the days of punk. Maybe it worked as late as the 1980s, with its deliberately fostered sense of hedonism and excitement – the very embodiment of the leisure society. But there came a point when it ceased to have quite that effect, and it just looked slightly vulgar. When Virgin Atlantic used the slogan 'Mine's Bigger than Yours', it began to feel a little tired. When Branson's PR man announced the new slogans for their alternative to Coca-Cola in 1999, one of them was 'Open your mouth, I'm coming'.[5] At which point the whole thing tiptoes towards the teeth-clenchingly embarrasing.

Taking off

But all that was some years in the future. Virgin was heading, as so often before, for its familiar financial crunch. The Sex Pistols broke up, the 1980 recession surged through the economy. Virgin's deal in France went wrong and was followed by a disastrous business trip to the USA in which Branson attempted to expand across the Atlantic. He lost around £1 million in an attempt to set up a London entertainment listings magazine called *Event* to capitalize on the strike which had silenced the alternative *Time Out*. He threatened to sue *New Musical Express* for publishing rumours of his financial difficulties.

As so often before and since, Branson tackled the financial problems in a counter-intuitive way: by expanding. He bought the Roof Garden in Kensington and the gay night club Heaven, both with interest-free loans from brewers. He also set up Palace Pictures. Virgin's trading losses for 1980 were £900,000.

Further difficulties followed. He had to find £1 million to pay off his old friend Nik Powell. He was forced to renegotiate the contract with the lucrative Mike Oldfield. But Virgin Records rode out the storm with Phil Collins, the Human League and nine hits in 1981 alone. Once again, it was a rebellious artist who really brought the money rolling in. Virgin signed Boy George's Culture Club and managed to hold the creditors at bay.

Already the projects were beginning to redouble. There was Virgin Books, destined to become – via Virgin Publishing – the source of a vacuous series of celebrity tomes. There was the film *Nineteen Eighty-Four*, which was saved from complete disaster by using a soundtrack by the Eurythmics. There was a failed court action against Stiff Records over broken sales agreements. After fifteen years in business, Branson had managed one major success, and some smaller ones. It needed something else.

Once again, the company was to find temporary salvation at least in a dramatic and ambitious expansion. In February 1984, a young American lawyer called Randolph Fields approached Branson and asked him if he was interested in setting up a transatlantic air service. Branson was the first to accept that, as a record producer, he was unlikely to have been the first potential partner Fields approached.

But the idea was tempting. It fitted with the Virgin idea of the leisure society, and there was a business opportunity: the Gatwick to New York route was available after the collapse of Freddie Laker's Skytrain venture in 1982.

Branson phoned People Express, which was the closest to a budget airline that existed in those days. He could not get through, and the entrepreneur's mind began to work. 'It was that continual engaged tone on my telephone throughout Saturday more than anything else which triggered my belief that we could set up and run an airline,' he said.[6]

He had lunch with Laker himself, who warned him against the might and behaviour of British Airways, and they came up with an original idea – a limousine to pick up passengers in business class. But Simon Draper and his other colleagues were absolutely appalled. Everything they had worked for in Virgin Records seemed now to be on the line. Branson's relationship with Draper never really recovered. Even so, much of the basic business was already in place. Fields had extracted an agreement from Boeing to lease an old 747. Former aircrew from the old British Caledonian airline had been tracked down. Former Laker executives were prepared to come on board. The plane was decked out in Virgin colours, but the first flight came close to media disaster.

There was a bang and smoke poured out of one of the engines. A new engine had to be fitted overnight, at the cost of £600,000, and once more Virgin was pushing at its overdraft limit. Worse, the smoke pouring out of the engine had been snapped by one of the press photographers on the ground. But there was a telling moment when the photographer from the *Financial Times* took the film out of the camera as Branson landed, and gave it to him. Branson knew the threat that the photos represented – he was the quintessentially media-savvy chief executive. He knew he was now living in the world of business hype where what you see is what you get. The photo could have killed Virgin Atlantic, but it never appeared.

Back from the inaugural flight the following day, Branson was greeted at home by his Coutts account manager, who said that Virgin's overdraft limit had been finally reached. The bank would bounce any further cheques. Branson threw him out, changed his bank and survived the immediate crisis to be able to reorganize the company structure. From then on, Virgin would have retail, music and 'vision' divisions, and Virgin Atlantic and Virgin Holidays would be separate companies. Branson was already beginning to think about solving the financial intractability, like so many of the pioneers in this book, by taking the company public.

But before that, he needed to force out Fields. He bought out his interest in the company for £1 million and a lifetime of free flights. Branson also needed to publicize the new service. There then followed the first of a series of risky pioneering ventures which, more than anything else, were to make Branson a household name.

The first was the 1985 attempted Atlantic crossing, with Ted Toleman, in a powerboat called the *Virgin Atlantic Challenger*, which tried to exhume the old Blue Riband for the fastest Atlantic crossing by an ocean liner. This ended in a humiliating sinking off the coast of Iceland. The second attempt in 1986 was rescued by the RAF, which – thanks to pressure brought to bear on Downing Street – used a Nimrod to drop new fuel filters to them in mid-Atlantic. Branson sailed, victoriously, up the River Thames with Margaret Thatcher, Bob Geldof and Sting on board. It was a public relations triumph.

It is easy to be cynical about the Atlantic crossings and the round-the-world balloon attempts that followed them.

Certainly Branson thrives on this kind of publicity, but there is no doubt also that he saw clearly that Virgin was a different kind of company. Lifestyle companies were a new idea. Virgin barely made anything. It required a strong profile among young people with time and money. The image was the company. It needed something like these life-threatening escapades to hone some kind of edge in markets which were dominated by more powerful players with deeper pockets.

But there was also something else. Branson seemed to be motivated, as much as anything else, by people's disbelief. His colleagues scorned the idea of Virgin Atlantic, so he had to prove them wrong. The press were cynical about the record attempts, so he had to prove them wrong, too. He also aspired to something more, and something more paradoxical. Virgin had got big by using anti-establishment rhetoric, but Branson was determined to be part of the establishment none the less. He wanted the prime minister as a guest on his powerboat. He wanted the RAF to bail him out in mid-Atlantic, just as – in the decade to come – he would fight tooth and nail to run the National Lottery.

There were times, especially before the decision to launch Virgin Atlantic, when he had become bored by business and was even considering a political career. Like any other political operator, Branson wants to be accepted and on his own terms. Virgin is many things, but it is also an aspiring political campaign. Equally, all this adventuring gave him ideas that were grist to the mill. Not content with being rescued from a frozen lake in Yukon, Canada, he decided to start a company that made balloons, provided balloon flight-training and sold balloon holidays. He tried to design and build small airships that would carry observers up to make traffic reports.

Still the same old pattern kept on re-emerging. Virgin Atlantic was a great success. Branson's attention to detail, when he is paying attention, can be ferocious and it paid off. Passengers were entertained with videos on the back of the seat in front. There were even the occasional live performances on board. The airline grew slowly by keeping costs low and by focusing on expansions with high profit margins, attracting the rage of long-established giants such as British Airways, which flew everywhere. By 1988, Branson still ran only two planes, but Virgin boasted the highest occupancy rate and greatest profit margins in the industry.

Even so, the debts and losses in other parts of the empire were mounting. It was the era of Big Bang and privatizations, and the sale of 34 per cent of the company to the public seemed like the logical next step. There was the predictable media blitz. One television advertisement included an executive in a pin-striped suit dancing on his desk (slogan: 'From the rock market to the stock market').

The sale was a success, but Branson was immediately unhappy with it. The non-executive directors cramped his style and insisted on paying big dividends to shareholders when he wanted to invest the money in the company. The share price also began to fall. Branson decided to buy the shares back, but in the meantime began to stalk the recording giant Thorn-EMI. The announcement of a formal takeover bid was due to happen, despite the implacable opposition of the non-executive directors, to coincide with Virgin's profits announcement.

But it was not to be. The day after the hurricane struck London in October 1987, a similar cataclysm hit the world's financial system. It was known as Black Wednesday, and it destroyed about a quarter of the value of most of the publicly quoted companies in the world. Branson took the opportunity and bought the rest of the shares back again. Virgin has been privately owned ever since, owned in fact by a series of family trusts registered initially in the Channel Isles, and – since 1993 – in the British Virgin Isles, where Branson owns the private island of Necker.

The idea of staying private is certainly not unique. The evidence of this book is that handing over ownership to speculators is a lucrative business, but it can corrode anything in the way of innovation or idealism. There are also less idealistic reasons for registering ostensibly British companies in tax havens, including minimizing corporation tax. We cannot look at Virgin's detailed accounts, because they are secret, so there will always be arguments about exactly what this represents.

There will also be arguments about Branson as a businessman. His technique was to run the whole empire from the end of a series of phones – he famously does not use a computer – while splitting the different businesses up into small units which could remain fast-moving and personal. Virgin is not one of those bureaucratic and hierarchical organizations. It makes for informality and flexibility. On the other hand, since so many of the business ideas have been his, or borrowed from other entrepreneurs and subsumed under the Virgin brand, it is hard to see how the imagination and entrepreneurial drive can be brought to bear in such an impersonal and distant way.

The structure of Virgin, like the basic accounts, stays in his mind and the minds of his closest associates, and does not filter much beyond them. But it is responsible both for Virgin's phenomenal speed and its supreme successes as well as for its multiple failures. The small units and informal structures were supposed to allow staff to innovate and, where necessary, to make mistakes. The problem was that, as in any large organization, the real entrepreneurial drive was endlessly watered down.

The BA business

One of the reasons that Virgin's drive was watered down was because of Branson's own shifting attention. He was once more contemplating giving everything up and going back to university in 1991, when suddenly Saddam Hussein invaded Kuwait, and the first Gulf War seemed set to erupt. The price of oil rocketed. Travellers cancelled flights. Virgin pushed perilously towards its £25 million overdraft limit. But Branson hit on the idea of overcoming the difficulties, and making a humanitarian gesture, by rescuing the British hostages who had been snatched off a British Airways 747 while the invasion was underway.

Flying to Baghdad was a risky business at the best of times. If the Virgin plane had been destroyed, the British government agreed to underwrite its insurance. But if it was just detained indefinitely, then Virgin Atlantic would very quickly have gone bankrupt. There was also the personal risk. When Branson's colleague David Tait was told about the plan, he said, 'There is one upside. They'll hold Richard there too and spare us any more of his hare-brained schemes.'[7]

The plane came home, and so did the hostages. Yet the whole venture also earned Branson a very powerful enemy. Lord King, the bad-tempered chairman of British Airways, was furious that Virgin had been given government backing to fetch home what had originally been BA passengers. He was outraged that Branson was acting, as he so often tried to do, as if he was some entertaining branch of the UK government. It was a harbinger for the future. Virgin was dependent on BA for servicing its planes. It was not an easy relationship and, when these maintenance bills tripled, it sparked a slow-burning showdown between the two British airline egos.

The perennial financial difficulties at Virgin were still as awkward as ever. They remained heavily overdrawn and Lloyds was determined that the company should lower the bank's exposure by selling Virgin Music. At the same time, the two airlines were battling over the right to spare slots on the route from the UK to Tokyo and a range of other issues. Worse, there were rumours of some bizarre behaviour by BA staff, apparently using the flight booking computer system to poach Virgin passengers, bad-mouthing Virgin in the press – though the financial difficulties were actually true – and even hiring detectives to follow Branson around and go through his bins.

The business of the British Airways dirty tricks department is confirmed by people outside Virgin.[8] There was the strange tale of the senior policeman who complained about his BA meal and was hounded mysteriously. This kind of paranoia and resulting behaviour happens sometimes in companies that get too big and too self-obsessed. It was never clear who was behind it. But then neither was it clear whether Lord King was more obsessed with Virgin or whether Branson was more obsessed with BA. Dressing up as a pirate in 1991 and dropping a Virgin logo over the tail of a British Airways Concorde, as Branson did, is not the action of somebody trying to cool a mounting dispute.

Inevitably, the battle with BA and the rumours about Virgin's precarious finances began to become threatening. The *Guardian* horrified Branson by running a full-page article with the headline 'Will Richard Branson's balloon burst?' Something had to happen. It is significant that it was the news that King had referred to him as a 'loser' which made up Branson's mind on legal action. He cannot bear criticism at the best of times. Thames Television had just broadcast a documentary about BA's peculiar behaviour and Lord King had denied it. Branson decided that this amounted to a defamatory slight. King was calling him a liar.

Branson took care to employ the formidable libel barrister George Carman, the man who made his reputation by getting Jeremy Thorpe acquitted for conspiracy to murder, and the prospect of being cross-examined by Carman was enough to end the case. British Airways settled out of court for £610,000 in damages. It was the biggest libel settlement ever awarded.

Even so, Branson was never quite able to let the grudge alone. He pursued BA in the American courts for dirty tricks. When British Airways was running into trouble lifting its hugely popular London Eye ferris wheel in 1999, Branson hired a balloon to fly over the Thames with the slogan 'BA CAN'T GET IT UP!' Innuendo again. They can't resist it.

Virgin Records was sold for $1 billion – a huge sum for a company started by students in a basement – and Branson and Draper went their separate ways. The money was used to underpin Virgin Atlantic, and then suddenly a new project was on the horizon.

The idea of Virgin Trains, like so many of the company's other departures, began as a distraction from the financial problems of the group. There was no available money to bid for a franchise, let alone invest in the line, but a few mock-ups of what a Virgin train might look like were enough to keep the creditors and commentators guessing. Nor was the prospect of the idea terribly bright at the beginning. Branson met Chris Green, the director of British Rail's InterCity service – and eventually head of Virgin's rail operation – and afterwards overheard another rail executive saying: 'I'll be in my grave before that fucker gets his logo on my trains.'[9]

That kind of remark is almost enough to shift the company's direction, and was easily enough for Branson to set about proving him wrong. With a successful airline under his belt, it was not difficult to imagine Virgin Trains, any more than it was difficult to imagine the other ventures that had been pouring forth – Virgin Holidays (1985), Virgin Megastores (1988), Virgin Books (1991), Virgin Radio (1993), Virgin Cola (1994), Virgin Direct (1994), Virgin Express (1995), Virgin Cinemas (1995) and so on. But it was already clear that the Virgin imprimatur was no guarantee of success. Virgin Radio was to be sold in 1997 (becoming Absolute Radio in 2008). The Our Price record chain (bought in 1994) was to become an albatross and sold in 2001. Virgin Cinemas were sold four years later.

These ups and downs were not going to pose any threat to the idea of Virgin and its whiff of hedonistic youth. But trains? At least air travel carried some of the exoticism of foreign places, but trains seemed to imply every bit of anal stodginess to which Virgin was intended as the antidote. To make matters worse, the track was out of date and the new trains were still some years off when Virgin Trains began life in 1997, running from Euston and St Pancras in London to Scotland, the West Midlands and north-west England.

There were immediate problems: delays, broken lavatories, people reserved in the same seats and seven times as many complaints as any other train operator. The service was measurably worse than it had been under British Rail and – as Railtrack unravelled in a series of disastrous and tragic incidents involving broken rails – things got even worse.

For some time, Virgin Trains became a byword for unreliability. Branson was frustrated. His executives believed they were just being singled out for criticism by those who were opposed to privatization. They pointed out that passenger numbers were still rising and the income for a privatized monopoly on Virgin's lines was all but guaranteed, but the company's reputation seemed to be haemorrhaging. 'Is Branson in a pickle?' asked one headline. Even the new trains, when they finally arrived, were just too slick for comfort. There seemed to be less space for luggage. There were too many intercom interruptions and there was irritating muzak as you came aboard.

Branson was becoming desperate to reinvent himself. Not only were there problems with the trains, but he had been turned down for a proposed knighthood by the new Prime Minister Tony Blair (who later changed his mind in 2000), who regarded Branson as an icon of the old Thatcherite regime. Worse, the markets were going crazy for the internet and Virgin seemed to be missing out. At the tail end of the dotcom boom, therefore, Virgin launched a whole flurry of new companies, including Virgin Active health clubs, Virginmoney.com, Virgin Travelstore, Virgin Student, Virgin Energy, V.Shop, Virgin Cars, Virgin Wines, Virgin Mobile Australia and the Australian budget airline Virgin Blue.

Most of these were to fall by the wayside or to be sold on. But Virgin Mobile, which launched at the end of 1999, represented a whole new direction for the company, which went way beyond immediate worries about dotcoms.

The leisure society myth

Virgin sometimes feels as if it is perched uneasily between two worlds, the mid-century world of industrial production – Coke bottles and Fords pouring down the new assembly lines – and the new world of brands, e-commerce and mobile money. It carries the implications of the first, even if this was primarily a background to react against. But somehow it pre-dated the whole business of e-commerce, and seemed to struggle to realize the possibilities.

What holds the company's various projects together – if anything does – is one big idea: the leisure society. This is not, in fact, a terribly new idea. It dates back to a speech by the scientist Julian Huxley, speaking to the Young Men's Hebrew Association in New York in 1926. There is a limit to how much of the products of this automation humanity can consume, he told them, which is why a two-day working week and a five-day weekend was inevitable.

Huxley started the ball rolling and soon the whole idea of a leisure society became a truism. 'When we reach the point when the world produces all the goods that it needs in two days, as it inevitably will, we must turn our attention to the great problem of what to do with our leisure,' he wrote in the *New York Times* on 17 November 1930. Two years later, a book called *The Challenge of Leisure* by Arthur Pack predicted the same thing, praising a man in Maine who had spent his leisure time building a three-mile model railway, and urging us to take up painting, stamp-collecting or public service. Soon every futurist seemed to agree. There was going to be less work, everyone seemed to agree. Work was running dry and the world where people worked forty-eight hours a week, forty-eight weeks a year for forty-eight years of their life, and died obediently within eighteen months of retirement, was almost over.

A spokesperson for General Motors promised in a 1966 BBC documentary, 'People will start to go to work at about age twenty-five. Six-month vacations would not be out of the question.' That had an element of truth: so did the prediction for the year 2001 in *Vogue* magazine, by the author of *2001: A Space Odyssey*. Arthur C. Clarke said that 'our descendants' might be 'faced with a future of utter boredom, where the main problem in life is deciding which of the several hundred TV channels to select'.[10]

The period of *A Space Odyssey* was the high point

of the idea of a looming shortage of work. It dovetailed nicely with the sense that we all deserved a little more tuning in and dropping out, the origins of the Virgin brand. When that light bohemianism was entirely subsumed into the burgeoning consumer society, that suited Virgin too, with its brand made up of what Branson called 'fizz fun and freedom'.[11] How much simpler if the badge of being a bohemian was just to buy stuff.

Even Virgin Atlantic, as we have seen, fitted into that sense of excitement and relaxation. The problem was that the leisure society did not really quite add up any more. For one thing, you only have to wander through any of our inner cities to see just how much work now is not being done. Looking after parks, visiting older people, watching over railway station lavatories – nobody does it any more, and not because the work has been automated or computerized, but because society has decided it cannot afford it. The work has not disappeared; it is just that, because it is not paid work, we forget it exists. Because these are not marketable tasks, they just do not get noticed any more.

But there are other problems for the leisure society. Some peculiarity of the economic system means that those of us in employment in the western world have actually been working harder than ever. Executives sometimes squeeze their sleep down to less than six hours a night to find time to go to a gym at 5 a.m. As many as 37 per cent of British people work on Sundays. Even children as young as eight have an hour's homework every night and formal tests in each area of school work every week – and they have so many CV-building after-school activities that 'windows' for play are often a week or so apart.

It is true that those who do not fit into the increasingly narrow economy, or those who have retired from it, face endless vistas of time stretching for years ahead of them.

There is a widening gulf between the increasingly busy and the increasingly marginalized, for whom time hangs heavy. The idea that somehow we are all part of an increasingly leisurely society is simply not accurate. It is part of the big lie that somehow we are only living authentically when we are not working. Maybe this is because of the failure of the leisure society to emerge, maybe it is despite it – perhaps leisure needs to be scarce to be marketed in the way it is. Either way, we have been encouraged by Virgin and others to think that the only real life is leisure. Reality is tourism or partying or both.

Except that it is not. This perception makes no sense, does not mesh well with reality, aligns itself with environmentally destructive conspicuous consumption and is liable to lead to depression or bankruptcy for the true believers. No wonder the Virgin brand began to wobble. The leisure society was just not enough.

Perhaps the peculiar story of Virgin Cola accelerated the demise of an idea that no longer quite worked. It was launched in 1994 with huge razzmatazz, after a link-up with the Canadian bottlers Cott. It never caught on in the USA and soon lost what market share it managed in the UK. At the moment, it is not even sold on Virgin Trains.

You win some, you lose some. The trouble was that, without the leisure society idea at the heart, Virgin seemed increasingly like an uneasy hodgepodge of businesses, bound together by Branson. The sale of Virgin Records, together with the contracts for Bryan Ferry, Janet Jackson and the Rolling Stones, left the company far more independent of banks than they had been before. After 1993, no bank would ever dictate to us how to run our business, said Branson.[12] But what did it all mean?

In fact, this was not entirely true, hence the sale of 49 per cent of Virgin Atlantic to Singapore Airlines. Nor did it put at rest Branson's hunger to be part of the establishment, which explains his involvement with an ill-fated environment initiative under John Major's government. It also explains his two expensive bids to run the National Lottery – one of them ended up in court on two occasions, once against rivals Camelot to overturn the decision by the regulator and once against the head of the lottery operator G-TECH, whom Branson accused of offering him a bribe.[13]

Perhaps it also explains why there was a growing suspicion of Branson and his endless parties as the century turned. It was not just the albatross of Virgin Trains or the tireless publicity – Branson spends about a quarter of his time on PR – it was the sense, said biographer Tom Bower in *Branson* (2000), of 'Britain's most visible entrepreneur, an eager recipient of hero worship, trying to influence practically every aspect of British society'.

Bower found himself uninvited from a trip to witness Richard Branson launch one of his balloon events as it became known he was planning a book about him. Later he faced legal action from Branson related to an *Evening Standard* article even as his book was being published. Bower won when the courts deemed as 'fair comment' his claim that Branson's bid to win the contract to run the lottery was motivated by, among other things, financial self-interest and the desire for free publicity for Virgin.[14]

When the book was finished and published, Branson was no happier. In fact, he was horrified, but not at a loss for words: 'What I have read has offended me on every single level. It is a foul, foul piece of work from the first words to the last – really rotten, nasty stuff.'[15]

But something has changed, too. Branson now has a majority stake in around 220 businesses and the ultimate owners of Virgin are a series of offshore trusts registered in the British Virgin Isles. Together those companies earn around £400 million a year, before tax. They include names like Virgin Spa, Virgin Health Bank, Virgin Festivals, Virgin HealthMiles, Virgin Holiday Cruises, Virgin Limited Edition, Virgin Wines, Virgin Balloon Flights, Virgin Galactic, Virgin Life Care, Virgin Limousines, Virgin Limobike, Virgin Money, Virgin Mobile, Virgin Active, Virgin Charter, Virgin Connect, Virgin Experience Days, Virgin Voucher, Virgin America and many others.

Virgin Group has also changed its role. It is now a kind of boutique venture capital company, putting in its own money to develop ideas. Each company is given its own chief executive and board of directors, with at least one member from Branson's seven-man advisory council. Virgin itself is a group of bankers, strategists and accountants who deal with the outside investors involved in each company. When the group needs the money, some of those investments are sold and the brand moves on.

The other big change is the strange virtualization of Virgin itself, starting in 1999 with the launch of its own mobile phone company. Virgin Mobile was not altogether a success, though it claimed to have attracted a million subscribers by 2001. Its phones were clunky and far too many people signed up and then stopped using them. What was interesting about it was that it marked an increasing pattern in the way Virgin invests. The company's headquarters and its telephone network were both rented from somewhere else.

What was at the heart of the operation – and increasingly at the heart of Virgin as a whole – was a massive database, operated within a few years by a call centre with a thousand seats and a huge piece of customer relationship management software, which measured and scripted everything, set up in just nine weeks by a sleep-deprived team from OneOffice.

These were wider trends. The decades on either side of the turn of the century saw the huge expansion of off-the-peg software – or hugely expensive tailored systems – which would ostensibly re-engineer the way corporations ran their whole operations, bringing whole departments together in huge back-office processing systems. Enterprise Resource Planning (ERP) software began in 1993 and is sold off-the-peg by companies such as SAP and Oracle. There are divided opinions about whether they ever save money, or ever will – because their purpose is to set business processes in concrete, script every sentence of conversations with customers and to lock staff into rigid control systems that monitor their actions.

The main impact of the ERP revolution has been to create the faceless systems that we interact with so frustratingly every day, dealing with call centres – often employed by an intermediate agency – operating customer relationships management (CRM) software that often has no space for the specific query or request we have so laboriously contacted them about.

This has been part of a parallel process of hollowing out, as the biggest corporations began to withdraw increasingly from the frustrating business of making things or dealing with customers, aware that financial operations were so hugely profitable that nothing else mattered nearly as much. Other functions were increasingly outsourced, mainly offshore. Often all this was done in the name of efficient customer service, but actually customer service grew steadily worse. The systems may have worked, but by chopping functions up into small units for processing no one staff member could see whole tasks or take responsibility for them.

Virgin Mobile may not have grown into the giant that Branson hoped for, but this new world of virtual corporations was one that Virgin could adapt to quickly. Soon the whole business of running a phone network was being virtualized even further, using voice recognition software. This was finally rolled out in the USA in 2002, outsourced to Virgin's customer service centre in Spokane, Washington. 'The call center reps have been very uniquely selected to match the profile of Virgin's target audience,' said Rudy DuBay, senior vice president of sales at ICT Group, in charge of Virgin Mobile USA's customer management, in a statement which reeked of Virgin's increasingly exhausting approach to sex.[16] 'They give good phone.'

Virgin Mobile never quite made the grade. Even in the USA, where it managed a successful leveraged buy-out in 2007, it happened amid weak growth and widening losses. Virgin Mobile USA has been fighting a legal action from angry investors ever since. It was sold to partners Sprint in 2009. Virgin Mobile Canada went to Bell Mobility the previous year, which promptly outsourced customer service to the Philippines. Virgin Mobile Singapore closed in 2002.

But in the UK, Branson was going through the next stage in virtualization. He sold Virgin Mobile to a new company formed out of a merger between NTL and Telewest, creating at a stroke the second biggest phone company in the UK. As part of the deal, the new company, Virgin Media, would pay at least £8.5 million for the right to use the Virgin brand name and Branson became the biggest shareholder (15 per cent). There were alliances with content providers such as Sky, because content is vital in this new world of 'convergence' – the coming together of computers, phones and televisions. Even customer service has now been outsourced.

Part of the answer to the question posed by this chapter – what lies at the heart of Virgin? – is this: a huge database that can be mined, sold and cross-sold. Virgin Media forged an agreement with the controversial software company Phorm, which had been accused of making spyware, to search into its customers' behaviour and buying habits. Phorm has since pulled out of the UK, but watch this space.

Is anyone there?

It is a truth universally acknowledged that a company in possession of a huge customer database, and with powerful customer relationship management software, must be in want of a bank. Huge databases are a business asset. The next stage from providing phones, internet and TV is to add financial services into the mix. With conventional banks absent in their own dream world of the speculative economy, it has been left to other corporate entities – all with databases – to start innovating with banking services.

This explains Virgin Money's attempted takeover of the failed bank Northern Rock, followed by its acquisition of a tiny bank called Church House Trust, to provide it with a banking licence it could use to operate some of the bank branches now being shed by the great failed megaliths, Lloyds and Royal Bank of Scotland. As we write, the American billionaire Wilbur Ross is now backing Virgin Money's £2 billion bid for the 318 branches of RBS that are up for sale.[17] Whether this turns out to be a breath of fresh air in the uncompetitive UK banking market or more exhausting database manipulation – or both – remains to be seen.

In the meantime, fun remains on the agenda. 'If you were able to trade places with any corporate chieftain, wouldn't it be Richard Branson?' gushed a *Fortune* profile of him in 2003. 'He simply has the most fun. Branson's greatest business feat, perhaps, has been to engineer a breathtaking life for himself.'[18] Branson still gives the impression that he enjoys life to the absolute full. He entertains his staff, family, investors or people such as Bill Gates on Necker Island, with the occasional slightly nerve-racking practical joke. When he is not using it, he rents the island out at $22,500 a day.

These days, his political interests increasingly over-shadow the activities of the company, as if they were the real purpose all along. Many of these initiatives are high-profile propaganda ventures to promote technological solutions. The Virgin Galactic project promotes the idea of space travel. Virgin Earth Challenge, a $25 million prize for 'a commercially viable design which results in the removal of anthropogenic, atmospheric greenhouse gases so as to contribute materially to the stability of Earth's climate', suggests that global warming can be tackled by a simple technological rescue for business as usual. Branson is supposed to have been talked out of climate-change scepticism by Al Gore.[19] Branson promised $3 billion to the Clinton Global Initiative (CGI) for renewable energy projects. He even promised to invest all future profits of the Virgin Group's transportation businesses – mainly airlines and trains – into renewable energy initiatives by his own companies and others. Even so, airline bosses will always have an uncomfortable time as environmentalists, especially as they also have to persuade prime ministers to go easy on airlines. And, typically, Branson fails to see any contradiction whatsoever between expressing concern for the environment and promoting lifestyles in which not just regular, long-distance air travel is a perfectly normal expectation, but so is space travel.

He has been on the outside of the debate about the inter-net. His wife Joan stopped him from putting up his hand at one high-profile conference when Bill Gates asked the audience who was still not using the internet. But the basic underlying business of becoming the establishment still applies. Getting the Red Arrows to fly in formation with a Virgin Atlantic 747 to celebrate the airline's quarter-century in 2009 was definitely a coup. But sometimes, when the establishment stays at arm's length, the best thing to do is to start your own. Sure enough, in 2007, Branson announced the formation of a group called 'The Elders' including people like Desmond Tutu and Nelson Mandela, which, in Virgin's own words, is 'a group of leaders to contribute their wisdom, independent leadership and integrity to tackle some of the world's toughest problems'.

The idea that the environment is a central cause at the heart of Virgin fails, for several reasons, to quite carry conviction. Branson's addiction to powerboats seems to militate against it. When Virgin Atlantic staff talk about the importance of recycling the newspapers passengers have used – when they have just burned tonnes of fossil fuel to get across the Atlantic – it points to a potential conflict if Virgin were to take green transformation really seriously.

The Virgin website says, 'We believe in making a difference. Virgin stands for value for money, quality, innovation, fun and a sense of competitive challenge.' There is no other statement of corporate purpose, no ethical credo, no cause beyond self – apart from the hint of fizz and sex, left over from the 1980s – and we are left wondering what there is at the heart of Virgin, which might guarantee its continued existence after Branson's eventual demise. Or is there anything there apart from a database and huge ambition? Virgin Atlantic is half-owned by Singapore Airlines. Virgin Trains is half-owned by bus operator Stagecoach. Only a tiny slice of Virgin Media is now owned by Virgin – so what is there at the core of it?

At his Millennium Lecture at Oxford University in November 1999, when most of Virgin's enterprises apart from the airline and trains were trading at a loss, Branson talked about the future of business in terms of branding. 'I believe there is no limit to what a brand can do,' he said.[20] There is no doubt that brand recognition has taken Virgin a very long way, but – despite all the energy dedicated to valuing brands and all the highly paid brand managers and brand consultants – the whole idea is something of an illusion. Brands are not, in fact, the new religions that people live their lives by, as the advertising agency Young & Rubicam claimed. The truth is that most people hate most brands, most of the time. They are deeply disloyal to them, and the very word 'brand' has come to imply something shiny, insubstantial and basically fake – something manipulated, without human values at its heart.

The result is that, despite all the hype, brands are not really foundations for the future. They facilitate communications but they fade so quickly. So what is Virgin? Branson's friend Peter Gabriel answered the question once: 'Virgin is becoming everything. You wake up in the morning to Virgin Radio, you put on your Virgin jeans, you go to the Virgin Megastore, you drink Virgin Cola, you fly to America on Virgin Atlantic. Soon you'll be offering Virgin births, Virgin marriages, Virgin funerals.'[21]

This was intended as a joke, but there is something chilling about it, and it says something about the future direction of business as rival models loom offering us different versions of the same of everything. Do we want the supermarket model of monopoly (Tesco or Walmart), or the internet model (Amazon or Google) or do we want the brand database model, like Virgin? Or do we want none of them?

CONCLUSION

A CORPORATE REFORMATION

If leaders of big companies seem to occupy a different
galaxy from the rest of the community they risk being
treated as aliens.

Richard Lambert, director-general of the
Confederation of British Industry, 2010

Economic historian Robert Heilbroner writes that for
much of the last millennium the 'notion that a general
struggle for gain might actually bind together a community
would have been held as little short of madness'.[1] Yet this
'struggle for gain' has become the culture and law of the
corporation. In his history of the East India Company,
Nick Robins writes that, 'across 400 years of modern corporate history, three design flaws in particular unite the
(East India) Company with the global corporations of
the twenty-first century: the drive for monopoly control,
the speculative temptations of executives and investors,
and the absence of automatic remedy for corporate abuse'.[2]
To understand how to progress, we need to know where
the corporation came from, where it went wrong and what
should replace it.

When Henry VIII broke away from papal authority, he
needed revenue and used his new nation state to give royal

trading rights to merchants in the City of London. In this way, the Levant Company, the Baltic Company and others emerged. The Levant Company would ultimately evolve into the British East India Company and help found the empire. Under Elizabeth I, out-and-out pirates operating in the Caribbean were legitimized by the crown so that the state could earn income from their international 'trading'. Adventurers such as John Hawkins and Francis Drake were knighted to pillage the Spanish Armada, colonize overseas territories and bring back gold and plunder.

This 'reformed piracy' evolved into mercantilism. It also did so in the space of just one generation, from the death of licensed pirates such as Henry Morgan in Port Royal, Jamaica, to the hunting of Blackbeard, Kidd and all the others over the next two decades. They had been replaced by respectable slave-traders and speculators because simple piracy had become too crass and unpredictable.

The main issue was how to issue charters most efficiently to bring in maximum income for the crown. The earliest form of corporatism therefore linked up big business and the state – much as it does today with, for example, the revolving door between supermarkets and the government. Monopoly rights in trade within empires came under Adam Smith's successful intellectual assaults. His deep antipathy towards large corporations is conveniently forgotten today.

Clearly, for maximizing profit, monopoly wins out against competition all the time. That is why the British monarchs preferred royal charters, as competition was a percentage cut of corporate profits. Smith, however, was the mouthpiece of industrialists, not the earlier mercantile capitalists in the City of London. His manufacturers were frustrated by the global trade barons. They could not 'get on' without breaking down the special interests in trade.

This was necessary in order to develop their own autonomy to trade their goods internationally.

Partly in response to the investment crash of the South Sea Bubble, a 1720 Parliamentary Act introduced into law the idea of limited liability, but only in a very narrow sense. Today, the privileges and the protection it provides are taken for granted. But company law is based on the notion that legal benefits are given in return for obligations. In this case, it was to restore investors' confidence and later so that they would put money into the growth of the railways.

So it was that the 1844 Companies Act enabled businesses to be incorporated without having to extract a royal charter and legal statute from recalcitrant legislators who were worried it would be abused, fearing fraud and 'moral hazard'. Real limited liability came only in 1862, allowing companies to take commercial risks without directors risking personal ruin as well, but the new privilege was really intended only for enterprises to benefit the public through major public works.

In the preface to his book *The Just Enterprise*, George Goyder quotes the historian Arthur Bryant, writing in 1940:

A limited liability company has no conscience. A Priesthood of figures cannot consider claims of morality and justice that conflict with its mathematical formulas; it must live by its own rules. Man, who once tried to model his life on the divine, came to take his orders from the lender of money and the chartered accountant . . . . It is not the profit motive which is to blame. Free men have at all times sought profit from their labour. It is its enthronement to the exclusion of other motives that is far more important.[3]

The modern corporations are increasingly considered too big to fail, their liabilities are still limited, their obligation in law is to privilege the interests of finance, and they are managed by a very small global clique of executives playing musical chairs, who expect and get astronomical and disproportionate rewards. It is hardly surprising that western capitalism almost destroyed itself, only to be rescued with breathless irony by the public sector mortgaging itself.

Today corporations' responsibility to investors comes before contributing to the good of the general public. In the wake of the financial crash of 2008, the notion of public interest being at the heart of regulating business enjoyed a renaissance. Such a test was proposed for foreign takeovers of British companies in the wake of Kraft buying up Cadbury. Tesco, for example, is a public limited company, though modern global financial structures also allow it to minimize the amount it contributes to the public purse through clever tax-avoidance strategies such as selling music, films and computer games from a special branch of the company in a Channel Island tax haven.

The most recent Companies Act forces British corporations to report on their wider social and environmental impact, but this is a complex and depressing business. It is hard to disconnect the damage companies such as BAA or Walmart do to economies and the planet from the central purpose of the company. The largest 300 corporations own somewhere between a half and a quarter of the world's productive assets, yet employ less than a quarter of 1 per cent of the global population. Such unsustainable disconnections are further signs that the days of great corporations might be drawing quietly to a close.

Many of the names in this book were not basically amoral to begin with. They started out with quite different agendas. There is also an emerging new sector made up of companies that have at their heart the objective to make the world a better place – not as an add-on, bunging a few charitable donations about before going back to pillaging the planet – but as their central corporate objective.

But the truth is that companies such as Cadbury started in exactly the same way, then found themselves blown off course by the implications of corporate financing. Handing over their destiny to the stock market and an overarching obsession with profit seem to give companies a different metabolism. Describing the changes accompanying the rise and deregulation of finance in recent decades, John Kay, the author and *Financial Times* journalist, writes:

> The more shareholder value became a guide to action, the worse the outcome. On the board of the Halifax Building Society, I voted in 1995 for its conversion to a 'plc'. We would allow the company to pursue the goal of maximising its value untrammelled by outmoded concepts of mutuality: in barely a decade, almost every last penny of that value was destroyed. In 1996, as my thoughts on this began to form, I went to the CBI annual conference and described how ICI, for decades Britain's leading industrial company, had recently transformed its mission statement from 'the responsible application of chemistry' to 'creating value for shareholders'. The company's share price peaked a few months later, to begin a remorseless decline that would lead to its disappearance as an independent company.[4]

Similar forces of change shaped Marks & Spencer for the worse, as we described earlier. Kay goes on to point out the irony of some of the most profit-obsessed firms such as the investment banks Lehman Brothers and Bear Stearns, who traded under signs which read 'Let's make nothing but money' and ended up, writes Kay, losing more money 'than they ever made'.

The late Anita Roddick bitterly regretted taking the Body Shop public and regarded it as her greatest mistake. She felt it clipped her wings. When she wanted to experiment with innovative new forms of trade and investment, the actual control of the company lay with those who determined the share price – people, as we have mentioned before, with no sense of history.

John Kenneth Galbraith wrote about the great crash of 1929: 'The sense of responsibility in the financial community for the community as a whole is not small. It is nearly nil.'[5] Little seems to have changed in the decades that led up to the 2007 sub-prime lending crisis, which in turn once again triggered the near meltdown of western economies.

Pointing out the vacuum where a moral sense ought to be has been one of the modern critiques of corporations. But equally important is the vacuum where a sense of history should be: a sense of what is likely to happen, what the wider effects are likely to be, a broader sense of a bigger picture. A visit to the City of London Business Library in the course of writing this book, in the very month of the disastrous crash, revealed that all its collected magazines and publications are disposed of after five years, and most after three years. The excision of history from business commentary and corporate life – and its replacement by mush – is one of the major causes of the current miserable economic climate.

Anita Roddick believed in the heroic entrepreneur who could imagine the world differently and make it happen. Many of the stories in this book – of Simon Marks, George Cadbury, John Reith – are about people like that. But they also confirm the fragility of that vision in the face of a corporate form that spreads its ownership to investors, but not to anybody else. The one exception is Virgin, which avoided the questionable embrace of the public limited company, but seems unable to articulate much of a moral vision.

The extraordinary way that productive business has been replaced by the sound and fury of the markets has been set out, among others, by the great investor John Bogle, founder of the Vanguard group of mutual funds in the USA. He describes the sad and pointless story of the car rental company Avis, founded in 1946 by Warren Avis and sold two years later to another businessman, who sold it to Amoskeag, who sold it to Lazard Frères, who sold it on to ITT. That was 1965, and Avis has now been owned by eighteen different entities. Each time the sale happens, the bankers and lawyers earn fees and there is another highly paid chief executive taken on.[6] But does it do Avis any good? Has it done Cadbury any good to be used, along with all its tremendous history, as a bolster to Kraft's share price? Did the 700 businesses acquired during the speedy rise of Tyco International, and before its swift and notorious demise, benefit from the deal?

Fortunately, there are many alternatives. Some are new, alternative models, but with others history can again be our friend. Co-operatives, for example, expanded noticeably in the vacuum of trust that conventional business found itself in after the market and banking failures of 2008. Co-op's roots are, though, much deeper.

Robert Owen, the nineteenth-century capitalist turned social reformer, went from being a mill manager to founding the Grand National Moral Union of the Productive and Useful Classes (possibly history's greatest act of economic naming) from which grew the English labour movement.

A group of twenty-eight weavers who became known as the Rochdale Pioneers took Owen's ideas and in 1844 created the consumer co-operative movement by setting up the Rochdale Society of Equitable Pioneers.

Instructively, their innovation was in response to economic hardship and market failure. As well as enduring appalling working conditions, many families in the growing towns and cities of northern industrial Britain found it hard to get good, unadulterated food at fair prices. Co-operative methods came to their rescue. Customers were members of the society and received a dividend in return for what they spent (a very early, and much more generous, precursor to the loyalty card – the difference being that the societies were run democratically for the benefit of members).

By 1863, the movement, largely based in Lancashire and Yorkshire, grew to 300 co-ops. By 1890, there were 1,400 societies, and by 1950 the co-operative movement supplied nearly one-third of the grocery market, and distributed the benefits. Today the combined turnover of the Co-op food, bank and insurance services is over £7 billion and its popularity is rising. The success in a time of recession of the Co-operative Bank, department store John Lewis and food retailer Waitrose, which are all owned by their staff, is evidence that the co-operative model still has the energy today to make a difference.

Yet, compared to their success in Scandinavia and many parts of continental Europe, co-operative models have been relatively marginalized in the UK, home to a more aggressive, individualistic variant of capitalism.

Mutual building societies, for example, where customers were the owners, were once dominant players in the UK home loans market. Yet most opted to demutualize in the period of increasing financial deregulation or did not survive an assault by the big banks. When it came to the point, the members did not rally round and support their organizations, mainly because ownership – by itself with no activity required – does not feel very important. It is different when the staff are the owners. After the 2008 crash, however, the mutuals that remained had the last laugh. More trusted, and more divorced from high-risk investment activity, they rode out the storm without bankrupting public finances in the way that the major high-street banks did.

Enterprises owned, not by distant shareholders who come and go day by day, but by the staff or the customers, or some combination of the two, seem both more resilient to external shocks and responsive to public concerns.

The co-operative movement in Europe retains powerful networks of small engineering businesses, while workers' co-ops have been a great success in northern Italy. Extensive farmer co-operatives are spread across Europe and other parts of the world. But the network of workers' co-ops in Mondragon, in the Basque region of Spain, has provided a model which may prove even more important.

It began with the first businesses set up by the local Roman Catholic priest after the Second World War. There are now more than 200 linked businesses in and around Mondragon, which trade with each other and underpin the area economically, producing a range of different goods. The combined network is now the sixth biggest company in Spain, with representatives and other factories all over the world. Its recent agreement with the American steelworkers' union USW to start launching similar networks of mutually supporting businesses around the USA marks what may be the beginning of a whole new business model in the Anglo-Saxon world. One of the giants of world football, the Spanish club Barcelona, is also run on co-operative lines. Its experience compares favourably to the turmoil surrounding English Premier League clubs whose ownership has fallen to private finance.

In the UK and the USA we have lived for more than a generation with the idea that the model of companies owned by shareholders is the most effective way of making things happen in the world. We forgot, or lacked the imagination to see, that other proven models are available.

Today, Scott Bader is a €220 million international firm with a workforce of 600. It started life in 1921 as a conventional capitalist enterprise in Wollaston, Northamptonshire. It dealt in specialist resins, adhesives and polymers – just a normal company that made stuff. Then, in 1951, Ernest Bader, the company founder, took a radical step. Disillusioned with conventional business, he handed the firm's governance over to its workforce using a model called the Common Trusteeship Company. Bader defined two challenges: 'how to organize or combine a maximum sense of freedom, happiness and human dignity in our firm without loss of profitability, and to do this by ways and means that could be generally acceptable to the private sector of industry'.[7]

He tried to implement this in a number of ways. For example, the maximum differential between highest and lowest paid is a ratio of one to seven. During a probationary period, new staff are told about the firm's ethos, and if the probation is successfully completed they become 'Members of the Commonwealth'. This allows individuals to engage in bodies that govern the business such as the Members' Assembly which represents members' interests and is the peak of the governance structure. Most members are elected and must hold to account the Scott Bader Group board and the Commonwealth board on behalf of the membership in line with the founding principles.

Instead of failing, as many predicted, when these changes were introduced, the company went from strength to strength. Scott Bader has no external shareholders, is immune to takeover and has long planning horizons – 60 per cent of profits are reinvested in the company. Each generation at the company is obliged to work to ensure the long-term sustainability of the firm, in order that future generations may benefit. Trusteeship as a form of economic governance was promoted by Mahatma Gandhi. The economist E.F. 'Fritz' Schumacher, in his classic book *Small is Beautiful* (1973), described the notion as applied by Scott Bader as developing 'responsibility for a bundle of assets – not ownership'. Bader's descendant, Godric Bader, points out that this has 'a direct parallel as to how we now urgently have to look at our earthly home'.[8]

The approach, writes Schumacher, overcame 'the reductionism of the private ownership system and uses industrial organizations as a servant of man, instead of allowing it to use men simply as means to the enrichment of the owners of capital'. The transformation of ownership into a sense of long-term trusteeship over common assets, rather than its mere changing of hands from company founder to workers was, though, he thought, a 'necessary, but not sufficient, condition for the achievement of higher aims'. Explicit tasks that are useful in economic, but also social and environmental, ways need to be written into the principles of 'commonwealth'.

As we have seen, the corporation was ultimately born out of a form of state-sanctioned, legalized piracy. This laid the foundations for the relentless rise of international trade. But even here, on the hallowed global trading grounds of the multinational corporation, practical alternative models have emerged. One type of mutual trade is practised by Just Change, a network of communities that creates trading links for mutual social and economic benefit domestically and between continents.[9] Tea grows well in India, but not in Britain. So, the south Indian Nilgiri tea-growing tribal organization Adivasi Munnetera Sangham trades directly, for example, with the working-class tea-drinking Marsh Farm Estate in Luton, England. This way of trading builds links, co-operation, understanding and economic literacy about how the world works between communities who might otherwise be complete strangers. But it is not just commodities and greater affinity that is shared. So is any surplus that results from the trade. It is a form of international trade which builds non-exploitative patterns of interdependence.

Another variant of these different models is the social enterprise, which looks like a company – and has to make a profit – but the idea of public benefit is written into its core purpose. In some ways this is an older way of organizing business. Chartered corporations began in the days of Elizabeth I. The BBC is, in some ways, no more than a huge chartered social enterprise, though perhaps it is anomalous in terms of its size and cultural significance. It was structured along the lines of the London Passenger Transport Board in the 1920s, and the same model was borrowed for the new town development corporations in the 1940s. It is a successful way of focusing resources on solving specific problems, and – thanks to the charter – such organizations are less likely to lose that powerful sense of purpose, whatever else happens.

The term 'social enterprise' emerged in the 1970s, and some of the first modern social enterprises were seen around Glasgow in the 1980s in the form of community companies whose main purpose was to employ local people. Now there are hugely successful social enterprises in the UK, like the Liverpool-based Furniture Resource Centre, which has spawned a range of new ideas in recycling and youth training, or the phenomenal Ealing Community Transport, which provides public transport all over the country. At one stage it was also running a railway in Devon.

But what so many of these alternative models have in common is that they are not public companies, listed on the stock markets of the world and wholly dependent on the whims of speculators, who are deeply sceptical of innovation – especially green or organizational reforms – which does not immediately impact on the single bottom line of maximizing returns to shareholders. This strait-jacket is the corrosive undermining factor for so many of the companies in this book, the main reason they have departed so far from the ideals of their founders.

This old-fashioned version of the leviathan corpora-tions, automaton-like in their pursuit of shareholder value and the power and prestige that come with size, looks increasingly out of step with the modern world. Complex social, economic and environmental challenges at the local and global level require a more deft and diverse approach.

The former merchant banker Jeff Gates set out one alternative as the 'Ownership solution', where smaller enterprises – owned much more broadly – can make those changes happen. It is a vision that draws on, for example, the network of co-operatives launched in Mondragon in Spain. It draws also on the network of small workshops that underpins the economic success of the former car-making regions of northern Italy.

It requires a different kind of financing infrastructure, with a whole range of different models co-existing, just as the new corporations are going to be more diverse and intricate. We should not forget that inside the vast belly of the monster that is now Barclays, for example, lives a whole range of other species it swallowed up over the years

– from family banks such as Martins to mutual building societies such as the Woolwich. They are still there, just dozing, ready to be reawakened.

The former corporate raider Shann Turnbull, an Australian, suggested a different kind of financing for corporate endeavour that was time-limited. Some government policies have 'sunset clauses' built in, so why not a 'time-limited corporation'? If investors look no further than twenty years ahead, then giving them ownership rights to their investment beyond that horizon is inefficient, he argues. The ownership could alternatively revert to the employees, or the neighbours, or the small developing country that has hosted the project, and the sheer noise of corporate gigantism, the clash of mergers and acquisitions – so much sound and fury signifying so little – might be a great deal reduced.

Previous attempts to deal with unhealthy shareholder dominance relied largely on reforming the board. There have been experiments with worker directors, while countries such as Germany have tried two-tier boards through which supervisory directors can represent wider interests. UK enquiries into board governance culminated in the Combined Code for stock market companies. Other voluntary codes emerged particular to different sectors, ranging from food to clothes and toys. Ideas such as the social audit, promoted in the 1990s by the New Economics Foundation, tried to change the culture within the private sector. Yet these experiments largely failed to tame the power of the capital markets. One way to do that would be to replace the annual shareholder meeting as the ultimate government of the company.

Instead of this largely supine body which typically nods through outrageous pay deals and ignores irresponsible behaviour, companies need a vibrant assembly in which the interests of all stakeholder groups can be represented – and

337

balanced. This could be a Stakeholder Council. It would meet at least annually, but perhaps as often as quarterly, to debate key issues for the company. It would not be involved in detailed operating decisions but would work as a policy forum, operating in ways which would be recognizable in the voluntary and public sectors, in the manner of school governors or charity trustees. The board would be left to run the company within the broad policy framework laid down by the Stakeholder Council – thereby meeting the balanced needs of customers, suppliers, employees, communities and shareholders. Initially, it could apply to the largest companies, for example the FTSE 350. Such a 'new model company' could be endowed with the legitimacy which most multinationals crave because it would embrace all sections of society and break the iron grip of the financial markets. Though attractive, a revolution in governance of this order seems distant.

As western economies languished in the long shadow of recession, some of the worst corporate excesses returned in terms of 'fat cat' pay – out of all proportion to adequately rewarding executive performance or providing necessary incentives. In truth, such practices never went away: even in full disgrace and saved only by nationalization, Britain's banks still threw billions in bonuses at senior staff.

In 2001, when the foundations for the later economic crash were being laid, just 392 people, some sitting on more than one committee, made up the remuneration committees of ninety-eight of the UK's largest companies. In 2003, Jean-Pierre Garnier, chief executive of GlaxoSmithKline, was set to get £22 million if he was fired, and thought himself 'pretty much at the bottom of the pile' among his peers. The defence of high pay has always been that it is needed to attract and motivate senior executives, and give mid-level executives something to aspire to. The reality has long been different.

A study by a UK management consultancy, Kepler Associates, found that in 2000 there was an inverse relationship between pay and performance in the FTSE 100. The typical boss of a poorly performing company was earning £175,000 a year more than a world-class player. Mergers and acquisitions, those manoeuvres which create both ever bigger corporations and ever higher-paid chief executives at their helms, also consistently destroy more value than they create.

More than a hundred years ago, the banker J.P. Morgan said no company should have a differential greater than ten between the highest paid and the lowest paid. He thought that was quite sufficient to motivate. The Royal Navy, for example, has had a de facto differential of eight. Yet neither theory nor experience seems capable of changing actual behaviour. The pay deal for Marks & Spencer's new chief executive in 2010 looked set to give him £15 million in his first year.

After the crash of 2008, all the banks, not just those actively privatized, were still in business only thanks to public intervention. So it was peculiar when John Varley, Barclays' chief executive, reacted in horror in 2009 to the suggestion of a BBC radio interviewer that some parameters should be put around pay and bonuses awarded to bank staff. It would, he said, 'interfere with the market'. And in less than a decade, we have gone from Jean-Pierre Garnier's prospective £22 million payout to learning in 2010 that Bart Becht, chief of Reckitt Benckiser, took home £92 million for a year's work. Just for comparison about current economic and social priorities, a nursery-school worker in whose hands rests the fate of the next generation and takes home around £12,000 per year would need to work for 7,666 years in order to equal the annual reward given to the public face of the detergent Cillit Bang.

That example may be extreme, though still a real and telling illustration of skewed economic priorities that are getting worse. According to Richard Lambert, director-general of the corporate-friendly Confederation of British Industry, the chief executives of the 100 biggest companies in the UK were paid eighty-one times more than full-time workers' average pay in 2009, and the ratio had increased over the decade from 'just' forty-seven times more in the year 2000. Lambert said, 'If leaders of big companies seem to occupy a different galaxy from the rest of the community, they risk being treated as aliens.'[10] Excessive pay and short-termism are both expressions of the same smash-and-grab culture that entrenches when corporations dance to a tune of self-seeking finance.

The existence of such inequality is embedded in the culture of modern corporations, as the ratios between highest and lowest paid grow ever wider, yet it remains unsupported by either business logic or economic necessity. It is also enormously socially and environmentally destructive. Ground-breaking work by social epidemiologists Richard Wilkinson and Kate Pickett, published in their book *The Spirit Level* (2009), reveals the degree to which a wide range of social and environmental problems, and the costs associated with them, go up as inequality rises. Not only are eminent corporations frequently failing on their own terms, the role models they set for the rest of us are also failing society.

Perhaps the real question is whether corporations can survive at all in their current form. Once in the grip of the stock market, they are lobotomized dinosaurs, making meals of their own tails, unable to feel any emotions except fear and greed. But now that the global finance system is discredited, and the system of non-executive directors as watchdogs revealed as dozing while the financial institutions galloped into disaster, these monsters may have no future. Perhaps it is just as well that they might be replaced by models that are smaller, more agile and more balanced in terms of objectives, and are differently owned, financed and managed. In such new model companies, innovative and heroic entrepreneurs, individuals, whole workforces or larger communities can once more put visions into practice and expect them to survive.

One reason that rot so firmly gripped the modern corporation is that economics in general, and business reporting in particular, draws little more than yawns from the general public. Corporate governance is an esoteric subject at best, and agonizingly dull at worst. But there is one area where the destructive influence of corporate finance has deeply touched and increasingly enraged the masses, and especially the male masses: football. Sometimes it is hard to distinguish the difference between the sports and business sections of newspapers as football commentary is dominated by the turmoil resulting from clubs which have become the playthings of private finance. It ranges from the world's greatest clubs such as Manchester United, which floats on a deep ocean of corporate debt, to lesser clubs such as Portsmouth that get relegated when points are deducted for entering administration when their finances collapse. In this area, at least, it is plain to the broader population that 'business as usual' is broken.

The issue became so contentious that in the middle of the 2010 general election campaign the sitting government saw fit (and saw advantage) in announcing a radical plan to enable fans to retake control of their clubs. Clubs would be required to give a 25 per cent stake to supporters in acknowledgement of their stake, and the stake of the local community, in the life of the club. Should a club be up for sale or go into administration, supporters would also be given the first chance to enact a takeover.

There is no shortage of potential legislation that could be applied to the three historically enduring design flaws of the corporation: the drive for monopoly control, the speculative temptations of executives and investors, and the absence of an automatic remedy for corporate abuse. This legislation could range from real competition policy with teeth to maximum pay ratios between highest and lowest earners which would allow the creative energies of executives to be redirected more productively.

Could the eminent corporation be sufficiently reformed without utterly changing the basis on which it operates? To rediscover the explicit public purpose of its original design probably involves creating a new corporate form that would be both unrecognizable and unattractive to the current financial system.

With suggested changes such as legal obligations to give equal or greater privilege to social and environmental goals compared to shareholder returns, or restrictions on the percentage of shares and therefore influence that any one investor may control in corporations above a certain size – the logical trajectory of reform quickly crashes head-on into the assumptions and expectations of the financial markets.

This, of course, is not a judgement against change. If anything looks more compromised in the modern world than our eminent corporations, it is our banking system. The market itself has delivered an overpowering case for the simultaneous reform of both company and banking law.

Possibly the simplest positive change we could make, however, is one of mindset. Adair Turner, former head of the Confederation of British Industry and subsequently head of the Financial Services Authority, believed that in the 1970s the balance between public interests and the private sector had swung too far towards the former. Now, he says, we have 'got the balance wrong in the other direction',[11] and that we need more collective approaches and a greater emphasis placed upon them.

The preservation and enhancement of the public sphere – which means much, much more than merely matters that obviously involve the state and local government – look like increasingly necessary pre-conditions for societies to survive and thrive in economically and environmentally challenging times. The assumption of recent decades that private sector ownership and management are automatically superior to public sector ownership and management has been shown to be false. This is especially so when the ownership is by huge faceless corporates, and it suggests we need to reverse their co-option of common resources into markets which are organized for and dominated by corporations.

How and where to do this requires open debate. But the public interest would seem to outweigh that of shareholders in areas such as: broadcasting for children; education, health and welfare systems; public spaces, parks, nature conservation and national parks; the police and judicial systems; the common natural resources of the biosphere from management of the atmosphere, polar caps and the oceans to biodiversity and our genetic heritage. In many countries, this issue is fought over, literally sometimes, in relation to the proper management of utilities ranging from water to energy and transport.

Change does not have to come from a single approach. We should investigate broad new philosophical approaches at the same time as reforming corporate governance.

Many such innovations are urgently needed, but regulators tend to get captured by the industries they oversee and quickly lose their verve, even if starting out with good intentions. The better way may simply be to encourage other models of enterprise to assume a more dominant role in the economy.

On the evidence in this book, old-style corporations are, in any case, doing a good job of gradually consigning themselves to history. Our children may gaze at their monstrous skeletons in our museums in wonder that such creations could have stomped the earth.

Yet we know that the human will to make things happen will continue. The drive to create organizations to allow good lives to be lived will be necessary. But what form those new institutions will take, whom they will benefit and how they will raise the necessary finance are matters that are likely to evolve a great deal in the near future. This book is an obituary, perhaps a memorial – not an entirely loving one it is true – to the days when corporations ruled the world. We may not see their like again. But we are already surrounded with numerous alternatives that are more in tune with the times – different models better able to respond to complex human and environmental predicaments.

The emerging new economy may have fewer eminent leviathans than the old one but, like a rugged, vibrant and diverse ecosystem compared to a vast and vulnerable monoculture, it will almost certainly be healthier, happier, more interesting and more resilient.

AFTERWORD

When we first thought of writing this book, capitalism was having a hell of a time, a good one.

Its sudden change of mood was captured by a single, small cartoon published in the *Financial Times* newspaper. Two forlorn businessmen are walking along Wall Street and one, long-faced, turns to the other and says, 'Capitalism was more fun when I was making lots of money out of it.'

Hard to believe that such a short time before, superficially at least, our eminent corporations, flagships of a certain kind of market system, and the financial institutions on whose conjured wealth they floated, seemed untouchable. But holding this height, the apogee of the system, was ephemeral. Now it has passed and the rush of air from its earthward hurtle has sucked the breath from many.

Architects of the old economic system, like Alan Greenspan, former head of the US Federal Reserve and, for decades, one of the most powerful men in the global economy, were left momentarily stunned and bewildered. Speaking to a congressional committee on Capitol Hill in Washington DC in October 2008, Greenspan offered an ideology-shattering insight: 'I made a mistake in presuming that the self-interest of organizations, specifically banks, is such that they were best capable of protecting shareholders and equity in the firms. . . I discovered a flaw in the model that I perceived is the critical functioning structure that defines how the world works'. He was left, he said, shocked and in disbelief. He wasn't, isn't, alone. As the mists still clear of the triumphal delirium that spell-bound western economies, in particular, after the Cold War, an awful lot of long-term wreckage and vulnerability lies in the wake of Greenspan's presumption about organizing our affairs according to the benign self-interest of organizations.

To see that, you only needed to look at the proposal from the in-coming Conservative–Liberal Democrat coalition government that all public spending departments should prepare contingency plans to make stunning cuts of forty percent. This came in the wake of the chancellor of the exchequer repeating in his first Budget statement that the need for cuts was due to the banks' failure and the financial market. Dark rumours circulated too, that the scale of cuts was driven also by fears that the banks might soon demand another round of massive public bail-outs.

In 2010, the 'flawed presumption' also lay across the Gulf of Mexico in the world's largest ever oil slick washed up on the Louisiana shores. Had the comments of BP's chief executive, Tony Hayward, been scripted by a play-writer to illustrate Greenspan's revelation, they might have seemed implausible. But Hayward really did point out that, 'the amount of volume of oil and dispersant we are putting into it (the Gulf of Mexico) is tiny in relation to the total water volume.' It was like saying that the amount of cyanide I put into your drink is tiny in comparison to the amount of gin and tonic. Arguing that the Deepwater Horizon spill was just a drop in the ocean seemed to justify a broader suspicion that the captains of our eminent corporations have become dangerously removed from most people's reality.

Richard Lambert's broader observation that: 'If leaders of big companies seem to occupy a different galaxy from the rest of the community, they risk being treated as aliens' seemed especially relevant to Hayward, and even more poignant given that Lambert was director-general of the trade body for big companies, the Confederation of British Industry.

The BP debacle was even worse because it turned out to be much more than just an environmental disaster. BP's share price tumbled, as its expected liabilities from the spill climbed so high that the financial markets gave the company's debt a 'junk' rating, meaning that you wouldn't expect to get your money back if you bought it. The liabilities may have been upward of $40 billion, but no one really knows.

The Pulitzer Prize-winning investigative news organization ProPublica revealed that there had been repeated internal warnings by senior BP managers that the safety and environmental policies were being ignored by the company. A BP report into the previous 2005 Texas City disaster, when a massive explosion at a refinery killed fifteen workers, concluded that there had then, too, been 'apparent complacency toward serious safety risk'.

Yet any schadenfreude concerning the economic impact on the company of its own failings was tempered by the realisation that our own livelihoods were deeply entwined with the company.

Around the time of the disaster, £1 in every £4 of dividends paid to UK shareholders came from just one sector – oil and gas – in which just two companies dominate, BP and Shell. BP alone accounted for about 12 percent or £2 in every £8, of British pension payments.

Correcting the 'flawed presumption', (as well as shifting from fossil fuels to renewables), then rapidly becomes not just a matter of protecting the environment and human rights, but also of ensuring our collective economic security.

The cost of banks and other eminent corporations becoming too big to fail now present systemic risks to public finances and the fabric of society. These have been our cacophonous wake-up calls. Yet, perversely, in the aftermath of the great financial collapse and recession, consolidation continues. The banks and other corporations merge and grow. The shaky future of Cadbury's British workforce in the aftermath of its leveraged buy-out by Kraft is one further unhappy footnote.

Largeness of scale and the absence of the human dimension is a widening faultline. In 1957, the economist Leopold Kohr concluded in his landmark book, *The Breakdown of Nations*, that 'Wherever something is wrong, something is too big.'

For the sake of our own security, survival even, it is time to reduce corporations to a size at which they do not pose systemic risks to our livelihoods and life support systems. But it is also time to acknowledge and act upon Alan Greenspan's flawed presumption. We need to have as our mainstream, default position, forms of enterprise in which social progress and a positive, equilibrium relationship with the environment are both the over-riding priority and purpose for doing business.

NOTES

Introduction

1. Lytton Strachey, *Eminent Victorians*, edited by John Sutherland, Oxford World Classics, OUP, Oxford, 2003.
2. Joel Bakan (2004), *The Corporation: The Pathological Pursuit of Profit and Power*, Constable, London.

Chapter 1

1. Archie Baron, *An Indian Affair*, Channel 4 Books, London, 2001, p.79.
2. Quoted in Romesh Chunder Dutt, *The Economic History of India under Early British Rule (1757–1837)*, Kegan Paul, Trench, Trubner & Co., London, 1908, p.29.
3. Thomas Babbington Macaulay (1886), *Hastings*, Chautauqua Press, New York, p.39.
4. Joseph Parkes and Herman Melville (1867), *Memoirs of Sir Philip Francis*, vol.II, Longman, Green & Co., London, p.18.
5. William Cowper (1913), 'Expostulation', in *Poetical Works*, Oxford University Press, Oxford, p.51.
6. Adam Smith (1994 edition), *The Wealth of Nations*, Book IV, Random House, New York, p.675.
7. Adam Smith (1994 edition), p.693.
8. Adam Smith (1994 edition), p.288.
9. Adam Smith (1994 edition), pp.681–2.

10. Adam Smith (1994 edition), p.170.
11. Adam Smith (1994 edition), p.692.
12. Ian Simpson Ross (1995), *The Life of Adam Smith*, Clarendon Press, Oxford, p.353.
13. Adam Smith (1994 edition), p.814.
14. Edmund Burke (1783), speech to Parliament, 1 December.
15. Edmund Burke (1783).
16. Stanley Ayling (1988), *Edmund Burke*, Cassell, London, p.162.
17. Edmund Burke (1788), speech on the impeachment of Warren Hastings, 15–19 February.
18. *Gentleman's Magazine* (1767), April, p.152.
19. www.theeastindiacompany.com.

Chapter 2

1. Margaret Ackrill and Leslie Hannah (2001), *Barclays: The Business of Banking 1690–1996*, Cambridge University Press, Cambridge, p.56.
2. J.M. Price (1980), *Capital and Credit in British Overseas Trade: The View from the Chesapeake 1700–1776*, Harvard University Press, Cambridge MA, p.72.
3. Anthony Sampson (1988), *The Money Lenders: Bankers in a Dangerous World*, Hodder & Stoughton, London.
4. David Kynaston (1995), *The City of London Vol.1: A World of Its Own 1815–1890*, Pimlico, London, p.15.
5. Margaret Ackrill and Leslie Hannah (2001), p.56.
6. Forrest Capie and Ghila Rodrik-Bali (1982), 'Concentration in British Banking 1870–1920', *Business History*, vol. XXIV, no.3, November.
7. P. Johnson (1985), *Saving and Spending*, Oxford University Press, Oxford, pp.168 and 192.
8. Margaret Ackrill and Leslie Hannah (2001), p.106.
9. David J. Jeremy and Christine Shaw (eds) (1984), *Dictionary of Business Biography*, vol.I, Butterworth, London, pp.321–4.
10. Margaret Ackrill and Leslie Hannah (2001), p.142.

11. Martin Vander Weyer (2000), *Falling Eagle: The Decline of Barclays Bank*, Weidenfeld & Nicolson, London, p.34.
12. Anthony Sampson (1965), *Anatomy of Britain Today*, Hodder & Stoughton, London, p.422.
13. *Economist* (1980), 14 March.
14. Margaret Ackrill and Leslie Hannah (2001), p.202.
15. Margaret Reid (1985), *All Change in the City: The Revolution in Britain's Banking Industry*, Macmillan, Basingstoke, pp.127–8.
16. Martin Vander Weyer (2000), p.195.
17. John Kenneth Galbraith (1975), *Money: Whence It Came, Where It Went*, Andre Deutsch, London, p.29.
18. Martin Vander Weyer (2000), p.85.
19. Margaret Ackrill and Leslie Hannah (2001), p.327.
20. *Financial Times* (1994), 11 March.
21. Martin Vander Weyer (2000), p.222.
22. Martin Vander Weyer (2000), p.138.
23. Martin Vander Weyer (2000), p.262.
24. Martin Vander Weyer (2000), p.238.
25. Nick Robins (2007), 'Quietly conquering the climate', *Ecologist*, May.
26. *Independent* (2007), 2 February.
27. Bloomberg (2008), 8 October.
28. *Independent* (2007), 10 November.
29. James Harding (2007), 'Well, Barclays, thanks for clearing that up', *The Times*, 16 November.
30. Abigail Hoffman (2007), 'Barclays and fear of the unknown', *Euromoney*, September.
31. *Daily Telegraph* (2009), 16 September.
32. *Evening Standard* (2009), 6 February.
33. *Evening Standard* (2009), 17 March.

Chapter 3

1. Iolo Williams (1931), *The Firm of Cadbury 1831–1931*, Constable, London, p.5.
2. Iolo Williams (1931), p.20.

3. Walter White (1852), 'Visit to a chocolate manufactory', *Chambers's Edinburgh Journal*, 30 October, quoted in Iolo Williams (1931), p.28.

4. Gillian Wagner (1987), *The Chocolate Conscience*, Chatto & Windus, London, p.36.

5. Quoted in Iolo Williams (1931), p.154.

6. Iolo Williams (1931), p.220.

7. J.B. Priestley (1934), *English Journey*, William Heinemann, London, quoted in Carol Kennedy (2000), *The Merchant Princes: Family, Fortune and Philanthropy – Cadbury, Sainsbury and John Lewis*, Hutchinson, London, p.89.

8. Carol Kennedy (2000), p.51.

9. Iolo Williams (1931), p.151.

10. Gillian Wagner (1987), p.91.

11. *Standard* (1908), 26 September.

12. Gillian Wagner (1987), p.99.

13. Gillian Wagner (1987), p.99.

14. Carol Kennedy (2000), p.80.

15. Carol Kennedy (2000), p.89.

16. Francis Williams (1960), 'The murder of the News Chronicle', *New Statesman*, 22 October.

17. Margaret Stewart (1960), 'The night the blow fell', *New Statesman*, 22 October.

18. James Cameron (1985), *Point of Departure: An Experiment in Autobiography*, Oriel Press, Stocksfield, p.80.

19. Carol Kennedy (2000), p.108.

20. John Bradley (2008), *Cadbury's Purple Reign: The Story Behind Chocolate's Best-loved Brand*, John Wiley, Chichester, p.233.

21. *The Times* (1981), 9 December.

22. *Financial Times* (1998), December.

23. Carol Kennedy (2000), p.114.

24. Christian Parenti (2008), 'Chocolate's bittersweet economy', *Fortune*, 11 February.

25. *Guardian* (2010), 19 January.

Chapter 4

1. Judi Bevan (2007), *The Rise and Fall of Marks & Spencer – and How It Rose Again*, revised edition, Profile, London, p.18.
2. Israel Sieff (1985), *The Memoirs of Israel Sieff*, Weidenfeld & Nicolson, London, p.52.
3. Goronwy Rees (1969), *St Michael: A History of Marks & Spencer*, Weidenfeld and Nicolson, London, p.63.
4. Corah (1966), 'Annual Statement', quoted in Goronwy Rees (1969), p.105.
5. Judi Bevan (2007), p.10.
6. Israel Sieff (1985), p.166.
7. Goronwy Rees (1969), p.250.
8. Israel Sieff (1985), p.196.
9. Lord Marks (1945), speech to M&S shareholders, quoted in Goronwy Rees (1969), p.141.
10. Judi Bevan (2007), p.43.
11. Goronwy Rees (1969), p.243.
12. Israel Sieff (1985).
13. Judi Bevan (2001) *The Rise and Fall of Marks & Spencer*, Profile, London, p.39.
14. Israel Sieff (1985), p.203.
15. *The Times* (1966), 18 May.
16. Judi Bevan (2001), p.71.
17. Judi Bevan (2001), p.52.
18. *Sunday Telegraph* (1999), 23 May.
19. Judi Bevan (2001), p.24.
20. Stanley Chapman (2004), *Socially Responsible Supply Chains: Marks & Spencer in Historic Perspective*, Nottingham University, Nottingham.
21. Judi Bevan (2007), p.287.
22. *The Times* (2009), 23 October.

Chapter 5

1. Baffour Ankomah (1999), 'The Butcher of Congo', *New African*, October.

2. *A Short History of Rover* (1970), Rover Company Limited, British Leyland, Solihull.

3. Dudley Noble (1969), *Milestones in a Motoring Life*, Queen Anne Press, London.

4. Michael Perelman (2005), *Manufacturing Discontent: The Trap of Individualism in Corporate Society*, Pluto Press, London.

5. Formally known as the Locomotives on Highways Act, 1865.

6. Roy Foster, 'Beep Beep Yeah', *Financial Times* (2003), 8 November.

7. Raynes Minns (1980), *Bombers & Mash: The Domestic Front 1939–1945*, Virago Press, London.

8. National Archives, memorandum, http://yourarchives. nationalarchives.gov.uk/index.php?title=Shadow_ Factories%2C_World_War_Two.

9. BBC News Archive, '1940: Germans bomb Coventry to destruction', http://news.bbc.co.uk/onthisday/hi/dates/stories/november/15/newsid_3522000/3522785.stm.

10. Kevin Phillips and Jan Phillips (undated), 'The Rover Car Company: Hindsight ... Reflections of the Past', www. rover.org.nz/pages/history.htm.

11. Miranda Bryant (2008), 'The gigolo, the German heiress, and a £6m revenge for her Nazi legacy', *Independent*, 3 November; BBC News (2007), 'Quandts to reveal Nazi-era links', 9 October, http://news.bbc.co.uk/1/hi/world/europe/7035485.stm.

12. Roy Church (1994) *The Rise and Decline of the British Motor Industry*, Cambridge University Press, Cambridge.

13. Roy Church (1994).

14. Roy Church (1994).

15. Roy Church (1994).

16. Roy Church (1994), p.71, quoting D.T. Jones and S.J. Prais (1978), 'Plant Size and Productivity in the Motor Industry: Some International Comparisons', *Oxford Bulletin of Economics and Statistics*, vol.40, no.2, May.

17. Roy Church (1994).

18. Roy Church (1994).
19. Roy Church (1994).
20. Chris Brady and Andrew Lorenz (2002), *End of the Road: BMW and Rover – a Brand Too Far* (second edition), Financial Times, Prentice Hall, Pearson Education Limited, London.
21. Chris Brady and Andrew Lorenz (2002).
22. Chris Brady and Andrew Lorenz (2002).
23. Tom Donnelly, David Morris, Kamel Mellahi (2003), 'Rover-BMW: from shotgun marriage to quickie divorce', *International Journal of Business Performance Management*, vol.5, no.4.
24. BBC News (2000), 'Rover bid timetable', 9 May, http://news.bbc.co.uk/1/hi/business/729267.stm.
25. Roy Church (1994).
26. KPMG, *Mergers and Acquisitions: Global Research Report* (1999); reported in 'Mergers destroy value, says KMPG', *Guardian*, 29 November 1999.
27. BBC News (2005), '15 arrested in Land Rover protest', 16 May, http://news.bbc.co.uk/1/hi/business/4550593.stm.
28. Dr Peter Wells (2006), 'The Suitability of Offroad Vehicles for Urban Environments', www.greenpeace.org.uk/files/pdfs/migrated/MultimediaFiles/Live/FullReport/7504.pdf.
29. Union of Concerned Scientists (2000), 'Pollution Lineup: An Environmental Ranking of Automakers', Cambridge, MA.
30. Andrew Rudin (1999), 'How Improved Efficiency Harms the Environment', http://home.earthlink.net/~andrewrudin/article.html.
31. Reuters (2003), 'Automakers rev up U.S. advertising spending', 12 May. Analysis by Merrill Lynch showed spending up from $8.5 billion in 2002 to $9.9 billion in 2003.
32. ANC (1977), 'Statement at the Meeting of the Special Committee Against Apartheid', 12 December, www.anc.org.za/ancdocs/history/aam/abdul-10.html.
33. Helen Close and Roy Isbister (2008), *Good Conduct? Ten Years of the EU Code of Conduct on Arms Exports*, Campagne tegen Wapenhandel, the Netherlands; Caritas,

France; ControllARMI: Rete Italiana per il Disarmo (Italian Network on Disarmament), Italy; Groupe de recherche et d'information sur la paix et la sécurité (GRIP), Belgium; Saferworld, UK; School for a Culture of Peace, Spain; Swedish Peace and Arbitration Society (SPAS), Sweden; Transparency International, UK.

34. 'Arms without Borders' (2006), Control Arms Campaign: Amnesty International, the International Action Network on Small Arms & Oxfam International, www.control-arms.org/en/documents%20and%20files/reports/english-reports/arms-without-borders.

35. 'Arms without Borders' (2006).

36. Jeanne Van Eeden (2007) 'Land Rover and Colonial-Style Adventure: The "Himba" Advertisement', University of Pretoria, South Africa, www.up.ac.za/dspace/bit-stream/2263/2538/1/VanEeden_Land(2007).pdf.

37. Clare Pillinger (2001), 'Land Rover's U-turn over "racist and sexist" advert', *Daily Telegraph*, 28 January.

38. PPA Marketing, Consumer Magazine Advertisement of the Year, 2004, Land Rover Freelander Maasai – Rainey Kelly Campbell Roalfe/Y&R.

39. K. Homewood, E. Coast, S. Kiruswa, S. Serneels, M. Thompson, P. Trench (undated), 'Maasai Pastoralists: Diversification and Poverty', International Livestock Research Institute, www.ilri.org/Link/Publications/Publications/Theme%201/Pastoral%20conference/Papers/Home woodet%20al.pdf.

40. Oxfam (2008) 'Survival of the fittest: Pastoralism and climate change in East Africa', www.oxfam.org/policy/bp116-pastoralism-climate-change-0808.

41. *Guardian* (2008), 'Indian firm buys Jaguar and Land Rover', 26 March, www.guardian.co.uk/business/2008/mar/26/automotive.mergersandacquisitions?gusrc=rss&feed=networkfront.

42. Bloomberg News (2008), 'China Should be Afraid of India's New $2,500 Car', 23 January, www.bloomberg.com/apps/news?pid=20601 039&sid=a.yeOh3ufMvg&refer=home.

43. World Resources Institute quoting: American Automobile Manufacturers Association (AAMA), 'World Motor Vehicle Data 1993' and AAMA 'Motor Vehicle Facts and Figures 1996'.
44. *World Health Statistics 2008* (2008), World Health Organization, Geneva, www.who.int/whosis/whostat/2008/en/index.html.
45. *World Health Statistics 2008* (2008).
46. *Motor Trader* (2008), 'Nanjing MG – To start producing bikes at Longbridge, UK!', 1 April, www.chinacartimes.com/2008/04/01/nanjing-mg-to-start-producing-bikes-at-long-bridge-uk/.

Chapter 6

1. Colin J. Campbell, 'The Oil Age – A Turning Point for Mankind', presentation for the Association for the Study of Peak Oil (ASPO), www.energieinstitut.at/HP/Upload/Dateien/Campbell_Colin_das_Oelzeitalter_nuechtern_betrachtet.pdf.
2. Ronald W. Ferrier (1982), *The History of the British Petroleum Company: Volume 1, The Developing Years, 1901–1932*, Cambridge University Press, Cambridge.
3. http://library-resources.cqu.edu.au/thesis/adt-QCQU/uploads/approved/adt-QCQU20050427.131849/public/11Conclusion.pdf.
4. Ronald W. Ferrier (1982).
5. Berrie Ritchie (1995), *Portrait in Oil: An Illustrated History of BP*, James & James, London.
6. Ronald W. Ferrier (1982).
7. Berrie Ritchie (1995).
8. Anthony Sampson (1975), *The Seven Sisters: The Great Oil Companies and the World They Made*, Hodder & Stoughton, London.
9. Ronald W. Ferrier (1982).
10. Anthony Sampson (1975).
11. Ronald W. Ferrier (1982).

12. Berrie Ritchie (1995).
13. Anthony Sampson (1975).
14. Anthony Sampson (1975).
15. Anthony Sampson (1975).
16. J.H. Bamberg (1994), *The History of the British Petroleum Company, Volume 2, The Anglo-Iranian Years 1928–1954*, Cambridge University Press, Cambridge.
17. Henry Longhurst (1959), *Adventure in Oil: The Story of British Petroleum*, Sidgwick & Jackson, London.
18. Anthony Sampson (1975).
19. Daniel Yergin (2008) *The Prize: The Epic Quest for Oil, Money and Power*, Free Press, New York.
20. Daniel Yergin (2008).
21. Berrie Ritchie (1995).
22. Daniel Yergin (2008).
23. Hugh Thomas (1970), *The Suez Affair*, quoted in Anthony Sampson (1975).
24. Berrie Ritchie (1995).
25. Berrie Ritchie (1995).
26. Andrew Simms, David Woodward, Petra Kjell and James Leaton (2006), *Hooked on Oil: Breaking the Habit with a Windfall Tax – The UK Exchequer's Dependence on Fossil Fuel Income*, NEF and WWF, London.
27. Ogilvy Public Relations Worldwide (undated), 'How do you rebrand a group of recently merged oil companies as a unified global energy company?', www.ogilvypr.com/en/case-study/bp, accessed 13 July 2009.
28. Ogilvy Public Relations Worldwide (undated).
29. *BP Sustainability Report 2004: Making the Right Choices* (2005) BP, London; Andrew Simms, David Woodward, Petra Kjell and James Leaton (2006).
30. 'Product Emissions', *BP Sustainability Report 2005* (2006) BP, London.
31. Friends of the Earth (2006), 'Shell vs. BP: Who is performing worst on climate change?', press release, 27 July, www.foe.co.uk/resource/press_releases/shell_vs_bp_who_is_perform_27072006.html.

32. www.bp.com/sectiongenericarticle.do?categoryId=14&contentId=2002063.

33. *Financial Times* (2002), 'Colombia holds out for a big oil find', 1 February.

34. Reuters (2006), 'BP shuts giant Alaska oil field on pipe damage', 7 August, www.reuters.com.

35. 'BP Issues Final Report on Fatal Explosion', 9 December 2005, www.bp.com/genericarticle.do?categoryId=2012968&contentId=7012963.

36. *Wall Street Journal* (2010) 'BP Suffers Setback on Containment Dome', 10 May, http://online.wsj.com/article/SB10001424052748704858104575232610208583340.html?mod=WSJ_WSJ_US_News_3; *Guardian* (2010), 'BP "facing £15bn loss" over Gulf of Mexico oil spill', 6 May, www.guardian.co.uk/business/2010/may/06/bp-oil-spill-gulf-of-mexico-deepwater-horizon.

37. Greenpeace (2008), 'BP Presented with 2008 "Emerald Paintbrush" Award by Greenpeace: Oil giant accused of using advertising to "greenwash" massive new investment in fossil fuels', press release, 22 December.

38. Ed Crooks (2009), 'Daunting tasks in prospect for new BP chairman', *Financial Times*, 11 June.

39. Ed Crooks (2009), 'BP finds "giant" US oil field', *Financial Times*, 3 September.

40. Olivia Boyd (2009), 'Ex-BP boss wants banks forced to invest in green power', *The Times*, 6 July.

41. Ed Crooks (2009), 'Daunting tasks in prospect for new BP chairman', *Financial Times*, 11 June.

42. Interview with the authors.

Chapter 7

1. Asa Briggs (1985), *The BBC: The First Fifty Years*, Oxford University Press, Oxford, p.29.

2. Asa Briggs (1985), p.44.

3. Asa Briggs (1985), p.46.

4. John Reith, Diary, 8 May 1926.

5. *Radio Times* (1926), 28 May.
6. Paul Bloomfield (1941), *BBC*, Eyre & Spottiswoode, London, p.213.
7. Jack De Manio (1967), *To Auntie with Love*, Hutchinson, London, p.140.
8. Paul Bloomfield (1941), p.20.
9. Paul Bloomfield (1941), p.80.
10. Asa Briggs (1985), pp.118–19.
11. Asa Briggs (1970) *The History of Broadcasting in the United Kingdom, Vol.III: The War of Words*, Oxford University Press, London, p.230.
12. Asa Briggs (1985), p.177.
13. Asa Briggs (1970), p.342.
14. David Boyle (2001), 'Why spin didn't help win World War II', *New Statesman*, 12 November.
15. Noel Newsome (1940), *A Plan and Basis for Propaganda: History as our Ally*, European Service Directive, 8 July.
16. Michael Cockerell (1998), *Live from Inside Number 10: The Inside Story of Prime Ministers and Television*, Faber & Faber, London, p.25.
17. Asa Briggs (1985), p.300.
18. Michael Cockerell (1998).
19. Chris Horrie and Steve Clarke (1998), *Fuzzy Monsters: Fear and Loathing at the BBC*, Heinemann, London, p.168.
20. Chris Horrie and Steve Clarke (1998), p.243.
21. Chris Horrie and Steve Clarke (1998), p.243.
22. Chris Horrie and Steve Clarke (1998), p.226.
23. Paul Bloomfield (1941), p.248.
24. Stephen Robinson (2009), 'Fear and loathing inside the BBC', *Evening Standard*, 12 October.
25. Andrew Gilligan (2010), 'PC-mad BBC where even church bells and Teletubbies are vetted', *Sunday Telegraph*, 10 January.
26. Asa Briggs (1985), p.331.
27. Asa Briggs (1985), p.244.

Chapter 8

1. Tom Bower (2000), *Branson*, Fourth Estate, London, p.13.
2. Richard Branson (1998), *Losing My Virginity*, Virgin, London, p.67.
3. Tom Bower (2000), p.2.
4. Tom Bower (2000), p.30.
5. Tom Bower (2000), p.327.
6. Richard Branson (1998), p.194.
7. Richard Branson (1998), p.285.
8. Martyn Gregory (2000), *Dirty Tricks: British Airways' Secret War Against Virgin Atlantic*, Virgin, New York.
9. Richard Branson (1998), p.359.
10. David Boyle (2003), *Authenticity: Brands, Fakes, Spin and the Lust for Real Life*, HarperCollins, London.
11. Richard Branson (1998), p.438.
12. Richard Branson (1998), p.433.
13. BBC (1998), 2 February.
14. *UK Press Gazette* (2001), 13 July.
15. Ally Carnwath (2008), *Observer*, 17 August.
16. *Connected Planet* (2002), 1 August.
17. *The Times* (2010), 4 April.
18. Betsy Morris (2003), 'Richard Branson: What a life!', *Fortune*, 22 September.
19. ABC News (2006), 22 September.
20. Tom Bower (2000), p.xiii.
21. Quoted in Richard Branson (1998), p.442.

Conclusion

1. Robert Heilbroner (1994), *21st Century Capitalism*, W.W. Norton & Company, New York.
2. Nick Robins (2006), *The Corporation that Changed the World: How the East India Company Shaped the Modern Multinational*, Pluto, London.
3. George Goyder (1987), *The Just Enterprise*, André Deutsch, London.

4. John Kay (2010), 'Decision-making, John Kay's way', *Financial Times*, 20 March, www.ft.com/cms/s/2/0daa1cf6-3164-11df-9741-00144feabdc0.html.

5. John Kenneth Galbraith, *The Great Crash of 1929*, Houghton Mifflin, Boston MA, 1954.

6. John C. Bogle (2009), *Enough*, John Wiley and Sons, New York, pp.111–12. Bogle credits the Avis story to an article by Michael Kinsley in the *New York Times*, May 2007.

7. www.scottbader.com.

8. E.F. Schumacher (1973), *Small is Beautiful*, Blond & Briggs, London; http://gandhifoundation.org/2008/07/10/schumacher-and-trusteeship -by-godric-bader/.

9. Andrew Simms (2007) *Tescopoly: How One Shop Came Out on Top and Why It Matters*, Constable, London.

10. Jean Eaglesham (2010), 'Chiefs risk being seen as "aliens" over pay', *Financial Times*, 31 March.

11. Interview with the author for *The World Tonight*, BBC Radio.

INDEX